SPECULATIVE REALI

Also available from Bloomsbury

AFTER FINITUDE
Quentin Meillassoux

POST-CONTINENTAL PHILOSOPHY
John Mullarkey

SPECULATIVE REALISM

PROBLEMS AND PROSPECTS

Peter Gratton

Bloomsbury Academic
An imprint of Bloomsbury Publishing Plc

B L O O M S B U R Y
LONDON • NEW DELHI • NEW YORK • SYDNEY

Bloomsbury Academic
An imprint of Bloomsbury Publishing Plc

50 Bedford Square
London
WC1B 3DP
UK

1385 Broadway
New York
NY 10018
USA

www.bloomsbury.com

BLOOMSBURY and the Diana logo are trademarks of Bloomsbury Publishing Plc

First published 2014
Reprinted by Bloomsbury Academic 2014, 2015

British Library Cataloguing-in-Publication Data
A catalogue record for this book is available from the British Library.

ISBN: HB: 978-1-4411-0887-6
PB: 978-1-4411-7475-8
ePDF: 978-1-4411-6367-7
ePUB: 978-1-4411-8802-1

Library of Congress Cataloging-in-Publication Data
Gratton, Peter, author.
Speculative realism: problems and prospects/Peter Gratton.
pages cm
Includes bibliographical references and index.
ISBN 978-1-4411-0887-6 (hardback) – ISBN 978-1-4411-7475-8 (paperback) – ISBN 978-1-4411-8802-1 (epub) – ISBN (invalid) 978-1-4411-6367-7 (PDF) 1. Realism. 2. Meillassoux, Quentin, 1967- 3. Continental philosophy. I. Title.
B835.G73 2014
149'.2–dc23
2013047466

Typeset by Deanta Global Publishing Services, Chennai, India
Printed and bound in Great Britain

CONTENTS

INTRODUCTION

Speculative realism is an area of philosophy declared just 7 years ago. Now it is a Continental philosophy splinter group with dedicated blogs, at least two online journals, numerous commentaries in articles both popular and academic, and yes, this book. To those critical of speculative realism, this quick movement is enough to deny its importance. Continental philosophy, with its creaky traditions and often-hideous nomenclature, is said to be in a time of transition. Philosophy, the fear is, has become even more of a bazaar of self-branding academics pumping out articles and books and pushing new systems of thought with clunky titles (neo- *this*, meta- *that*) buttressed in a few cases by nothing more than a few months of thinking, a couple of blog posts, and an adorable ability to insert the words "what I like to call" before the most prosaic of ideas. ("What I like to call physicality, as opposed to physics . . .") We hearten ourselves by saying other disciplines may be worse, even as we measure if we've made it by our number of citations in those departments. (Did you know my *work*—drop an octave to give the appropriate gravitas—is often cited by sociologists and gardeners?) Gone are the days when careers were made by reading The German Thinker, making his translated verbiage your own, and then spending a lifetime tossing out repetitive essays saying the key to his work is to be found on some slip of paper you discovered on the floor of his archive. Gone is the time when you could make a career ventriloquizing the words of the Thinker so much that you would quote him (and it was invariably a "him") in every chapter or essay you wrote—as well as love letters and the occasional holiday card. Sure you can still get by with obsequiousness to whoever is still alive in France and Germany after the deaths of Derrida et al. But to make it for real these days, the cynical will claim, you must have a *system*, and it better come with a ready-made politics. Which, *of course*, you'll say, it *does*, since it's the subject of your forthcoming book; anyone can have a book *forthcoming*, and it is best to have several to have a trump card to throw into any conversation at conferences: "I too have a chapter on *that* in a book I'm writing, you know." No need to be shy, some among us say about new movements in academia. Those thinkers before you were monumentally wrong anyway, and you'll invent some new word for describing how their thought led to Nazism or cancer or some other malady you are free to dream up. Be fearless in building your opponents in the history of philosophy with straw and setting them ablaze. Fortune favors the bold, not the sucker who has to read everything before saying anything.

Better, too, to have that system as soon as possible: Plato gave his philosopher kings some 50 years to develop their chops; he obviously never had to upload his CV to Interfolio. You'll need *bona fides* for applications for jobs that no longer exist in a discipline funded off, it seems, bake sales and whatever change falls out of the pockets of the Dean of Business. Books have to be pressed and nobody is waiting for the next Gadamer to publish his first major work at sixty. Despite the poverty, you will find this liberating, this new age of uploaded treatises and downloaded podcasts. You are no longer a pre-given label—so strange it must have been to be known by someone else's name: Derridean, Foucaultian, Deleuzian, Arendtian. . . . You can make up your own label—though pro tip: best not to end your catchphrase with "-ology," which tends to make even the most tantalizing field sound like a melanoma. If you're having trouble with a label, just throw "post," "trans," or "meta" in front of a name you've already heard—postmaterialism, metanaturalism, and so on are just there for the taking. But you must write in a tone that no one has thought this before, and treat readers as if they didn't know familiar things about the contemporary world: computers, brain scans, cell phones, and so on. And worry little about changing labels every few months; you should peel them off as often as inveterate shoplifters pull off price tags. Tell those who think it's inconsistent with your older, now months-old work they didn't understand your work in the first place.

Am I not giving into this whole cynical viewpoint here with this book? A few years in and we have a "movement"? Is someone, somewhere negotiating the merchandising rights, too? No doubt you'll tease me for my gullibility. I don't doubt there's good reason for the cynicism outlined above. The loss of numerous teaching jobs in philosophy has happened at the same time as scholars have had easier access to publishing options online, which has meant a heavier burden to identify oneself quickly, to make a name before one even has a name on a regular paycheck. Ray Brassier, who came up with the term "speculative realism" and ever since has told anyone with ears to listen that he has burned his membership card—one gets the idea he would rather be revealed as a member of Campus Crusade for Christ—insinuates that speculative realism is just one more marketing label, as can be seen from an interview given a couple of years ago:

> The "speculative realist movement" exists only in the imaginations of a group of bloggers promoting an agenda for which I have no sympathy whatsoever: actor-network theory spiced with pan-psychist metaphysics and morsels of process philosophy. I don't believe the Internet is an appropriate medium for serious philosophical debate; nor do I believe it is acceptable to try to concoct a philosophical movement online by using blogs to exploit the misguided enthusiasm of impressionable graduate students. I agree with Deleuze's remark that ultimately the most basic task of philosophy is to impede stupidity, so I see little philosophical merit in a "movement" whose most signal achievement thus far is to have generated an online orgy of stupidity.[1]

Some scary scare quotes there. And lurid details of an "online orgy of stupidity." By now, you're waiting for me to pivot here and begin chastising Brassier for being too young to shake his cane at the hooligans endangering his lawn; where I discuss the brilliance, the world-historical innovation of Graham Harman, Quentin Meillassoux, or whomever from a movement you might have just heard of when you picked up this book. Where I detail my conversion experience and describe my penitence before the holy trinity of speculative materialism, object-oriented ontology, and "pan-psychist metaphysics."

But though we might disagree with parts of what Brassier says, it's hard to doubt his claims about the internet if one has seen the trolling on websites identifying themselves for and against the speculative realists. The internet's promise of some vaunted exchange of ideas has given way in too many cases to the exchange of put-downs and pile-ons. Let us thus make Brassier's analysis our starting point. A movement should have to prove its staying power and importance, not just get name-dropped in art catalogues and cloying treatises. Any early book on it should investigate just what is being sold to the "impressionable" and the incredulous alike. Whether you'll be one or both by the end of these pages will depend on the alert appraisal of the claims, arguments, and interpretations these philosophers, including Brassier himself, provide—all the while avoiding the trolling that is a mark of too many online discussions.

But I've delayed long enough. What is speculative realism anyway? Giving a precise answer is like trying to say what's the same for all animals in a zoo.

Indeed, some mentioned in this book may think they, too, are held captive by the term. Nevertheless, let's tell the story found frequently in essays on speculative realism. In April 2007, Ray Brassier, from the American University of Middlesex, Iain Hamilton Grant, from the University of the West of England, Graham Harman, from the American University in Cairo, and Quentin Meillassoux, from the École normale supérieure, presented a series of talks under the title "Speculative Realism" at Goldsmith's College, University of London, which were published later in the heretofore unknown journal *Collapse*. They seemingly agree on but one thing: that European philosophy since the time of Kant has stopped talking about reality, since it's stuck thinking about how we *know* reality—just endless stuff on demonstrations, discourses, dialectics, and deconstruction. The label, imparted by Brassier in *Nihil Unbound*, takes off—though let's be frank, we're not talking Ke$ha's latest album here—even as non-philosophers are baffled that only in such a discipline could you gain a name by talking about reality. Other philosophers are as nonplussed: who said we weren't talking about reality?

Questions about the relation between thought and being are as old as the earliest Greek philosophers and as deceptively simple as a Chinese finger trap, and one has been caught with the other for seemingly an entire tradition. Let's keep things comically simplistic for now—we'll ramp up soon enough. For Plato, the forms were real, but because the word for forms was *Idea*, he was the West's original idealist, taking the world around us as unreal and unworthy of study. Aristotle is trickier. Forms, for him, were immanent to the things around us, but he also teaches that the greatest happiness is found off in contemplation, away from the sales pitches and haranguing political talk of the agora, all while turned away from the things of the world. Skipping long bits of history, we get Catholicism and the view that the most real entity, God, rules over a fallen world, so again the attention is on the supernatural over the natural. It's not until the development of empiricism in the modern period that philosophy begins to knock back against the idea that it's not reason's insight or faith in the otherworldly that provides the best knowledge of the world. But that opens the door to David Hume's skepticism, which denies certainty about reality and even the relation between any cause, say, a billiard ball hitting another, and its effect, its precise trajectory from there. Before long Kant wakes from his famed dogmatic slumber, arguing that cause and effect and indeed time and space are not "out there," but are concepts of the understanding that we place over the world or the "in-itself." From there, goes the story, we philosophers were less interested in reality itself.

Rather, our focus was on how we come to know the world, or the ideas we form about it, or the relationships among these ideas, or the cultural and linguistic filters that block us from reality as it is. Then it's said we fell more than a few steps downhill, arguing there is no truth since all is socially constructed: my culture says there are gods and whispering winds and yours says there are concealed pleasure-giving beings called endorphins—who's to say? From there, it's another step or two and you're arguing that since the philosopher can't tell us what is real, no one can deny with certainty that the "in-itself" beyond the shadow of our thoughts isn't God. Who am I to tell you that your love of God is unrequited and your hopes for eternal play with your dog Skippy are just delusions? Thus relativism and faith, supposedly opposed when the evangelical rightwing attacks liberal relativism, are bitter twins born of the failures of philosophy to claim the real, midwifed by what we'll see gets called "correlationism."

This is where speculative realists come in, arguing it's time to give the real its due. You'd be excused for hearing a rising score in the background, since their punchy prose often brings to mind the heroic sight of gallant defenders of reason routing the postmodern constructivists and relativistic hordes from the academic citadel. The real will finally be saved from them and if we're lucky we won't see their likes again. Once more this is a simple story, simpler than any speculative realist would ever tell. Like any tale, it gets far more complicated as you bore deep into the details. You will find out about the different characters and hidden rivalries—for example, the object-oriented people versus the process people—and before long, you will realize that perhaps there is much to learn from this movement, even if you just figure out how better to rouse your defenses the next time they are in your midst.

There is also something to the fact that the speculative realist writers and their interpreters all come from the generation that arose after the peak (or nadir) of post-structuralism and various forms of discourse studies, and some of the invective of writers in speculative realism would be familiar to those who've read the dismissal by the post-structuralists of Jean-Paul Sartre and the existentialists. Many generations of philosophers suffer from an anxiety of influence, and the speculative realists are no different. But, of course, this is not to suggest that there are not true philosophical differences and important philosophical critiques; this book would be a waste of your time if this were the case. Instead, we set out to sharpen these differences. But just as a first meeting can shape very much the relationship to come, we recognize that this volume—perhaps to the chagrin of those writers we cover—will have its own place in how people come to think about speculative realism. We will wed together under this heading—whether it will be happy nuptials is anyone's guess—disparate thinkers questioning "correlationism," including thinkers not among the four at the original conference in 2007. If Graham Harman is right in the only agreement among the original four speculative realists was a critique of correlationism, years later we find this a common thread linking different thinkers in the second decade of this century and see no reason to exclude important philosophers such as Elizabeth Grosz, Jane Bennett, and Catherine Malabou.

But as your narrator, I must confess to what my friends already know: I can't chronicle anything without commenting as I go along. A simple story about how I enjoyed a book I bought turns into a tirade against the new age books blotting the philosophy section in Barnes and Noble. A flight home for Christmas makes a stopover in a soliloquy about the national security state and the implicit racism of passport lines. (I do have more pleasant commentaries, too.) Thus with the thinkers I present here, I offer my own views about their problems and the prospects, as the subtitle of this book says, but all to introduce better their claims as well as potential connections with other authors not normally listed alongside them. However, whatever my analysis, there's an undeniable point here: I wouldn't write at such length—I couldn't spend so much mental time with—authors I don't greatly respect and with whom I feel the need to think through problems of the utmost philosophical import, and I think by the end of each section, you'll agree. In Chapter 1, I begin with the problem of correlationism, following closely behind as Quentin Meillassoux chases down the post-Kantian era of philosophy that he believes had taken the wrong path. As characterized by Meillassoux, correlationism is a straightforward view: there is no thinking of reality without *thinking* of it. Thus the job of philosophers is to map out the myriad ways in which thought and being are always correlated, while neglecting reality as it is, like fantasy sports players who spend endless time setting up their league, memorizing the stats of virtual players, and so on, but who can't tell you the result of the real championship game. As the philosopher Lee Braver puts it well, "[W]hat does it profit a philosopher if he gains knowledge but loses the whole world? In the course of the last two centuries of philosophy, these thinkers believe, we have indeed lost the world, and it is a world most badly lost."[2]

Meillassoux describes different kinds of correlationism—like coffee, they come in strong and weak varieties—and we will learn to distinguish them, as well as several different forms of idealism. We will also find out the link between the critique of correlationism and "speculative realism." Speculation has a specific meaning deriving from the work of Kant, whose task in his *Critique of Pure Reason* (1781) was to describe the conditions of possibility for our knowledge of the world. There is, for him, the world as it is "in-itself" (*an sich*), which he calls the "noumenal," and the world as it appears to us, the "phenomenal." For Kant, speculation occurs when we attempt to think the world as it is beyond what appears to us. Thus speculative realism—here they agree—argues that we can know there is a reality and that we can speculate about it.

This brings us to Meillassoux's critique of correlationism, which is based on what he calls his "ancestral argument," described in Chapter 2. We'll wait to define it until then, but little noticed is that a similar line of reasoning was pursued several years before Meillassoux by the Anglo-American philosopher John Nolt, and the comparisons between them will show how Meillassoux differs much from other arguments for realism. This will also allow us to keep touch with debates over realism and anti-realism that were prominent in Anglo-American or analytic philosophy in the 1970s and 1980s. But a critique of correlationism doesn't get us to the real on its own. In published writings from his dissertation until recently, Meillassoux has offered one of the boldest arguments in Continental philosophy in some years. For Meillassoux, what is ultimately real is pure chaos. We'll show how he gets there, but the real audacity is in Chapter 3, when he charts the path that follows from pure chaos to the promised land. For Meillassoux, everything is possible from moment to moment. This means there is no necessary being, no God, since God, perfect as it is, would be fixed and thus not up for changing moment to moment, or ever. But if everything is possible, then we can't rule out that God won't come to be and raise the dead and provide for justice in the world—this would be a God demonstrably not around us today. For Meillassoux this fact not only gives us hope—he is not another Frenchman dissolute over the absurdity of existence—but makes claims on us for how to act before God may get here.

But if what is real is chaos, then what of the aspirin bottles, lamps, coffee cups, and other objects around us? Are they not real? This is Graham Harman's criticism of Meillassoux, that he leaves out the very stuff of our world. Harman's work has been a powerful voice for not neglecting the world of things, a voice that is now heard in many different fields. For Harman, all that is real are objects, but with a twist. Unlike readers who have set up Harman in terms of philosophers such as Martin Heidegger, I think his genuine model is Emmanuel Levinas. It's true that Levinas is less known for his ontology than his ethics, since he argues that the self is always already a hostage of and responsible for the Other. This last term is used to point out the singularity of those who come before us. Harman modifies this structure of a relation to Otherness. In an intricate approach, he attempts to show that only an aspect of objects appears to us, just like the one I love only approaches me through the delicacy of her face, her bountiful depths forever hidden from me, yet always drawing me closer. This will eventually give him a four-fold model of objects, and we will also see how other object-oriented ontologists—the name goes back more than a decade, but Harman started using this label for his version of speculative realism in 2009—take off from this claim.

But in Harman's accounts of objects, a certain thought that had been niggling at me when writing about Meillassoux became more apparent. Meillassoux could not do his work, as we'll see, without the mathematics of set theory. I began to wonder if we weren't returning to Platonism, the view that what is ultimately real is outside of time. I won't lead you into this thicket now, but there would be no Continental philosophy in the twentieth century without endless attempts at shedding Platonism. But Harman argues that objects as they are in themselves are not in time, since time is embedded in appearances, which seems to repeat Plato's account. We will ask if this is a major problem with his work.

Against this specter of Platonism, we will have on hand those who think objects are produced by ongoing processes of becoming. These realists, Iain Hamilton Grant, Jane Bennett, and Elizabeth Grosz, also work through how the human, not just objects, is a product of natural forces. Each is a critic of social constructivism and argues for a realist naturalism to overcome the years of not-so-benign neglect of nature by Continental philosophy. This has the effect of an important reversal in political thinking. Previously, it was viewed that political differences hid under the alibi of being natural—class and social differences, such as between women and men, are thus said to be part of the order of things—but these thinkers argue the defeat of these faux naturalisms should be done with a better naturalism, not a retreat from the real through analyses of social discourses. Both Bennett and Grosz argue along similar lines against correlationism. Bennett posits humans as embedded in assemblages working in and around them and Grosz argues for what she calls a "chaotic real." That they also have a political thinking to match their realism is important, too, which gives us a chance to discuss why naturalisms were critiqued in Continental philosophy in the first place. After all, wasn't the whole problem of racism and sexism the fact that people describe as natural the products of racist and patriarchal cultures? Why go back to that? This is the first question asked by many political thinkers when reading the speculative realists and a problem that these three thinkers continue to engage. But also importantly, we will need to see how this view of nature is different from the one commonly depicted in the modern period. For Grant, in particular, this means seeing a certain idea of nature available in such figures as Schelling and Plato.

The problem is not just a supposed avoidance of nature. As we'll see, some speculative realists are also arguing we have disregarded new studies of the brain, which is not only important to many Anglo-American philosophers, but has also changed how many think about themselves in everyday life. We will have three chapters on those tangling with these neuroscientific insights. First up is Ray Brassier, who argues that we must discard previous views of the self in favor of neurology-based descriptions while keeping the rationality of the subject. Brassier discusses this in terms of his nihilist position that there is no meaning to nature: God is dead, good riddance, and now let's cast overboard the soul, spirit, and mind, too. But just because existence is meaningless does not imply that there is no truth, a point justifying his "transcendental nihilism." Brassier is still building his sophisticated structure of thought, under the influence of the Anglo-American philosopher Wilfrid Sellars, but I suggest part of his task is to think another "death of man" long after the funeral orations of structuralism in the 1960s, since in his work we begin to see a glimmer of something beyond the folk psychologies that gave us "man" in the first place. This does not mean silencing the voice of reason in all of us; Brassier may be a nihilist but for him philosophy is not for nothing.

Adrian Johnston's work moves in a similar direction as Brassier towards a Continental naturalism, but he cautions us to apply the brakes before sending the subject off the cliff. History and nature make subjects, he argues, but it's not the case that subjects make nothing. His political theory, focusing on how events can come about even in the most moribund systems, makes this clear. Catherine Malabou, the focus of our last chapter, agrees with Brassier in unexpected ways, describing recent neuroscientific work as the final deconstruction of the human. But she also argues one can develop an ontology and even a politics out of the models of brain plasticity. What she dubs the "deconstructed real" is nothing but plasticity itself. Like the brain depicted in popular accounts in recent years, as a network with different centers throughout the cranium, she calls for a politics of networked communities without center, molding and unmolding themselves.

But let's begin to wrap up these summaries—the most tedious parts of any introduction. A red thread runs through this book, whether it's Meillassoux's "time without becoming," or Harman's objects forever in the present, or Malabou serving notice, citing the neurophilosopher Thomas Metzinger, that without a first-person point of view, there would be no temporality. In the final chapter, I want to play off a thought experiment that Harman has used on occasion before turning to time. Often enough, books like this end by opening onto future avenues for research. In the final chapter, we shift this approach slightly by asking what would happen if speculative realism becomes the dominant force alongside philosophies influenced by Gilles Deleuze in post-Continental philosophy. Since this is a movement still growing, this obviously will seem a bit hasty, like thinking of names for your grandkids on a first date. But this will allow us to emphasize the scope of speculative realism, as well as its problems and prospects.

My hunch is this: speculative realism may stand the test of time, but only if it takes the reality of time as a test to pass. The reader no doubt thinks me a fool: who would deny the reality of time? Time passes, we all die, and the sun goes round—such is the stuff of life. Yet, from the point of physics, the differences between past, present, and future are insubstantial, and a number of neuroscientists argue that time is but a mirage invented by the brain for some sort of evolutionary adaption—better to avoid prey and fuck before dying and so on. Anglo-American philosophy, too, has had a strong current of anti-realisms about time. And philosophy as such began with Plato declaring the temporal order to be the lowest form of being; the task of philosophy was not to look to the reality of time, but to shift upward, to move from the temporal world to the eternal reality of the forms. My view is that those critiqued by the speculative realists, such as Martin Heidegger, Jacques Derrida, and several others, were not "correlationists," but were after a realism of time—Being *as* time, as Heidegger put it, a claim that made his project and the later deconstruction possible. It may look like a rear-guard action, an attempt to go back in time and deny the correlationism we know to be true. I will quickly show why this is not the case, why a temporal realism is an implacable safeguard—not that anything is safe from time—against anti-realisms that do not speak their name. You need not worry I will detain you long with this—time marches on after all—but I will also show why scientific naturalisms, which seem the surest route to the real and true in these fast times, fail in just this regard. After all, is not the fact of the future, denied as real *now* in so much writing on time, the ultimate non-correlation—not *experienced* and therefore not able to be correlated to a thinking subject, but nevertheless real?

You may worry—good grief, what new movement is *he* trying to push? But the chapter itself is but a conclusion, a sort of *petit four* before sending you on your way. In any case, it's about time for a temporalism of philosophy, even if it's to be temporary, as all things ultimately are. But philosophy is not just about point scoring, about the recriminations and back-and-forth among philosophers. It's about what is *real*. Thus we have also written this book for those less interested in this or that school of contemporary philosophy than in joining an exciting conversation about where philosophy is heading, all while, as the kids used to say, keeping it real.

**

As a relatively new movement with authors working from so many influences—there's almost no match in the bibliography from my last book—I could not have written this book without the gracious people answering late-night emails and meticulously going over drafts and offering comments. First, let me thank the Humanities Centre at Australia National University in Canberra for offering me the space and time as a research fellow to write much of this book. The leadership of Debjani Ganguly makes it an exciting place to be and I presented parts of this work to researchers and students there. I especially want to thank ANU's Thomas Ford, who was something of an SR counselor—allowing me to bounce ideas off him as I no doubt began sounding mad, talking about future gods, hidden objects, and all. Thanks also to Vincent Bruyer and Karen Pinkus, who were great discussants at that time. I thank my hosts at the University of New South Wales, University of South Pacific, La Trobe University, and the University of Tasmania for memorable experiences and feedback on talks where I presented some of these ideas. I also thank my colleagues at Memorial University, who are available seemingly at any time if I have questions about their specialties; it's one of those rare places where philosophy is *done* and is a way of life, out there on the edge of the sea. I thank Memorial's Michael Austin, who was the impetus for reviving a project I had first thought about a couple of years ago, but had put aside. Michael, an editor at *Speculations*, knows the scene well and I enjoyed all of our discussions, many parts of which made their way into this book. I would also like to thank Jack Reynolds, Sean McGrath, Jay Foster, Gil Shalev, Seamus O'Neill, Michael O'Rourke, Graham Harman, Ray Brassier, Martin Hägglund, Devin Shaw, Richard Sebold, Paul Ennis, Adrian Johnston, Marie-Eve Morin, Daniel Sacilotto, Pete Wolfendale, and finally, Robin James, who gave me the subtitle for this book.

CHAPTER 1
CORRELATIONISM AND ITS DISCONTENTS

> This question—which is really the question of speculative realism—is that of knowing whether it's possible to access an absolute that's capable of being thought, not as a relative and cloistered outside, but as a Great Outdoors whose essence is irrelative to the thought of the knower?[1]
>
> Quentin Meillassoux

> [But] what precisely is meant by saying that the world existed beyond any human consciousness? An example of what is meant is that the world originally issued from a primitive nebula from which the combination of conditions necessary to life was absent. But every one of these words, like every equation in physics, presupposes our pre-scientific experience of the world, and this reference to the world in which we live goes to make up the proposition's valid meaning. Nothing will ever bring home to my comprehension what a nebula that no one sees could possibly be.[2]
>
> Maurice Merleau-Ponty

In these two quotations, you see at its most basic level the argument between realists and anti-realists concerning our ability to get to what Meillassoux calls the "Great Outdoors." But part of the back and forth is also just a question of meaning: Merleau-Ponty may simply be giving a version of the answer my son gave me when I asked him the old chestnut, trying to explain this topic, "If a tree falls in a forest and no one is around, does it make a sound?" His considered reply: "If we're not there, who cares?", which truth be known, discouraged my writing for a couple of hours—not least because he thought we should care instead about a zombie movie. Merleau-Ponty thinks that scientists only flatten out what is the reality of lived human experience, while Meillassoux wants to think what is real beyond this experience. In this sense, Meillassoux questions the priority given to the human in phenomenology and thus much of twentieth-century Continental philosophy. I became interested in speculative realism because, writing about critiques of all forms of sovereignty, I wondered about this last privilege of the human: to say that what is outside its view is without meaning. But it's also the case that speculative realism is joined by larger movements in the academy critiquing anthropomorphism and therefore human sovereignty: ecological studies, animal studies, neuroscience, and , let alone critical race theories and feminist accounts that have long questioned the sovereignty of a certain thinking of "man." To understand where speculative realists wish to take us, we must first map out how we got here and where we are. This means getting you up to speed on at least 200 years of philosophical work in just under a chapter. Luckily, this task is made easier by the fact that the speculative realists have judged a whole era of philosophy as "anti-realist" using criteria discussed below. We show, looking at both the Anglo-American and Continental traditions, why the question of the real is not as easy as knocking on a table and saying, "it's here." Meillassoux opens *After Finitude* by arguing that at least since Kant, philosophy has been caught in the problem of "correlationism." Let's begin with his definition:

> Correlationism takes many forms, but particularly those of transcendental philosophy, the varieties of phenomenology, and post-modernism. But although these currents are all extraordinarily varied in themselves, they all share, according to me, a more or less explicit decision: that there are no objects, no events, no laws, no beings which are not always-already correlated with a point of view, with a subjective access. Anyone maintaining the contrary, i.e., that it is possible to attain something like a reality in itself, existing absolutely independently of his viewpoint, or his categories, or his epoch, or his culture, or his language, etc.—this person would be exemplarily naïve.[3]

"Correlationism," Meillassoux argues, "rests on an argument as simple as it is powerful." This "simple" argument is "there can be no X without a givenness of X, and no theory of X without a positing of X."[4] The correlationists, Meillassoux argues, think that the "world is meaningful" only if it is "given-to-a-living (or thinking)-being."[5] If a human has never seen it, heard it, talked about it, and so on, then it's not meaningful. Thus the community of all humans has marked out a line where we cannot go. "Correlationism," he writes, "consists in disqualifying the claim that it is possible to consider the realm of subjectivity and objectivity independently of one another."[6] Realism, for most people, simply means a belief that there is a world independent of our minds or cultural beliefs. This is different from epistemic realism, which posits the belief that we can *know* this independent world, too. We will see both of these uses at work in the speculative realists. Before turning to this term, let's quickly set out the positions we will be highlighting in this chapter:

1. Naïve realism: this is the view that real things exist and that we can have direct access to them, as we do in our "natural attitude" about the world. You never question the existence of the oven while cooking, or this book while reading it. You simply take it for granted that it is there. There is not a thinker we will review in this chapter who, despite the fact that naïve realism seems to be our default common sense way of conceiving the world, does not find this form of realism untenable—hence this realism's depiction as "dogmatic" or "naïve."[7]
2. Weak correlationism: the view that reality exists and we can *think* it, that is, that it exists and that it is non-contradictory, but we cannot *know* about it given the filters through which reality is understood. The speculative realists' chosen representative will be Immanuel Kant.
3. Strong correlationism: there is no thinking about what is outside our own being in the world, as Merleau-Ponty argues in the opening quotation to this chapter. Meillassoux's examples are the phenomenologists such as Merleau-Ponty, and we'll discuss Edmund Husserl, Martin Heidegger, as well as the Anglo-American philosopher Michael Dummett.[8] But one could also add social constructivists such as Nelson Goodman and his considerations of culture as "worldmaking," or even Graham Harman's favored sociologist of science Bruno Latour, who said that the Pharaoh Ramses could not have died of tuberculosis, since that was not discovered until 150 years ago.[9] Others, like Ian Hacking, try to split the difference, discussing the human sciences, such as psychiatry, as "making up people" through a "dynamic nominalism"—simply put, social construction—while increasingly he shields the discoveries of physics from this view.[10]
4. Absolute or speculative idealism: Hegel is Meillassoux's example here, where there is a necessary relation between being and thinking, since for Hegel, the dialectic or relation between thinking and being *is* the absolute—the "and" here is what is ultimately real. This idealism is "speculative" in that it advances into thinking reality as it

> is: the correlation is taken as the absolute in-itself.[11] It is against this "infinite" dialectical movement of the absolute that the modesty of the strong correlationist appears valuable. Rather than positing, as Meillassoux describes it, an infinite and necessary being, the strong correlationist rejects metaphysics, defined by Meillassoux as any positing of a necessary being, and stresses our human finitude as well as our inability to establish assorted grounds for being, whether it be the Hegelian spirit, Leibniz's monad of monads, or the other necessary entities of metaphysics.

We know what "correlation" means in everyday language: putting your hand on a fire is correlated to a decent amount of pain, lax regulations are correlated to pretty bad oil spills, and so on. In fact, this is a standard for scientific knowledge. Are higher incidents of cancer correlated to higher uses of tobacco? We use this kind of inductive reasoning all the time: you didn't need a textbook to know not to touch the stove, or to know the correlation between applying the brakes and having your car stop. The problem is when people mistake correlations for causation. Being a Cubs fan is correlated to sitting at home in October watching other teams play the World Series, but you know that your being a fan hasn't caused their repeated postseason failures—though it surely hasn't helped. Meillassoux will thus argue that for too long we have never given the real or "absolute" its due. It is generally argued that to count as real something must be independent of human thought processes, language, or culture. (We could take up the fact that, of course, this leaves aside the "reality" of cultures, languages, and human thought processes, but let's take this up later.) For Meillassoux, we've had two dominant relations to reality: "correlationism" and "idealism." This is not to say that the philosophers he critiques don't take the "correlation" or ideas *to be real*, a point that Meillassoux will take to be the center of his own move from correlationism. Correlationists argue rather that reality and human beings go together like conjoined twins: where you find one, you find the other. On the face of it, this view seems absurd: obviously you don't think the room around you disappears when you leave it. But the correlationist, according to Meillassoux, simply rules out of bounds any discussion of "reality" *as it is* outside of human access. For this reason, Graham Harman calls correlationism the "philosophy of access." And, as suggested above, a naive idealist goes one step further than the correlationist: to be is to be perceived, and thus what we perceive has existence *because* of this perception. Thus what is real is but a projection of ideas we as humans hold. However

Plato, no one's idea of naive, was famously an idealist because he held that the "Forms" were the most real.[12] George Berkeley in the eighteenth century argued that the material world around us was a simple projection and no amount of intellectual proof could give us any evidence of it, since that would mean that we're thinking about it. Here's Berkeley's argument, which, Meillassoux suggests, has remained stubbornly with us:

> [S]urely there is nothing easier than for me to imagine trees, for instance, in a park, or books existing in a closet, and nobody by to perceive them. I answer, you may so, there is no difficulty in it; but what is all this, I beseech you, more than framing in *your* mind certain ideas which you call books and trees, and at the same time omitting to frame the idea of any one that may perceive them? But do not you yourself perceive or think of them all the while? . . . When we do our utmost to conceive the existence of external bodies, we are all the while only contemplating our own ideas. But the mind, *taking no notice of itself*, is deluded to think it can and does conceive bodies existing unthought of or without the mind, though at the same time they are apprehended by or exist in itself.[13]

In sum, we have the tiresome conundrum: if there is something outside of thought, how do you know without thinking of it?

In this chapter, we'll move through the categories Meillassoux uses in *After Finitude* to discuss correlationism: weak and strong correlationism as well as speculative idealism. We're not asking the reader to agree with Meillassoux on each point. Rather, the task is to see how he sets up his own arguments for thinking "after finitude." We will look at the strength of the correlationist positions as well as their prominent representatives, and at the end of this chapter deal with Meillassoux's path out of what he calls the correlational "*aporia*."

Weak correlationism and the case against naïve realism

Let's begin with the weak form of correlationism, which is fairly intuitive: you are reading this book and have certain thoughts about it. You now look around you and see a world that you take to be quite different from the way other beings do. As a human being, you take it for granted that others don't perceive the world completely differently: we can disagree over different perceptions we have, but generally we think that we're all seeing the "same" world. But, for you to describe this world, it first has to be "given" to you. Hence, while you take it to be the case that the world has reality, you also recognize that there are things that have to be "given" to you for you to have knowledge of them, that is, all you can know about the world comes through how that world is given to you. To have any knowledge of the French Revolution, you must first have read a book about it, and one presumes one can't speak to the reality of some proposed history of an alien race without that being "given" to you in some similar way. The weak correlationist argues that while all of one's knowledge must come out of one's relationship with and access to the world, one can still think about the fact that there is a world beyond subjective perceptions.

Immanuel Kant is the paradigmatic case here, though we will also turn to the Anglo-American philosopher Michael Dummett below. Kant's three *Critiques* in the 1780s were to re-establish certainty about knowledge after David Hume's skeptical arguments earlier in the century. What Kant wanted to understand is how *a priori* knowledge of the world is possible, given that Hume had argued that cause and effect as we experience it only comes to us as a form of probability: it's highly likely the sun will rise tomorrow, but not a metaphysical certainty. Past performance, as business people say when they get you a deal that works only for them, does not determine future results. Kant's theoretical counter-move would have to be confronted by every philosopher writing after him. Rather than simply collecting more empirical data, Kant argued that certainty was based on the shared sensible "form" of experience. In other words, as he argued in the "Transcendental Aesthetic" sections of the *Critique of Pure Reason*, as human beings we cannot *not* perceive the world except in terms of time (even our dreams have a before and after) and space (the gremlins of your nightmares do move around a bit). Thus while we are right to be skeptical that *what* we perceive is actually there, as when you see a mirage, *how* you perceive the world does provide you a measure of certainty. This is why Meillassoux also calls this "weak correlationism" a "transcendental one," since for Kant, "there are some universal forms of the subjective knowledge of things"[14] that transcend and make such experiences possible.

Kant was not simply looking to answer Hume's skepticism, but also those, like John Locke, that he deemed "dogmatic realists." Locke, following Descartes, understood that things had what he calls "primary" and "secondary" qualities, a distinction Meillassoux resuscitates. The primary qualities of a thing are those parts of a substance that comprise its independent reality. What Hume argued against Locke and the "dogmatic realists" was that they could never jump over thought to that supposedly independent reality. Primary qualities are those things you take to be "objective": size, shape, time, and so on. Secondary qualities would be those produced through experience. In fact, for centuries, philosophers debated what categories fall on either side of the line between primary and secondary qualities. The size of this book in terms of width and height would seem to be a "primary" quality, but what about its color? We can agree that its softness is something you perceive, but a color is part of our "subjective" experience (is this page off-white? Egg white? Sea foam white?) while there is also a mind-independent frequency of waves that are described in terms of the color function. In other words, is "color" dependent or independent of your perception, a primary or secondary quality? Kant's argument is that both primary qualities *and* secondary qualities are developed in cognition, and thus we can't ever say what they are independent of human knowledge. Meillassoux revives the primary and secondary qualities in order to have us retrace our steps back to the path not taken because of Kant's transcendental idealism. We'll see that, for Meillassoux, mathematics provides us with the "primary qualities" of the absolute or real.

This brings us to the Kantian distinction between the phenomenal and the noumenal, briefly touched on in the introduction. For Kant phenomena are things as they appear to us, not as they are "in-themselves." Kant argues that from the basic concepts of the understanding, time and space, we can have quite a bit of knowledge "*a priori*" to any empirical experience. Based upon the concept of space, for example, reason is able to develop, without having ever "seen" anything in the empirical world, geometry, mathematics, and a whole slew of other categories. Based on the category of time, a whole other set of concepts spring forth, including cause and effect. For Kant, what provides certainty is not perception, but these categories as they are applied to perception. Thus, they are the "conditions of possibility of experience," and what philosophy always deals with are not the things-in-themselves, but their representations. Kant writes, before him, "it has been assumed that all our cognition must conform to objects."[15] Kant reverses this formula: things-in-themselves are presented to us and conform to our manner of experience. In this way, cognition is a correlation of empirical sensation and the concepts of the understanding. "What we call external objects," he writes, "are nothing but mere presentations of sensibility" and "its true *correlate*, i.e., the thing in itself (*Ding an sich*), is not cognized at all through these presentations and cannot be."[16] This is Kant's "Copernican Revolution": to argue not, as had been previously the case, that the task of philosophy is to *conform itself* to exacting descriptions or representations of reality (however different these would be for different philosophers), but to bracket out the reality of things *as they are* as unknowable.[17] "All we know," he writes, "is the way in which we perceive" objects in themselves.[18] This is not to say that Kant isn't a realist about these forms of cognition: they are an undeniable fact, since, without the subject, there would be no experience as such.

But Kant is not an idealist in the traditional sense. He is not denying that things in themselves *exist*, though we only access the phenomenal realm. "Appearances are not things in themselves,"[19] but there is some unidentifiable *X* that in fact is presented to us, and for this reason our sensibility is "passive." In the same way that you could rationally deduce, indirectly, that there are more color wavelengths than you can see with your eyes, perhaps by noting how animals are able to see objects that are dark for you, so too Kant argues that we know there is an in-itself, but we are limited in the way the thing-in-itself is filtered by the concepts of our understanding. In sum, we can think it, but not know the in-itself. Berkeley was a "dogmatic idealist" who argued that any external world was "impossible," and hence the thing in itself was a mere illusion.[20] For Kant, it's not that it merely "appears" that things are outside of us, but that they do exist externally.[21] In this way, like someone embarrassed by intolerable relatives, Kant works to distance himself at all costs from his "idealist" predecessors.[22] Moreover, for Kant, "even our inner experience," our inner thoughts, "is possible only on the assumption of outer experience."[23] Later in the *Critique*, Kant also argued that not only are there independent things in themselves, but that we can deduce one further fact: these entities are "non-contradictory"; they can't both exist and not exist at the same time.

The upshot of "weak correlationism" is that knowledge of reality is a correlation of subject and the objects of its experience. "[S]ince Hume and Kant," Meillassoux argues, "the philosopher regards the notion of the knowledge of things-in-themselves—that is to say, knowledge of things thought to exist as absolute, independent, and not relative to the subject—as a kind of dogmatic realism (a 'moth-eaten realism,' as Kant put it)."[24] These philosophers accordingly prohibit any knowledge of the in-itself, since the categories of the understanding cannot be applied beyond intuition in transcendental philosophy. However, we can *think* the noumenal in that we can know *a priori* that the in-itself not only exists but is also non-contradictory. Now, for an extra step, which we mention because it's crucial to Meillassoux, as we'll see in a bit, the reality of the correlation itself is contingent or not necessary.

Let us turn to what Kant and his heirs mean by finitude, given its importance in the next chapter and the title of Meillassoux's *After Finitude*. The term is used in a variety of ways, and Meillassoux's *After Finitude* takes on several meanings. For Kant, epistemological finitude is reflective of the limits of human knowledge: there's only so much we can know and attempts to project what we experience onto the "in-itself" oversteps the bounds of reason. A similar "limit" has been suggested in Anglo-American or analytic philosophy from its development in Gottlob Frege to the work of Michael Dummett and Hilary Putnam in the 1970s. Both in Continental and Anglo-American philosophy, there appeared a "linguistic turn," as termed by Richard Rorty, a change in emphasis to the linguistic or logical systems in which knowledge claims are made. (In recent years it's notable that both traditions are turning against taking philosophy of language as first philosophy.) These philosophers differ over just about what to make of this, but the everyday practice of using words to refer to the things of the world means that language mediates our experience of the world. Though this "linguistic" correlationism is different in many ways from Kantianism, it similarly begins with our representations and how they are produced—and argues, for Meillassoux, that this production blocks access to the real as such. This is not to say that certain Anglo-American philosophers deny reality, but that the philosophy of language trumps ontology and metaphysics as some philosophers' starting point. Just as Kant argued we must first deal with the problem of knowledge before we discuss "what is," many philosophers during the linguistic turn argue that we must deal with the problem of how ideas are represented in language before turning to what is represented. In Continental philosophy, this has meant, more often than not, taking up the cultural systems and structures in which language is produced historically, while for Anglo-American philosophers, the point has been to produce coherent "conceptual schemes" that would be universal (seen as valid by anyone who reasons through them) and not intrinsic to given cultures.

For this reason, Anglo-American philosophers have critiqued their French and German counterparts for a supposed "social constructivism." Basically, to be a social constructivist would mean that one thinks all "reality" is produced by cultural systems or forms of power. But for most of us, the question isn't whether or not the social matters, but, in these and many other questions, just *how much*. The "conceptual schemes" of Anglo-American philosophy, though, are different in that they are to be coherent and the philosophers' task is to rend these schemes dry of any "folk philosophy" or cultural beliefs. We will return to something like this view in Ray Brassier's work, where the task is to use science to put us in touch with reality, while still holding onto the rational coherence of concepts.

As noted, for these correlationists, before we can ever take up "what is" we must first answer the question of how we can be said to "refer" to something in the first place. We use language to refer to things: we use car signals to refer to the fact that we plan to turn, and we use the word "dog" to refer to an actual dog. We also engage in language with "sense": we might not be referring to Skippy, but use the word "dog" to talk about dogs in general, as in "I prefer dogs to cats." This sounds rather uncomplicated, but philosophers such as W. V. O. Quine spent a lot of time (rightly) noting just how difficult this idea of "reference" is: Quine argues that in order to make any "reference" we must know the language we are using quite well. We tend to think reference is the simplest thing in language and Quine is convincing that in fact it might well be the most complicated aspect of language; the last step you can make in a language is knowing that the general word "dog" refers to some entity right in front of you. Why is this important? Well, if we are engaged in realism, one might say that we are just using language to "refer" to what is "obviously" right there in front of us.

One of the most formidable "anti-realists" in Anglo-American philosophy in recent decades had been Michael Dummett, who argues that the difference between realism and anti-realism is really a question of language, in other words, how we speak—a neat way to import that whole problem into the investigation of conceptual schemes. Where Kant and previous philosophers had dealt with the problem that by thinking about reality, you are, well, *thinking* about it, Dummett derives the linguistic variant of this: to speak of anything is to be caught up in language. Thus, if I am saying that independent of any mind, there is a set of entities freely existing, I am saying that my discussion of it "correlates" to a state of affairs independent of language. Let's say you've been convinced already that realism is an important philosophical problem and you head to the philosophy section in your local bookstore or library (or more likely, through a Google search) to check out the topic, you'll soon find out that there are all sorts of realists in Anglo-American philosophy (the word, until recently, all but disappeared in so-called Continental philosophy—thus providing the fallow ground in which "speculative realism" took root): moral realists, psychological realists, mathematical realists, and so forth. Even "materialists" are really "matter" realists and Dummett's work, though often unwelcoming to the novice reader (indeed, even to the expert one), makes the important point that each of these realists are producers of statements, and what concerns us is whether these sentences are "verification transcendent." That is, Dummett argues that a statement only has a given truth value or meaning if it can be said to be true or false, which requires that we use some constructive procedure for telling the difference. He argues that most philosophers tend to be realists about certain entities and anti-realists about others, though Dummett himself aimed at a totalizing anti-realism. Dummett's work is, incidentally, not just instructive for those thinking about the link between language and reality; he is also incisive for a way to read (at least in a preliminary way) philosophical differences. A typical philosophical move is not to claim that your opponent is "wrong" or just a clumsy thinker—though that might be. Rather, philosophers in conversation through books and at conferences (should) practice the "principle of charity." You don't presume your opponent is just some naïve simpleton—not out loud anyway—but instead try to think through the premises that set their work in motion. At some level, this usually means that they are taking the reality of certain entities for granted. To take a classic example, Karl Marx is a moral "anti-realist." Moral realists have very different accounts, but, as the name suggests, they take what is morally right or wrong to be something real whatever we humans think about it: morality is something independent of human existence. But Marx argued, influentially, that what we consider to be moral is a result of class structures. Accordingly, what is real is the dialectics of class struggle, which is for Marx the motor of history. Capitalist morality is but a fool's game: don't steal (a great principle to teach the masses if you have property), be humble (great for getting those masses to bow to the needs of the upper classes), and so on until we all think freedom is the freedom to buy and equality means equality of "opportunity," not material equality. Those critiquing Marx, in turn, argue that he is being "reductive," that he takes very different human phenomena, such as morality, and reduces them to economic history. In the philosophy of mind, there's a similar argument. "Eliminative materialists" argue that our "folk" ways of discussing the mind is a mistaken theory of what is real, and a more adequate one would be linked to the material processes of the brain. Thus propositional attitudes, your depression, how you are happy, your problems with your mother, and so on, are derivable from a set of neural processes. And of course, this in turn gets them labeled as being "reductive" in the everyday sense of the term.[25] Don't they understand that hope, fears, evil, and so on, are not just brain synapses firing off?[26]

But, Dummett argues, all of these arguments still take place at the level of differing inferential systems, series of statements tied together by logic. Realism, he argues, isn't about existing entities, but is rather a statement about other sets of statements: my economism trumps your moralism, and so on. As he puts it, "realism is a *semantic* thesis."[27] The major claim of his work is about the nature of truth, namely that realists hold that truth is "evidence-transcendent." I could produce a whole realism of unicorns, for example, which is a set of statements set to prove that the ultimate reality is made up of magical horned beings that subtend everything. But Dummett notes that *this* set of statements would be the same whether or not unicorns were real. If you are a materialist or unicorn-ist—surely one can be found on Google—what you are saying is all this about unicorns *and* one more thing: there are unicorns *and* they exist in reality. And what you say about their existence can be "true or false," which is what Dummett means by "bivalence." "The primary tenet of realism, as applied to some given class of statements," he writes, "is that each statement in the class is determined as true or not true, independently of our knowledge, by some objective reality whose existence and constitution is, again, independent of our knowledge."[28] To take an example, an "eliminative materialist" who hears a Freudian provide a set of statements about the superego, ego, and Id will concern herself less with the coherence of this conceptual scheme than with the fact that, for her, it doesn't "correlate" to reality. "Reductivists," for Dummett, are in essence arguing not that some set of statements is true or false, but rather that one set of statements, say unicornism, is better explained if you "reduce" it to another set of statements, those about fantasy animals. Without using the term, Dummett accepts that, in the end, all realism is ultimately a "correlationism," where there is a relation between a knower and the objects of knowledge. To think seriously about any state of affairs, you work on how it is logically coherent within a given set of statements.

Kant and Dummett hence share a critique of "dogmatic" realism: the belief that we can just simply point to beings in the world and access their reality. Kant argues that we must work out the conditions of possibility of knowledge, the concepts of the understanding, while for Dummett we must work out the coherence of our statements about the real in the first place. In the end, Kant says that all we can know about the in-itself (*an sich*) is that (a) it is not available to us through experience, (b) that it exists, and (c) that it is non-contradictory, that is, the in-itself is amenable to the principle of bivalence: what is true of it cannot also be false at the same time. For Dummett, there are all kinds of realists, who in turn are often "anti-realist" about other objects. For him, it is the philosophy of language (how concepts are made and how we put these concepts in relation) that trumps Kantian epistemology. This is why Dummett argues that realism is unnecessary for a theory of what is true or false, since we simply don't "need to invoke the notion of reference" in order to say whether it is true or false. In other words, he is arguing that in philosophy, we can work out concepts that should be non-contradictory and at the end of the day we can say whether they are true or false without having to worry about whether these concepts are "correlated" or "referring to" an independent existence. This is where one could argue that anti-realism falls into relativism, since if one's system is not anchored in an independent reality, then one can produce perhaps endless consistent systems, all equally "true." John McDowell wryly calls this "a frictionless spinning in the void."[29] Dummett for his part writes, "the naive realist's notion of immediate awareness, consisting in direct contact between the knowing subject and the object of his knowledge, is probably in all cases incoherent: it is certainly difficult to formulate it intelligibly."[30] Each philosophy, in a sense, has its own "first" principle that it must take for granted for its arguments to get underway: that matter or the mind or some such exists. And the major method of arguing in philosophy for centuries, not incidentally, was not a positive move to prove your first principles, but rather to show that your opponent—for a millenia, the atheist—had premises that led to all sorts of conclusions that seemed undeniably "false" (this is the *reductio ad absurdum*).

In any case, the non-naïve realist, for Dummett, is Kantian: she knows that we must have mediated access to the real and that what we can say about the in-itself independent of this "access" is that it is non-contradictory. Dummett says that a realism should be able to work out better how we can "access" the real, but he claims that there is simply no way to have knowledge of things as they are, and thus he is an "anti-realist" because he argues that even the realist is engaged in a logical argument. Here, he takes up the example of a naïve realist who believes memories give us direct sensations of past events:

> The naïve realist faces a twofold difficulty. He has, first, a problem to explain how we ever come to make a mistake in making a judgment on the favored basis: if memory is a direct contact with past events, how can a mistake of memory occur? Secondly, [s]he has a problem

> about the connection between our mode of coming to know the truth of a statement and the consequences we take it to have: if memory is a direct contact with a past event, which must, therefore, still exist in some manner if I am to be able now to apprehend it, how can I know that the event has not changed somewhat since it originally occurred?[31]

As Hilary Putnam puts it in a similar vein, "What is wrong with the notion of objects existing 'independently' of conceptual schemes is that there are no standards for the use of even the logical notions apart from conceptual choices."[32] Philosophy, therefore, progresses for them, not through a gamesmanship over who points better to some set of external objects, but through those adhering to logical laws *within* conceptual schemes. There is, indeed, an "external" reality to which our knowledge, for Kant, or our conceptual schemes, for Dummett, are *responding*. But we need to leave behind the dogmatists whose only argument is a non-argument ("but . . . but . . . *this* is real") and claim universal knowledge where we can. Anything else, for him, is hubris or illusion, or both.[33]

Strong correlationism: Husserl, Merleau-Ponty, and Heidegger

While "weak correlationism" argues that we can know only what is phenomenal or in language, while the "in-itself" is thinkable, strong correlationists posit, according to Meillassoux, that thought and world are like the married couple that you just couldn't imagine being apart, such they've even started looking alike. Meillassoux defines this "correlation" as the "idea according to which we only ever have access to the correlation between thinking and being, and never to either term considered apart from the other."[34] Strong correlationism doesn't just deny that we know some "in-itself" independent of us, but that, simply, there is no "in-itself" independent of us. The idealist, on Meillassoux's account, is different in reducing everything to some set of concepts. The correlationists think, Meillassoux's argues, that there is some X out there, but it's always "for us," as he puts it. As Meillassoux describes it, they argue that we are so trapped on this side of the correlation that cannot even think the *noumenal*. All we ever have is the pure givenness of the phenomenal, or, for supposed social constructivists, linguistic or cultural structures. Ultimately, he argues, the "weak" correlationists, given that they can never speak to the in-itself, are no better than the "strong correlationists." This is the "catastrophe," as he puts it, left in Kant's wake. The in-itself is left to magical thinkers and their fantasies of a great puppeteer beneath the phenomenal marionettes of appearances. We will see how the object-oriented ontologists, while arguing for a sustained realism, also agree that objects in themselves are forever concealed from sense experience.

Meillassoux's category of the "strong" correlationism is targeted at phenomenology and its post-structural heirs. Phenomenology is a type of philosophy inaugurated by Edmund Husserl in his *Logical Investigations* (1900–01). He called for a return "to the things themselves" and thus would seem a proponent of realism. But Husserl argued that we were to study "phenomena," that is, how reality appeared "for us." He wanted to make phenomenology an exact science, and for him this meant "bracketing" out the reality of things in studying them, which seems a strange move. But if you want to know what a number is, or what is the essence of this book in front of you, he argued that you need to first set aside the "natural" attitude in which you are reading the book, are turning its pages, and are simply at sea in the world. You need to take it out of that space in order to think about it with the mind's eye, and in this way, the "reality" of this book is no different than figuring out the meaning of any other idea. From there, Husserl argued for a further bracketing that would allow us to turn to the form of "intentionality" itself. Consciousness is always "consciousness of something," he argued, and this "of" is really a correlation of consciousness with some object. The basic fact of existence, for Husserl, is intentionality, and he provided many incisive analyses of the "pure Ego" that is involved in this relating to objects, which included, for Husserl, ideas in the mind's eye. Studying phenomena, therefore, means setting aside any external or independent reality, since that is not what is available to internal consciousness. Meillassoux's diagnosis of strong correlationism is based on the symptom that Husserl denies *any* reality independent of our correlation with the world as it is given. Even his later development of the notion of the "life-world" defines the world as what can be thought by the collection of those who have intentionality, though paradoxically, it seems, this lifeworld is what *precedes* any given act of intentionality, as Husserl notes in the *Crisis*. If it is not "for us," then it simply does not exist, at least on Meillassoux's account.

The problem is perhaps more clear in the work of Maurice Merleau-Ponty. His phenomenology is best known for attempting to undo mind-body dualism, and thus the primary apparatus of correlationism after Descartes. Hence, he would seem a hero to realists, since he returns us from the supposed idealisms of the mind to thinking about how our material body is the site of human experience. For this reason, he was critical of certain Husserlian insights, but on the key test of realism, his work could be found wanting. Readers of Meillassoux often presume that his critique of "correlationism" is but another critique of mind-body dualism, and to the extent that's correct, then Merleau-Ponty would be an ally. After all, doesn't Merleau-Ponty begin *The Visible and Invisible* by arguing, "it is the things themselves, from the depth of their silence," that philosophy "wishes to bring to expression"?[35] But Merleau-Ponty's work demonstrates that one can deflate dualism into a single embodied relation of body-world and still have a rigid correlationism, locking out any reality that is not within the direct circuit of particular bodies (humans) and the world. Merleau-Ponty is just not interested in a radical exteriority to human being and he is dismissive of any attempts to think it. To use an example that is important to my own conclusion to this book, "Time is not a real process, an effective succession that I should limit myself to recording," he argues in *Phenomenology of Perception*. "It is born of *my relation* with things."[36] In short, as Meillassoux puts it, the world is "meaningful only as given to a living (or thinking) being."[37] But what about science and its descriptions? For Merleau-Ponty, science is but a drying out of the "lifeworld (*monde vécu*)" that has its basis in the human perceptual relation, however complicated this becomes in his unfinished last work, *The Visible and the Invisible*. Merleau-Ponty thus critiques the "reflective attitude" that supposes a reality as external to this correlation, which is reductive of our original being-in-the-world. Philosophy is to investigate our fundamental openness of the world, the "conditions of possibility" of it being "for us,"[38] and in this way concern itself with the experience of the world. The world is thus the word for what forms a circle around this place of "contact"; anything but this lived world might as well be dead to us.

Heidegger will be our last example of a strong correlationist, despite the fact that his critique of Husserl's version of phenomenology is in many ways similar to Meillassoux's. For example, Heidegger argued that what Husserl dubbed our "natural attitude" was not some secondary phenomenon, but rather was a description of our being in the world; it was his "theoretical" attitude that should have been seen as secondary. For Heidegger, Husserl is right (in the wrong way) when he states that our first mode of being in the world is not separate from the world or from the objects around us. Our dealings with the world are primarily *not* theoretical (what he dubs "present-to-hand" [*vorhanden*]), but practical (or ready-to-hand [*zuhanden*]): you have read this book for some pages now without needing to work out *what* a book is and what makes it work. You haven't needed to inspect the binding or consider the essence of a book. You've simply been (hopefully) engrossed in the matters at hand. And next to you is perhaps a cup of coffee that you reach for without a second thought and without theorizing about coffee's difference from tea and so on. Even closer, you're sitting in a seat which you haven't even considered until now. In other words, *Dasein*, Heidegger's term for our existence, is engaged in the world of things and not engrossed primarily in theorizing through the correlation. But for Meillassoux, Heidegger argues for an "ontological" correlationism: unlike in Husserl or Kant, what is primary is not *what we know* or *how we know* reality, which is an epistemological correlationism, or, as in Dummett, how we speak of reality, a linguistic or logical correlationism, but rather our *way of being* in the world. This is what Heidegger calls our "care" (*Sorge*) for the things of the world. Heidegger's *Being and Time* (1927) delineates three types of beings: (1) *Dasein*, his word for those beings that can ask about the meaning of their own being; (2) beings that are ready-to-hand, that is, the equipment that is all a complex of handy entities for *Dasein*; and (3) beings that are "present-to-hand," that is, beings that reduce them, as in Husserl, to a set of ideas. Heidegger's famed tool analysis argued that the Husserlian "theoretical" glance is really just about broken tools: only when things break do they come to our theoretical attention. We'll discuss in Chapter 4 how Graham Harman has extended Heidegger's tool analysis to think the reality of the things of the world. But for now, it's enough to note that, despite the fact that Heidegger thought he was undoing every previous "dualism" of the thinker (or linguistic subject) and being, Meillassoux holds him to be a "strong correlationist." His reasoning is that Heidegger denies reality to beings outside the circuit of their relation through *Dasein*. As any reader of Heidegger knows, *Dasein* itself is not some "spatial" point over *here*, but a being out in the world among the things, without a "separation" from the hammer or the car or this book while it is existing. But Meillassoux argues that if "realism" means finding room to describe things *as they are* when they are utterly independent of our being, and if this means not just independent of how we think or produce language about them, then it is also about our "circumspective concern" as Heidegger discusses it. Marie-Eve Morin puts this well:

> For Heidegger Being is only insofar as there is a Dasein that relates meaningfully to entities, and Dasein is only insofar as it displays this essential relation to Being. In a similar way, the world is only insofar as Dasein exists.... Truth also exists only insofar as Dasein is, since the

> uncoveredness of entities that serves as the basis for a true assertion is dependent upon Dasein's understanding of Being, which lets these entities manifest themselves. Hence, as Heidegger will say, Newton's laws were not true before Newton's discovery, but neither were they false. Rather, it is Newton's assertion of the laws of motion that made entities accessible as obeying (and as having always obeyed) these laws.[39]

Partisans of Kant, Husserl, and Dummett could defend them from charges of correlationism, but because of Heidegger's import to many speculative realists besides Meillassoux, we will spend more time on his work. We will also see how a "realist" or even "speculative realist" perspective helps to shift debates over oft-discussed philosophers.

There has been much work to bring Heidegger into contact with the work on realism and anti-realism in such figures as Hilary Putnam, where Heidegger, as often as not, is made into a pragmatist describing our relation to objects as one of engagement and care. Michael Cerbone argues that Heidegger doesn't fit easily into these discussions of realism: "a persistent difficulty in interpreting Heidegger's *Being and Time* has been the question of whether, and to what extent, his position is amenable either to realism or idealism."[40] While some scholars, such as William Blattner, argue that he is a "dogmatic idealist," since his discussion of time always comes back to the discussion of the human,[41] others in the Continental tradition have suggested that after Heidegger realism and anti-realism is a "non-problem." Realism has been traditionally premised on two claims, as we've already discussed: (1) the *independence* of some set of (or all) entities of the human consciousness, cultural constructs, conceptual schemes, structures, and linguistic signs; (2) that these entities exist. We can get more precise in terms of Hilary Putnam's oft-cited definition:

> On the [metaphysical realism] perspective, the world consists of some fixed totality of mind-independent objects. There is exactly one true and complete description of "the way the world is." Truth involves some sort of correspondence relation between words or thought-signs and external things and sets of things. I shall call this the *externalist* perspective, because its favorite point of view is a God's Eye point of view.[42]

In this "externalist" perspective, independence marks those properties that are extrinsic to the experience of any such entities—primary qualities in

Descartes' language. Thus, many forms of realism attempt to short-circuit linguistic systems in order to jump over our own shadows by describing the world in such a way as to be independent of human description. Putnam, at least up to the early 1980s, agreed, at least broadly, with Dummett, since he argued that the attempts made by the "metaphysical realist" to detach conceptual schemes from the real also go the other way: even an "ideal theory," one that would satisfy every imaginable theoretical constraint and offer absolute completeness, might still be "untrue" in its relation to the (external) world.[43] Putnam's "conceptual relativity" means that even concepts such as "existence" have different meanings and thus cannot be used as absolute referents. As Cerbone notes, Heidegger's work, by attacking first and foremost the dualisms of subjects and objects, language and world, beings and Being, fits uneasily against these analytic concerns. In fact, Heidegger's critique of the "realist" responses to skepticism gives rise to the most dismissive passage in *Being and Time*:

> That Kant demands any proof at all for the "Dasein [or existence] of Things outside of me" shows already that he takes the subject—the "in me"—as the starting point of this problematic. . . . Kant presupposes both the distinction between the "in me" and the "outside of me," *and also the connection between these* [my emphasis]; factically he is correct in doing so, but he is incorrect from the standpoint of the tendency of his proof. . . . The "scandal of philosophy" is not that [proof for the in itself] has yet to be given, but that *such proofs are expected and attempted again and again.* Such expectations, aims, and demands arise from an ontologically inadequate way of starting with *something* of such a character that independently *of it* and "outside [*außerlaub*]" *of it* a "world" is to be proved as "present-at-hand [*vorhandene*]."[44]

A veritable "scandal," Kantianism leaves us to take "things" "on *faith*,"[45] and thus we feel the ground tremble beneath our feet as many have replaced this "faith in things" with all manner of theological leaps.[46] Heidegger argues that *prior to* any Kantian *a priori* is the being of the entity that we are (*Dasein*), which is always already in the world. Thus Heidegger claims that embedded in Kant's epistemology ("what can I know?") is an ontological dualism, which in turn takes time itself to be founded within the subject, that is, as not really existing. Ontically, we may reduce ourselves to such beings over and against one another, but ontologically we are structured by care (*Sorge*), which is the "founded mode of *access* to the Real."[47] As a consequence, the whole set of questions that have themselves founded realism and anti-realism debates over the last thirty or more years is sidestepped by Heidegger, as William McNeill[48] and others argue: the "externalist" position is *a posteriori* to *Dasein*'s being-in-the-world, there is no "God's-eye-view" from *outside* of the world, and truth as a "correspondence" between the subject and object thus always arrives late on the scene to an original unveiling or "access" that is the site of *Dasein*'s being-in-the-world. As a result, while the later Putnam argues, "the time has come for a moratorium on the kind of ontological speculation that seeks to describe the Furniture of the Universe and to tell us what is Really There and what is Only a Human Projection,"[49] Heidegger held that what is presumed in such a bifurcation of the "Furniture of the Universe" and "Human Projection" is a correlation of presence grounded in a "primordial temporality" that his project sets out to describe. Here he turns to *Dasein*'s "phenomenological access" to the "things themselves" in one of the most straightforward passages in *Being and Time*:

> This is the way in which everyday Dasein always *is:* when I open the door, for instance, I use the latch. The achieving of *phenomenological access* to the entities which we encounter, consists rather in thrusting aside our interpretive tendencies, which keep thrusting themselves upon us and running along with us, and which conceal not only the phenomenon of such "concern," but even more those entities themselves *as* encountered of their own accord *in* our concern with them.... In addressing these entities as "Things" (*res*), we have tacitly anticipated their ontological character. When analysis starts with such entities and goes on to inquire about Being, what it meets is Thinghood and Reality.[50]

In *Being and Time*, Heidegger describes the "things" of the world as appropriated within the circuit of *Dasein*'s care-structure, that is, as equipment, and outside of this referential, pre-cognitive circuit, there is no sense in terms of *Dasein*'s Being-in-the-world to ask about the *reality* of things without first attending to the fundamental ground of *Dasein*: "Reality," he writes, "is referred back to the phenomenon of care."[51] When Heidegger writes that "reality" has no priority in his work, it's because "reality" has been caught up in epistemological correlationisms that abstract out the referential totality of that which is ready-to-hand or handy (*zuhanden*) in terms of theoretical entities "present-to-hand" (*vorhanden*): "whenever we encounter anything, the world has already been previously *discovered*, though not thematically."[52]

For these reasons, Heidegger argues that previous "realisms" were reductive, granting existence only to "external" entities whose reality could only be dogmatically and faithfully asserted—and thus would dissolve *Dasein*'s existence as a being "always also absorbed in the world of its concern [*Besorge*]." Lee Braver notes, "realism," as Heidegger thinks of it, "insists that only one kind of Being is real, while everything else gets relegated to bastard status."[53] Heidegger was working against reductionism, which he believed occurred whenever Husserl and others bracketed out the existence of things to inspect the idea of them. This also gives rise to his deconstruction of "onto-theology," the argument that existence is reducible to one given being (in most instances God, as the name suggests). In the end, this is what Heidegger means, if a thumbnail sketch is needed, regarding entities that are "present-to-hand [*vorhanden*]": they are taken out of their referential whole and considered not as they are, but only in terms of their "outer aspect" (here he cites the origins of the Greek *Idea*).[54] Again, your concernful engagement with this book and your reading space is practical and worldly, not something "outside" of you as a mere flash of ideas. *Vorhandenheit* or "presence-to-hand" means that the things of the world are *presented* to thought as something external to *Dasein*, not as some entity ready-to-hand or handy (*zuhanden*), and Heidegger will later in *Being and Time* bring out the full temporal meaning of this "presence," a point that will return in our final chapter. For Heidegger, in any event, the entities that we encounter in the world are "equipment [*das Zeug*]," which is never one thing among others, but is rather a complex set of "assignment[s] or reference[s] of something to something."[55]

This is where Heidegger often gets reduced to an esoteric pragmatism, since objects have a "functional" status for *Dasein*.[56] But this reading is too loaded, since our care-structure, on Heidegger's account, places us always alongside entities that are not merely there for our mastery and use, as the pragmatic reading suggests, and our being-in-the-world is never *present* in the fully temporal sense of the term, since *Dasein* is futural as always out-ahead-of-itself.[57] The question that Graham Harman asks is what this "referential totality" would look like if we simply removed the reference to *Dasein* from this equation—and thus any hint of the idealism William Blattner finds. This may seem quite un-Heideggerian, since Heidegger was specifically concerned with the "Furniture of the Universe" in terms of *Dasein*'s being-in-the-world; to speak otherwise would be like trying to think of a play without actors. But Heidegger himself once wrote to Elisabeth Blochmann, in 1931, that this was a "fundamental question" for him: "I often ask myself—this has for a long time been a fundamental question for me—what nature would be without man. Must it not resonate through him (*hindurschwingen*) in order to attain its own-most potency?"[58]

Much of what subtends both sides of the realism/anti-realism debates, as we've seen, is a correlationism, at least for Meillassoux, that is, a co-presentation of one set of entities (subjects, discourses, conceptual schemes, and so on) with another (the external world, objects, references). Let's watch as Heidegger moves past the impasse that has taken up much work in Anglo-American philosophy:

> [T]he fact that Reality is ontologically grounded in the Being of Dasein does not signify that only when Dasein exists and as long as Dasein exists can the Real be that which itself is. Of course only as long as Dasein *is* (that is, only as long as an understanding of Being [*Seinsverständnis*] is ontically possible), "is there" ["*gibt es*"] Being. When Dasein does not exist, "independence" ["*Unabhängigkeit*"] "is" not either, nor "is" the "in-itself" ["*An-sich*"]. In such a case this sort of thing can be neither understood nor not understood. In such a case even entities within-the-world can neither be discovered nor lie hidden. *In such a case*, it cannot be said that entities are, nor can it be said that they are not.[59]

In this way, only what is given (*geben*) phenomenologically *to Dasein* can be understood (*verstehen*) in our pre-ontological relation to the world: "the Being of those entities which we encounter as closest to us can be exhibited phenomenologically if we take as our clue our everyday Being-in-the-world, which we also call our 'dealings' ['*Umgang*'] *in* the world and *with* entities within-the-world."[60] Against Kant, then, the in-itself of any such beings is not external or independent, but is "ready-to-hand" as "defined ontologico-categorially."[61] And unlike Husserlian phenomenology, which for Heidegger reduced all such beings to epistemological correlates, the "appropriate access [*angemessenen Zugang*]" is not seeing, considered either literally or through the "mind's eye" of the theoretical glance, but by way of our ontological being-in-the-world as equipmental concern.[62] Hence, for Heidegger, "phenomenology is our way of access" to "the things themselves [*zu den Sachen selbst*]."[63]

As such, for Heidegger, the "world is only if and as long as *Dasein* exists."[64] It is *only Dasein*, he makes clear—not animals, who are poor in world (*Weltarm*), not rocks, which are worldless (*Weltlos*)—who can "go along [*Mitgang*] with others in their access [*Zugang*] to things and in their dealings [*Umgang*] with those things"; this is the "*fundamental feature* of man's own immediate experience of existence."[65] It is *this* being who is "world-forming (*weltbildend*)"; it is *Dasein* who "step[s] out beyond itself, *ex-sistere*," and the projection of the world "belongs to *Dasein*'s being."[66] This is why we're proceeding cautiously here with the words "existence" and forms of the word "being," since for Heidegger: "to exist" has a specific meaning that neither denies nor affirms the being of other entities outside *Dasein*'s "access." As he explains, true to his phenomenological heritage, "the substantive problem with which we are concerned is precisely that of *accessibility itself*."[67]

However, this is not the end of the story for Heidegger. Later, in his Bremen lecture (1949) and the essay "*Das Ding*," Heidegger sought a more "realist" conception of the things of the world as falling within the four-fold of Being. Heidegger's famed jug (*der Krug*) is neither a piece of equipment brought back to the hands of *Dasein*, nor is it "present-to-hand" in terms of its scientific qualities (size, temperature, and so on). The question that is open, given that "mortals" are one element of his "four-fold" ("*das Geviert*") of Being, is whether or not real things have a certain autonomy that is irreducible to the three ways of being set out in his earlier work: (1) *Dasein* as existing in the world, (2) the handiness of equipment, and (3) the theoretical grasp of entities as present-to-hand.

We can now turn to Heidegger's question in "The Thing": "What is near is what tends to be called things. But what is a thing?"[68] The punchline that Heidegger provides in the following is justly (in)famous: "the jug's essence is the pure, donational gathering of the simple fourfold into an interlude of time. The jug holds sway as a thing. The jug is a jug as a thing. But how does the thing hold sway? The thing things."[69] And the "thing things" by appropriating the four-fold (earth, sky, mortals, gods). The "realist" questions—does the jug exist? Is it independent of human understanding?—are not those that interested Heidegger. He argues, from *Being and Time* to the end of his career, that realisms are representational and treat the world not as "standing in-itself (*Insichstehen*)" or "independent (*selbstständiges*)," but as an "object (*Gegenstand*)" presented to or correlated to a subject engaged in theoretical understanding.[70] That is, Heidegger's view was that realisms founder on the shores of correlationism: as an object, the jug would stand over and against a given subject, and we reduce the object to its "outward appearance."[71] Accordingly human beings at once open up things to language and referentiality, in a word, to a world, but at the same time it is these same human beings that reduce the beings to some outer aspect or quality. Heidegger wrote, in his introduction to "What is Metaphysics?":

> The being that exists is the human being. This being alone exists. Rocks are, but they do not exist. . . . The proposition 'the human being alone exists' does not at all mean that the human being alone is a real being . . . the human being is that being whose Being is distinguished by an open standing that stands in the unconcealedness of Being, proceeding from Being, in Being.[72]

Here we can watch the movement in Heidegger of the thing in and out of the encircling of mortals' concern:

> Thinging is the nearness of the world [*Dingen ist Nähern von Welt*]. . . . Inasmuch as *we* conserve [*schonen*] the thing as thing, *we* dwell [*bewohnen*] with nearness. . . . When and how arise the things as things? They do not arise only through the machinations [*Machenschaften*] of men. They arise, though, not without the vigilance of mortals [*Wachsamkeit der Sterblichen*]. The first step toward such vigilance is the step back [*der Schritt zurück*] from representational thought [*vorstellenden*], that is, which explains, to thinking that responds. . . . [E]ach thing, modestly compliant, fits into its own being [*je weilige Ding ring*]. Inconspicuously compliant [*Ring*] is the thing: the jug and the bench, the footbridge and the plow. But tree and pond, too, brook and hill, are things, each in its own way. Things, each thinging from time to time in its own way [*je weilig*]. . . . Men alone as mortals by dwelling, attain to the world as world [*Erst die Menchen als die Sterblichen erwohnen Welt als Welt*]. Only what encircles [*gering*] itself out of the world becomes a thing.[73]

Heidegger, like Merleau-Ponty after him, among many others, critiques the logic of representation, and in this way he too is a critic of correlationism—at least those forms linked to epistemological realisms. Indeed this is why his writing from this period is often opaque (the "thing things" and so on) since language is not to represent a given object ("jug" stands in for the object jug), but to open up ways of being that are not simply about describing the essence of a jug or what have you. Thinking representationally requires thinking of truth as a correlation of the representation to what is represented *out there*. Heidegger's strategy is, in his early work, to ground these "present-to-hand" representations in a prior being-in-the-world, thus removing any skepticism about reality since we are no long concerned with the "truth" of representations.

In this way, speculative realism follows Heidegger to the extent—this is particularly clear in Harman's work—that it rejects thinking the real through its representations found in linguistic and epistemological correlationisms, while also not grounding reality in an *a priori* relation of access described under the phenomenological being-in-the-world. For all their differences, Brassier's transcendental realism and Harman's object-oriented ontology agree that reality cannot be represented, but this is like saying that the US and Soviet Union agreed there was a Cold War; it didn't mean they weren't otherwise engaged in attacks on one another.

What then of idealism? Where correlationism argues that the absolute is unknowable outside human access, the idealist argues that the absolute is ideal. As with the above thinkers, we are only interested in setting up the discussions used by speculative realists, and thus a thumbnail sketch of how Hegel is used will have to do. Hegel critiques Kant's weak correlationism, arguing that Kant cannot know the boundary between the phenomenal and the noumenal without contradicting the transcendental enterprise. In the Hegelian structure of the co-implication of thinking and being, Hegel marks the "ideal" as real in and through the movement of the in-itself. As we noted earlier, this idealism is called speculative since it advances from the phenomenal to the in-itself, and it remains metaphysical in the sense that it posits an absolute that is necessary, for Meillassoux, namely the relation between thinking and being.

Meillassoux will argue against Hegel in an important way (that is, against the positing of the necessity of the correlation itself), but what's striking about *After Finitude* is that Meillassoux, frankly, has little to combat idealism as such. He expends a lot of energy on correlationists but, as we'll see, his method has nothing to say about idealisms that simply *deny* any correlation at all. Berkeley, for example, may be a subjectivist, but since he doesn't posit any correlation of thinking and being, anything Meillassoux has to do to critique correlationism will not, strangely, affect realism's most avowed enemy, idealism. It's also notable that in terms of subjectivist idealism, Meillassoux also counts such thinkers as Nietzsche, Bergson, and Deleuze, since he argues that their "will to power, duration of time, and account of life" respectively, export onto the in-itself these all-too-human qualities.

Now, the difference between the speculative idealist from the dogmatic idealist, such as Berkeley, is that the former attempts to find a rational means for thinking the real as within the circle of the correlation itself. Thus Hegel argues that the dialectic of thinking and being is the in-itself and is absolute and necessary. What Meillassoux borrows from Hegel is not just his critique of Kant, but also his use of the "speculative" procedure to reason from within the correlationist circle to reality as it is—hence without abuse, he can take up the label of speculative realism. Where Hegel circled back to the dialectical process of the ideal, Meillassoux tries to reason his way to the "principle of factuality": the utter contingency of being, not its necessity.

This focus on contingency—and his apparent critique of the necessary being that subtends all onto-theology—would seem to bring Meillassoux in the range of his hermeneutic and existential predecessors, whom he excoriates at length in his publications. As we proceed, though, we will see how his realism upends not just these previous thinkers' views on the question of reality, but also on politics, theology, and ethics. But first, we must take up Meillassoux's argument against correlationism, the subject of the next chapter.

CHAPTER 2
MEILLASSOUX'S PIVOT FROM CORRELATIONISM TO THE ABSOLUTE

What all speculative realists share in common, as we have seen, is their rejection of correlationism, which Harman notes is "the central polemical term of speculative realism."[1] While the last chapter sought to tease out multiple ways in which realism has been discussed in the past century, all as a means for later outlining the specific difference of *speculative* realism, the task in this chapter is to highlight Meillassoux's arguments against correlationism. This means we will cover his argument from the ancestral. As I will point out, Meillassoux was not the first to use this philosophical countermove against anti-realism, and I will discuss one approach from within the Anglo-American tradition that builds on that part of the literature. We will then turn to Meillassoux's lesser known argument against correlationism, which takes up the question of death as a possible correlate. There we will begin to see the path Meillassoux finds out of correlationism towards the "Great Outdoors." But we will also find in this argument an emphasis on providing a thought that goes beyond "human finitude" in the everyday sense of that term. This chapter takes us to the edge of what Meillassoux calls hyper chaos, and in the next, we will see how this hyper chaos is not the darkest of any possible existential plight—nothing matters since all can be washed away, even the very laws of nature—but as the path to a conception of immortality. Along the way, we will note criticisms that can attach to Meillassoux's arguments, so as to set up claims by other speculative realists in the coming chapters.

The ancestral argument

Meillassoux's critique of correlationism is his argument from ancestrality, which is described in the opening pages of *After Finitude* as well as in several later publications. For Meillassoux, the ancestral is "any reality anterior to the emergence of the human species—or even anterior to every recognized form of life on earth."[2] Meillassoux's tact is to argue that "arche-fossils"[3] provide evidence of the origin of the universe, the formation of the earth, and so forth, all prior to human being and thus any possible correlation of thought and world. Meillassoux's strategy is to think a fact whose provenance would have to be outside the correlationist circle. It so happens that two years before the publication of *After Finitude*, John Nolt, a University of Knoxville philosopher, published a similar argument confronting anti-realism, which we will quickly discuss below in tandem with Meillassoux. We do this for two reasons: first, Nolt takes on Anglo-American anti-realisms that Meillassoux largely leaves aside, and secondly, Nolt's solution to the problem of the ancestral differs in important regards and allows us to isolate the radical dimension of Meillassoux's thought. Finally, it should be said that there has been a longstanding divide between Anglo-American and Continental philosophy, and speculative realists often promise a move beyond this divide.

Moving forward to Meillassoux's argument, while empirical science can tell us, say, the date of the origin of the universe 13.5 billion years ago and the date when *homo habilis* took its first steps 2 million years ago, Meillassoux depicts the correlationists as always undercutting scientific claims with caveats that speak in a tone of modesty and are anything but. The scientist is said to be dogmatically realist, but the philosopher knows that the arche-fossil—the evidence for any ancestral event—is something *given*, either to a particular human subject or to a community of scientists, depending on the specific form of correlationism. The ancestral event would stand, then, for a "retrojection of the past on the basis of the present."[4] The correlationist, according to Meillassoux, cannot take the ancestral statement—the accretion of the Earth occurred 4.56 billion years ago—in its "literal sense." The event is not in the past, for the correlationist, but happens through the "givenness" or manifestation "for us"; thus the correlationist's denial of reality, he says, "is exposed."[5] The arche-fossil stands as a continual frustration of the correlationist worldview: "there is no possible compromise between the correlationism and the arche-fossil; once one has acknowledged one, one has disqualified the other."[6] Here is how Nolt economically puts his own form of the argument:

1. The cosmos existed and had structure before we existed, and during some of this time, it was possible that we would never exist.

2. From these premises it follows that the cosmos has a structure that would have existed even if we never had.
3. Therefore the cosmos has structure that is independent of our cognition—i.e., intrinsic structure.[7]

The best way to read Meillassoux's version is to take *After Finitude* as a critique of *previous* correlationisms in order to provide the basis for *another* correlationism anchored in the real, despite Meillassoux's claim to "refute" all correlationisms.[8] Meillassoux argues for moving "after" finitude so that we no longer see the limits of knowledge in the phenomenal: philosophy can say more than that there is the in-itself and we can think this; there is, he says, certain knowledge of the absolute. Meillassoux's work, consequently, takes us beyond the finite limits of the phenomenal realm, though in the end it will not question the phenomenal-noumenal split that orients Kantian philosophy. This is perhaps why Meillassoux differentiates between "refutation" and "disqualification" in the following, though frankly it's an impossible distinction to make out: "I can access a speculative realism which *clearly refutes*, but *no longer disqualifies*, correlationism."[9] He also writes, "My goal is simple, I attempt to refute every form of correlationism."[10] Elsewhere, he denies even that his argument from the ancestral is a "refutation"; thus his goal is anything but "*simple*" vis-à-vis correlationism: "in the first chapter of *After Finitude*, I simply try to lay out an *aporia*, rather than a *refutation*."[11] Meillassoux's ambiguity on this point is telling, since we will argue that he works his way out from the correlationist circle and thus must take the reality of that circle as the hidden premise of his argument.[12] More importantly, because he keeps primary and secondary qualities, Meillassoux remains a dualist in separating out the different modes through which the absolute, via mathematics, and phenomena are accessed.

In any case, this refutation or isolation of the *aporia* of correlation will not mean a return to a "naïve" realism, which is but our "natural attitude."[13] The naïve or dogmatically realist philosopher presumes an unmediated access to beings, which is just not tenable after Kant, German idealism, and the linguistic turn. This all means, on the one hand, that Meillassoux argues that correlationism must denude itself of any relation to the "great outdoors"; on the other, it is this relation that becomes the starting point for any future speculative metaphysics.[14] For this reason, Meillassoux's approach to correlationism cannot be as knockdown as his rhetoric suggests, since if correlationism is completely defeated, there would be no ground where he sows the seeds of his own project. The path to the real, from within the subjective-objective correlate, will be mathematics. The "hidden passage," he argues, is through the "Cartesian in-itself,"[15] which "presents itself to us as non-relative to us, and hence capable of existing whether we exist or not."[16] As he put it in his 1997 dissertation, *L'Inexistence divine*, mathematics is "the language of being *qua* being."[17] This claim is ambiguous and is at the heart of arguments over so-called Platonic realisms: is it that this math "represents" some extra-numerical reality? Or is the eternal language, say, of set theory, that which truly exists?

Let's first recall that Descartes had practiced a dualism between two types of substances, the thinking thing (*cogito*) and the embodied existence of things. This mind-body dualism is often interpreted as inaugurating a subject-centered view of the world, no matter that Descartes himself never used the French or Latin words for subject. Meillassoux is right to emphasize the real dualism that Descartes and other early modern thinkers bequeathed to the modern world: on the one hand, the non-temporal thinking thing, and on the other, the mathematical in-itself that gave rise to the scientific revolutions unleashed these last four hundred years. The idea that reality as such was approachable through mathematicization was not entirely new, but when wedded to scientific inquiry, indeed, it was, and the Cartesian privileging of the thinking thing changed little in terms of the influence the other part of his work would have. For example, however different philosophically, Newton, too, found that the mathematical was the in-itself, the unchanging language beneath appearances, and this would have profound consequences for physics for centuries. The "Cartesian" in-itself is an external world that is fully mathematical, a view Meillassoux believes is championed by modern science—as opposed to the Kantian in-itself, which is external to the mathematizable concepts of the understanding provided by the subject. It is this external world that is "measured" when we speak of events millions or even billions of years before the advent of living beings, and thus Meillassoux returns us to a thinking that is pre-critical in the Kantian sense.

Against this, correlationism holds, as we have seen, that "we only ever have access to the correlation between thinking and being, and never to either term considered apart from the other,"[18] and hence "a world is only meaningful as given-to-a-living (or thinking) being."[19] Meillassoux's claim is that what he calls the "arche-fossil" is unthinkable by correlationism in its absolute reality. This fossil is not just a set of materials "indicating traces of past life," but signifies "the existence of an ancestral reality or event; one that is anterior to terrestrial life."[20] The correlationist must make, if one follows

Meillassoux, the following claims, depending on the type of correlationisms we've thus far reviewed:

1. the origin of the universe appears *to us* as 13.5 billion years ago, but as it is in-itself, we cannot know. (Kantianism)
2. What is knowable is founded in the human "intentionality," and knowledge is what is *given* in the noetico-noematic correlation. (Husserlian phenomenology)
3. Science aims at objectivity and our task is to present coherent conceptual schemes that are "internally" consistent. (Putnam's early internal realism)
4. Scientific practice is caught in regimes of power. Its claims to reality are nothing other than an attempt to naturalize systems of authority within a given society. (supposed social-constructivisms)
5. One must first take account of the "co-propriation (*Zusammengehörigkeit*) of man and being," which is the *Ereignis* or event. Neither human beings nor being "can be posited as subsisting 'in-themselves,' and subsequently entering into relation."[21] Rather, there is an "essential togetherness" of Dasein and being, and to think one without the other is to escape into representational thinking that reduces everything to that which is present-to-hand. (Heidegger)

Numerous other philosophical strategies are possible, but the point is that for Meillassoux, each tells "the scientist that his ancestral statements are illusory,"[22] that they are without any meaning except as from the point of view of human being. In this way, he argues, every correlationism, with regard to the arche-fossil, "is exposed as an extreme idealism"[23]:

> Correlationism will generally maintain—because it is subtle—that ancestral statements are true in a way—i.e., as universal statements, bearing on some present experiences about specific materials (starlight, isotope). But if it is consistent, correlationism will have to deny that the referents of these statements really existed as described prior to any human or living species. For the correlationist, ancestrality cannot be a reality *prior to the subject*—it can only be a reality that is said and thought by the subject as prior to the subject. It is a past for humanity which has no more effectiveness than that of a past of humanity that is strictly correlated with actual humans.[24]

By dictating that these ancestral statements are filtered through the subject, language, or human being-in-the-world, correlationists can only think the time of the "givenness" or access itself, according to Meillassoux, but not the actual anteriority of the time of the ancestral itself: these events must have occurred before any such a relation between being and thinking existed. Correlationists, thus, end up reducing everything, including the ancestral, to its appearance to conscious beings, yet the ancestral is precisely that which is *not* given to any consciousness or language, a point Nolt makes as well. This represents, Meillassoux says, a wearisome self-justification certain philosophers use for their own existence: the work of science is good *so far as it goes*, but philosophers understand the relative place of these statements within a general givenness of being to the subject, linguistic systems, or *Dasein*. At best, science offers objective and universal statements for the inter-subjective community of rational subjects. (We will see, however, that Meillassoux is doing anything but leaning on science as the arbiter of the truth of the real.) Nolt for his part argues there is always an assumption of an "anti-realist 'we,'" that is, some presupposed "set of actual beings whose cognitive [or linguistic] peculiarities the structure of the world is supposed to depend,"[25] which Meillassoux dubs the "for us."

Thus for the correlationist, the scientific discovery that the Earth accreted 4.56 billion years ago does not mean that we know *not* when it happened, but only as it *appears to have happened* for us. As Peter Hallward nicely sums it up, at the moment science after Copernicus was opening up a wider cosmos for our discovery, philosophy turned inward: "Post-Copernican science had opened the door to the 'great outdoors'" and "Kant's own so-called 'Copernican turn' should be best understood as a Ptolemaic attempt to slam this door shut."[26] Meillassoux and Nolt argue, however, that scientific statements make no sense if one refuses this temporal anteriority. The use of radioactive isotopes to carbon date arche-fossils from prior to human consciousness is not in need of any supplement (this statement *plus* the correlationist's "as given to human consciousness"). It stands for a temporal proof of a non-correlated reality.[27] In other words, it is not merely that we have found some event that has just now come to be given to human beings, but that, in itself, is "*prior to givenness in its entirety*."[28]

> [T]he time at issue here is the time wherein *consciousness* as well as *conscious time* have *themselves emerged in time*. For the problem of the arche-fossil is not the empirical problem of the birth of living

> organisms, but the ontological problem of the coming into being of givenness as such. More acutely, the problem consists in understanding how science is able to think—without any particular difficulty—the coming into being of consciousness and its spatio-temporal forms of givenness in the midst of a space and time which are supposed to pre-exist the latter.[29]

If one reads into this a certain "scientism"—namely, that science is the mediator of all truths—then one has grasped at least the affect, if not the ultimate result, as we'll see, of Meillassoux's prose. His concern is not just to defend the honor of science by taking away all the asterisks correlationists would put on ancestral statements. He is more troubled by the return of fideism in much Continental philosophy, which has filled the void left open by correlationist agnosticism about the in-itself.

> It then becomes clear that this [correlationist] trajectory culminates in the disappearance of the pretension to *think* any absolutes, *but not in the disappearance of absolutes*, since in discovering itself to be marked by an irremediable limitation, correlational reason thereby legitimates *all* those discourses that claim to access an absolute, *the only proviso being that nothing in these discourses resembles a rational justification of their validity*. . . . The end of metaphysics, understood as the "de-absolutization of thought," is thereby seen to consist in the rational legitimation of any and every variety of religious (or "poetico-religious") belief in the absolute. [Thus,] an exacerbated return of the religious.[30]

In other words, once the correlationist refuses to deal in reality, those religious believers of various stripes can fill in the gaps that these philosophers have left open. One can ask whether or not this is Meillassoux's strongest claim. It's true that many religious thinkers have found safe passage under the cover of phenomenology, hermeneutics, and even deconstruction, but pre-Critical realists about the in-itself such as Newton and Descartes were also no strangers to God, though they argued it was a matter of reason, not faith. Despite the work of the new atheists, such as Richard Dawkins, it is simplistic at best to bifurcate those who have a scientific worldview from those who are open to a theology of the absolute. The new Continental philosophies of religion are not just simple straw men easy to burn with the light of the fire of scientific thought.[31] Nevertheless at each turn, when an atheistic thinker such as Derrida or Badiou is used for religious purposes, one should question the bad faith of theologies using such thinkers for faux-radicalism and the dressing up of old doctrines in the newest fashions.

Ancestral questions

Is his refutation of the correlationist as knockdown as Meillassoux argues? In a word, no. First, Meillassoux is in danger of portraying Kant et al. as particularly daft philosophers who can't distinguish between ontological and epistemological claims. Kant isn't asserting that the in-itself doesn't exist, but rather that what we know can't simply be accounted for by some unmediated access to the in-itself. Indeed, as we've discussed in the last chapter, Kant's project is in part to provide for the ability to use mathematics for the reality that comes to us—hence the categories of the understanding. Meillassoux also suggests that the correlationist is making the idealist assumption that what is represented requires the act of representation, a relation of dependence of the "ancestral" on the very act of thinking, which is the fallacy at the heart of Berkley's view that "to be is to be perceived." If thinking stops, one presumes, then there is no ancestral being. Here, Markus Gabriel sums up the transcendental, that is, post-Kantian, position in a manner quite different from Meillassoux:

> Transcendental ontology investigates the ontological conditions of our conditions of access to what there is. It sets out with the simple insight that the subject (in whichever way conceived) *exists*, that the analysis of the concept of existence is, hence, methodologically prior to the analysis of the subject's access to existence.[32]

For example, I recognize that my radio "constitutes" the sound waves it brings in through a century's old mechanism, but this doesn't mean I think the sound waves weren't in the air before the radio was turned on, or that the actual people whose voices I hear are relying on my radio's battery power for continued existence.[33] Yes, it's *given*, but nothing Meillassoux argues changes any of that, and it's telling Nolt, Alain Badiou (in his preface to *After Finitude*), and Ray Brassier[34] use the word "dependence": the correlationists hold, as Nolt points out in this vein, "that the structure of the ancient cosmos existed not intrinsically but in a way that *depends* somehow on *our* cognition."[35] Or as Badiou puts it in his preface to *After Finitude*, against the correlationist, "yes, we can think what there is, and this thinking in no way *depends* upon a supposedly constituting subject."[36] But, as Peter Hallward points out, one can say such and such are the epistemological or linguistic conditions for knowledge of the ancestral without ever believing that things in the world "depend" on thinking for existence. "All the correlationist demands is an acknowledgment that when you think of an ancestral event, or any event, you are indeed thinking of it. I can think of this lump of ancient rock as ancient if and only if science currently provides me with reliable means of thinking it so."[37] Merleau-Ponty dealt with this question long before any speculative realist put pen to paper:

> What, in fact, do we mean when we say that there is no world without a being in the world? *Not* indeed that the world is *constituted by consciousness*, but on the contrary that consciousness always finds itself *already at work in the world*. What is true, taking one thing with another, is that there is a nature, which is not that of the sciences, but that which perception presents to me, and that even the light of consciousness is, as Heidegger says, *lumen naturale*, given to itself.[38]

This is not to say this isn't correlationist, but this view is perhaps not simply collapsible into the crude idealism Meillassoux suggests. Nathan Brown, in a spirited defense, argues that Meillassoux's critics haven't understood the relation between logical and temporal succession as it operates in *After Finitude*.

> [T]he correlationist cannot think ancestral objects are prior to the thought that thinks them. Meillassoux's argument is simply that if we accept the priority of the *logical* over *chronological succession* . . . we will be unable to assess scientific statements regarding ancestral phenomena without destroying the veritable meaning of those statements, which concern chronological priority of that which came before thought, regardless of any temporal retrojection performed by thinking. What is at stake here apropos of thinking and being is a disagreement regarding the priority of the *logical* correlation between thinking and being *over* the chronological disjunction of thinking and being.[39]

This may be true, but critics, such as Adrian Johnston, as we'll see in Chapter 7, claim that Meillassoux's rationalism trumps any rhetoric about adhering to science. We will see that Meillassoux's thinking of hyper chaos as time follows from his rationalism and is left out of Brown's summary above, since he would have to note that the laws of the universe that make scientific claims possible simply do not exist for Meillassoux. For the moment, perhaps an analogy will help here regarding his rationalism, an analogy that will help us as we explore neo-Spinozisms in later chapters. The rationalist Baruch Spinoza has been occasionally critiqued as something of a transcendental monist,[40] rather than someone who argues for the immanent, material space outside of which nothing exists. In the *Ethics*, Spinoza works out rationally, from his definition of God as nature, the specific modes human beings and other entities take, and then finally, our own particular psychologies. Thus, while later readers of Spinoza, such as several key thinkers in Chapter 5, find in him a "materialism," fair or unfair, his rationalist method has been viewed to trump any ability to move back from his logical working out of the divine substance to the material reality of our bodies; his "transcendental" apparatus produces its own view of the ultimate substance. (Again, Spinoza may indeed be an immanentist, but the focus is to his rationalist side for a point of analogy.) In a similar way, Meillassoux's rationalism *does not* work backward from the empirical, but merely takes anteriority as a logical problem. Paul Ennis has come closest to this point: "Meillassoux's rationalism is a pure form of rationalism—arguably he is even a nomological thinker. His principle does not make sense unless one accepts that, *contra* strong correlationism (phenomenology in particular), it does not deal with appearances."[41] This is precisely why Hegel in his *Logic* moves from *speculation* (the method) to the *Ideal*, or must dictate that the "real is rational" and the "rational is real," since to think reason is to think the real, for Hegel. But once one separates the two (the real and the rational), as in Meillassoux's speculative materialism, how does one move from the purely rational (the mathematical) back to the real, not in terms of application but as seeing the "world" as a given in mathematical sets, as we will see?[42] At least to Hegel, this raises a genuine question of whether "speculative realism" has an internal scission that it cannot suture. In some sense, this is what Hallward is getting at when he says that Meillassoux's use of set theory trumps any "applied measurement," that is, it can't move from the purely mathematical to the very existence in which the ancestral takes place.[43] Thus despite his claims that *other* philosophers delegitimize scientific claims, it is not clear, as we'll see, whether or not Meillassoux is any better, since his mathematical realism, *qua* "reductivism," to use Dummett's language from Chapter 1, means that he may be ultimately founding a scientific anti-realism.

Meillassoux could not be clearer about the conflation of epistemology and ontological claims on behalf of correlationists: "[A]ll that correlationism can say about ancestrality is that it is a subjective *representation* of such a past—but that this past couldn't really have *existed* in itself with all its objects and events."[44] In any case, as Peter Hallward notes well while providing a good hermeneutic principle for reading Meillassoux, the latter's tact is often to take the weak point of an argument, for example, the very correlation presumed by the correlationists, and take it as a point of strength for his own argument. As we'll see, the (arguable) weakness of his argument from ancestrality—whether he "refutes" or merely points out an *aporia*, depending on the moment in which he describes it—becomes a strength: as we keep noting, he works from *within* the correlational circle, not from the outside.

Though Nolt's argument depicts the conflation of correlation and dependence we've suggested is problematic, I want to turn to his conclusion quickly to differentiate his approach from that of Meillassoux. The basis for Nolt's argument is that the anteriority of the ancestral is indicative of a structure, that is, laws of nature discoverable by empirical science, which makes possible any possible *a posteriori* interpretation of the given. While we recommend his article as a whole, let's move to his closing paragraphs, where he posits, in agreement with Meillassoux, that we should no longer allow anti-realists to claim Lockean primary qualities (he doesn't use the term, but that's what's meant), such as mass and quantity, as mere concepts. "While it is true," he writes, "that our understanding of objects is always mediated by concepts, it is *not* true that the objects themselves make no contribution to our understanding."[45] We will see how Harman's work will make much of what is *left over* from any possible understanding, and Nolt is right, as Harman will be, not to conflate the *idea* of some X with X itself. For Nolt, the ancestral shows "it's not concepts all the way down."[46] Then he turns to the example of stars, which he could have noted are precisely given as that which was there before thought, since of course, the light of many stars was sent many years before the advent of the human, even if the signal is only received now. Below, he notes the early failure of the British philosophers G. E. Moore and Bertrand Russell to prove that we can identify pure sense data coming from the outside world without already implicating our concepts of them. This is what we'll see in Wifrid Sellars' "myth of the given," which becomes a powerful tool in Brassier's arsenal. But this failure does not mean, Nolt argues, there is no reality beyond correlationism that provides the sensations in the first place:

> Though in all meaningful perception there is interpretation, there is also something that we do not create and cannot change by our conceptions. When we look at the night sky, for example, we find the stars positioned in arrangements not of our making. These arrangements are among the sorts of things that G. E. Moore, Bertrand Russell and others tried to distill out of the flux of interpretation and reify as sense-data—the uninterpreted given in perception. They failed. Such arrangements must be interpreted even to be recognized as sense data. . . . But that does not mean that the way they appear to us is *only* the result, for example, of our engaging in a certain type of discourse, or even of the kinds of eyes and brains we have. . . . We may *reinterpret* the arrangements of stars, we may "form" them conceptually into different gestalts. . . . But this malleability is limited; there is an *arrangement*, a matter, a *structure* that persists.[47]

This structure is important, since for Nolt, it is the condition of possibility for any knowledge in the first place, and it is one that "persists"; we will see soon how radically Meillassoux undercuts this whole notion of a structure to the world, one that underlies Nolt's proposed solution to the problem of correlationism. For now, we can note that Meillassoux argues there is an "invisible reality of things" that is only approachable through "intellectual" or "dianoetic" "intuition."[48] Ray Brassier has critiqued this notion of "intuition" in Meillassoux's work, suggesting that it is another form of correlationism between an intellectual intuition that represents reality through mathematics and the represented, the primary qualities of the in-itself. But it's also crucial to see how Meillassoux's method requires showing what the correlationist, the only genuine other position on realism for him, must take for granted in her arguments, which he uses as the premise for his work.[49] In any case, here is how Nolt ends: "The existence of an ancient cosmos in which it was possible that we would never evolve has never been adequately explained—anti-realists—who hold that all world-structure (past, present, and future) somehow *depend* conceptually on *us*."[50]

But where Nolt discerns a structure of temporal succession that makes any "givenness" possible, Meillassoux argues for giving precedence to the "time of science" over the "time of the given,"[51] even though this is all upended in giving priority to the absolute time of chaos. The correlationist may sidestep the time of science, whose evidence is the arche-fossil, by saying that she is discussing "transcendental" conditions or the "conditions of possibility" of any such givenness, for example, modes of representation that make such dating possible, but Meillassoux asserts, "we are also raising the question of the emergence of the temporality of the conditions of instantiations, and hence of the taking place of the transcendental as such."[52]

Meillassoux's strategy, in line with Nolt, is to point out that the material reality of the ancestral is temporally prior to any such "transcendental" structures. We must be embodied beings prior to thinking any such concepts as Kant would have them, and prior to our embodiment is a set of real, even ancestral, realities that are absolute and unquestionable.[53] This temporality is the "condition of possibility," he argues, for ancestrality itself, and thus *anteriority* marks an absolute that is prior to any Kantian "conditions of possibility" of knowledge, an argument also found in the first respondents to Kant, including Schelling.[54] Moreover, it's notable that Heidegger, a supposed strong correlationist who uses a similar argument concerning temporality, goes in precisely the opposite direction as Meillassoux—away from the "logic of succession" to what we could call the reality, the *Es Gibt* (the "there is" of Being), of the original gift of time: "earlier than any possible earlier of whatever sort," is temporality, "because it is the basic condition for an earlier as such."[55] Thus, for Heidegger, rather than the concepts of the understanding providing for temporality, as Kant argues, it is a "real" temporality that is the model for any succession and, in precisely this way, would be "logically" prior to any "logical priority." For his part, Meillassoux writes,

> How could one give sense to the idea of a time preceding the subject, or consciousness or Dasein; a time within which subjectivity or being-in-the-world itself emerged—and perhaps will disappear along with humanity and terrestrial life—if one makes of time, and space, and the visible world, the strict correlates of this subjectivity? If time is a correlate of the subject, then nothing can actually precede the subject—as individual or more radically as human species—*within* time. Because what existed before the subject existed before the subject *for* the subject. Appeals to intersubjectivity are of no account here, since the time in

> question is not the time preceding such and such an individual—this time is still social, made up of the subjective temporality of ancestors—but a time preceding all life, and so every human community.[56]

As we conclude this book, we will argue that a rethinking of the reality of time is the royal road to any future realism. For now, let us cite Nolt's final sentence in line with what Meillassoux writes above, which could act as a credo for the disparate speculative realists, who if not anti-humanists, are at least offering an approach beyond humanism: "I have tried to show that *we* (whoever *we* are) are not *that* big a deal." Meillassoux's version is in a footnote to *After Finitude*: "The world can do without humanity."[57] And in Graham Harman: "However interesting we humans may be to ourselves, we are apparently in no way central to the cosmic drama, marooned as we are on an average-sized planet near a mediocre sun, and confined to a tiny portion of the history of the universe."[58] It hasn't gone without notice that this apocalyptic affect pervades speculative realism, from Meillassoux's depictions of the end of humanity[59] to Brassier's nihilism. This, at least, forms part of Adrian Johnston's critique,[60] which is in line with Slavoj Žižek's discussion of Alan Weisman's *The World without Us* (2007):

> This is the fundamental subjective position of fantasy: to be reduced to a gaze observing the world in the condition of the subject's non-existence—like the fantasy of witnessing the act of one's own conception, parental copulation, or the act of witnessing one's own burial, like Tom Sawyer and Huck Finn. "The world without us" is thus fantasy at its purest: witnessing the Earth itself regaining its pre-castrated state of innocence.[61]

Meillassoux's deadly argument

Whatever the strength of Meillassoux and Nolt's accounts of the ancestral, they are right to argue that it highlights a problem for thought and its limits.[62] In particular, Meillassoux calls attention to a real time that cannot be correlated to a subject or particular historical community. By beginning with ancestrality, Meillassoux posits a respect for scientific discoveries he says are oft-disparaged as of secondary importance in Continental philosophy, and his work is part of an important turn in recent years that joins with such thinkers as Catherine Malabou, Elisabeth Grosz, and Adrian Johnston, who see their work as in many ways informed by the latest work in biology and other sciences. Meillassoux also isolates the manner in which scientific discourses have long thought a time anterior to any givenness to human beings.[63] How then, is "thought able to access the uncorrelated," that is, that which is "real" beyond something being given "for us"?[64] For Brassier, following Sellars, this will be the scientific image of man in the world.

But Meillassoux's turn to a "non-metaphysical absolute" gives the name to his speculative (in every sense of the term) realism. The strong correlationist, for him, argued that *all* thinking and being are co-related. But because *all* thinking and being are co-related, there is one part of this "correlationist" circle that cannot be said to be inescapable, namely the relation itself. As Kant argued, the *fact* of this *relation* is itself *contingent*. There is no being that made this so, reality could have gone on without us, and thus strong correlationism, Meillassoux states, marked the "end of all absolutes."[65] A metaphysical "absolute," according to Meillassoux, presumes a necessary being. Heidegger called this type of metaphysics "ontotheology," and in this way, Heidegger argued not against the divine, thought as highest or most universal being, but against *any* being that is said to found all others.

Let's explain this more clearly. Recall from the last chapter that the idealist argues that through human thought alone we are granted access to the in-itself. While "weak" correlationism argued that we can think the in-itself but not have knowledge of it, the strong correlationist emphasizes the finitude of human existence: we are always within the limits of what is given to us and thus we are forever precluded from absolute knowledge. Meillassoux's "speculative materialism" is not the first philosophy to take seriously this relation between thinking and being. Hegel's "speculative idealism" took the *an sich* as such to be this relation. But for Hegel, the relation itself was necessary; there could *not* not be thought, which also pretty much sums up his view of double negation as the positive elaboration of the movement of the concept. Against this strong anthropic principle, Meillassoux argues that this correlation is contingent and the fact of this contingency is the absolute that realist philosophers have sought. That is, the contingency of the relation, which is the centerpiece of all correlationisms, on Meillassoux's account, becomes his own starting point for his speculative project.

When one says "life is contingent," one means that it didn't need to be. For this reason, in the modern era, after the "death of God" and the loss of all certainties, we may give ourselves over to Camus's existentialism and think of our existence as absurd. It didn't need to be this way and the future (the death of others and ourselves) is equally contingent as to the time and places of its occurring. Camus himself noted that in the modern era we are dual beings: on the one hand, we are thinking beings fully aware of ourselves and in this way, separate from the goings-on around us; on the other hand, we are physical beings given over to the scientific laws of cause and effect. In short, "physical laws remain indifferent as to whether an event occurs or not."[66] The word contingency is often used interchangeably with "facticity," which is usually used to refer to our mortal lives in this or that given historical setting. Meillassoux, for his part, defines "facticity" as the "structural invariant" of our particular being-in-the-world. However Kant, Husserl, or Heidegger may disagree, they nevertheless posit a "relation" of "access" between the thinker and being that does not vary from point to point. You don't wake up one day with Kant's concepts of the understanding and the next with Heidegger's care structure, and the next in Husserl's intentionality. These forms, Meillassoux argues, "are fixed."[67] Thus, "if contingency consists in knowing that worldly things could be otherwise, facticity just consists in not knowing why the correlational structure had to be thus."

Like a detective looking for the one clue that will put the whole scene of death in place and solve the crime, Meillassoux, too, begins with our ultimate demise, offering his speculative argument from the fact of death in order to solve the problem of correlationism. "I try," he writes, to give "correlationism its most rigorous form—to isolate the fundamental argument in it."[68] The thinkers of finitude have long related two kinds of finitude: the limits of our knowledge and the limit of our death. We are neither omniscient nor omnipotent nor eternal. "Human thought" has a "most remarkable power—its capacity to access the possibility of its own non-being, and thus know itself to be mortal."[69] This is what gives the title to *After Finitude*: Meillassoux takes the thinking of finitude—an "incapacity of thought"—and makes of this "power" an ability to "make our way towards the absolute."[70]

Directly halfway through *After Finitude*, Meillassoux isolates a pivot point through a *mise-en-scène* of a discussion among five people regarding the existence of God and the possibility of the afterlife. Here's the *dramatis personae*:

1. The dogmatic atheist: this person has views akin to the dogmatic realist. She knows what is real and takes for granted a material reality that excludes any necessary being, God.

2. The dogmatic theist: this person is akin to the dogmatic idealist. He knows what is real, and this reality is but an extension of anthropomorphic conceptions of the soul. There is an eternal being watching over us, answering our prayers, and so on. The dogmatism shared between this theist and the dogmatic atheist is why one often hears that "atheism" is but another religion. And in this limited sense, this would be right.
3. The strong correlationist: this person, Meillassoux suggests, is the non-judgmental friend who never takes sides and tries to play the peacemaker. The second person argues that there is no God, no benevolent being who will provide us an afterlife; the first believes just as strongly that there is. The correlationist basically throws up her hands and argues for agnosticism: we can only know what is *given* to us, and any certainty about the afterlife is illusory. Just as an embittered couple come together in their hate for their relationship counselor, so too the dogmatists are deeply unsatisfied by the correlationist, since her view is patronizing at best: I know that your certainty is wrong. But this agnosticism comes at a cost. "All beliefs," Meillassoux writes, "strike" the correlationist "as equally legitimate given that theory is incapable of privileging one eventuality over another."[71] Then he shows how agnosticism is another correlationism: "For just as I cannot know the in-itself without converting it into a for-me"—if I think the unthought, it is at the very moment made thinkable—"I cannot know what will happen to me when I am no longer of this world, since knowledge presupposes that one is of the world."[72]
4. The subjective idealist: there are atheistic idealists and theistic idealists, but they would agree on the inseparability of thinking and being in Meillassoux's depiction. For the idealist, the correlationists and dogmatist are wrong and inconsistent: they "believe that there could be an in-itself radically different from our present state," whether it be God and the afterlife, or sheer nothingness. But, for the idealist, "I cannot think of myself as no longer existing without, through that very thought, contradicting myself."[73] So much, then, for the Stoic dictum that "I fear not death, since if it is not here, I am, and if it is, I am not." Hence, the idealist argues, "I cannot but exist, and always exist as I exist now," according to Meillassoux. In other words, for the idealist, there is no "in-itself" that differs from the "for-us."

Then, completing the scene, Meillassoux calls forth the speculative philosopher, who argues that the agnostic correlationist has "managed to identify the absolute."[74] What does the agnostic correlationist *know* (despite Meillassoux's constant depiction that she is a know-nothing)? Here the speculative philosopher comes close to repeating the Socratic dictum that he knows only that he doesn't know. Meillassoux argues that in the face of the defeatism of the correlationist, the speculative philosopher knows why there is this unknowability: our "capacity-to-be-other," and thus to always face death. Here are the steps of his argument:

1. In order to think of myself as mortal, I must conceive myself as able to be *other*.
2. This thinking of mortality only has a real possibility if it is not simply the correlate of my thinking. (We will see a cosmic version of this in Brassier.) If it were not a real possibility, then as the idealist holds, it would be a thought that would depend on me for its continued existence.
3. Subjective idealism holds that, indeed, continuing to think of death always placates it. You would "agonize indefinitely," Meillassoux puts it, "without ever passing away." In order to refute the idealist, the correlationist must grant at least one fact: that of the pure, uncorrelatable possibility of annihilation. It is not a matter of ignorance of the afterlife (for or against) but a *real* possibility that the correlationist must take as absolute, or be left with subjective idealism. Put another way, by thinking the capacity-to-be-other under the guise of death—the uncorrelatable "possibility of one's impossibility," as Heidegger describes it—one has "touched upon" an absolute that is *knowable* but not *given* to thought, since death is the indirect, speculative result of the fact of the capacity-to-be-other, but is not representable as such.[75]

The correlationist hence comes upon a decision: either the correlation is not absolute (and thus one can die) and the idealist is wrong, or one argues that the speculative philosopher is wrong and one "de-absolutize[s] facticity," meaning that everything one thinks, including death, must be a correlate of thought. But doing this gives the victory to the idealist, Meillassoux argues. The correlationist thus holds (a) there is no necessary being (God, prime mover, and so on), and (b) there is an "absolute necessity that every entity might not exist."[76] Keeping in mind Hallward's remark that Meillassoux's *modus operandi* is to flip judo-like any argument's weakness into a strength, this is not a mode of ignorance, but for Meillassoux a positive fact—indeed, one that is necessary. This is the first principle of his speculative realism: the principle of unreason. As Ray Brassier nicely summarizes it, correlationism:

> finds itself confronted with the following dilemma: it cannot de-absolutize facticity without absolutizing the correlation [the idealist move]; yet is cannot de-absolutize the correlation without absolutizing facticity [the speculative materialist move]. But to absolutize facticity is to assert the unconditional necessity of its contingency.[77]

Hence, correlationism must assert positively one unconditional, that is, one absolute fact or condition: the facticity of contingency, and in particular, the contingency of the relation.

Factiality versus contingency, or the virtual and the potential

Let's begin this section with a somewhat long quotation, one that I think won't risk your patience, since it paints a powerful portrait:

> If we look through the aperture which we have opened up onto the absolute, what we see there is a rather menacing power—something insensible, and capable of destroying both things and worlds, of bringing forth monstrous absurdities, yet also of never doing anything, of realizing every dream, but also every nightmare, of engendering random and frenetic transformations, or conversely, of producing a universe that remains motionless down to its ultimate recesses, like a cloud bearing the fiercest storms, then the eeriest bright spells, if only for an interval of disquieting calm. We see an omnipotence equal to that of the Cartesian God, and capable of anything, even the inconceivable; but an omnipotence that has become autonomous, without norms, blind, devoid of the other divine perfections, a power with neither goodness nor wisdom, ill-disposed to reassure thought about the veracity of its distinct ideas. . . . . It is a Time capable of destroying even becoming itself by bringing forth, perhaps forever, fixity, stasis, and death.[78]

Here we arrive at *After Finitude*'s subtitle: the "necessity of contingency." Speculative realism takes its first steps beyond correlationism by arguing that the latter's position, that we cannot know the necessity of any being, including ourselves, tells us, as Brassier puts it, "that only contingency necessarily exists."[79] Firstly, it's not clear to us how convincing Meillassoux is, as yet, on this account. He may indeed be right that correlationists can deny all sorts of things, and that they must accept the facticity of the correlation itself. And he may be right that through this we have " 'touched upon' nothing less than an absolute, the *only veritable one*," namely that this relation is "factial."[80] But Meillassoux inflates *this* contingency, this literal contingency or "touching" of the real, to Being as such. We see this in *After Finitude*, where in one page, he provides the quotation above. He then discusses again how this defeats idealism, which argues that the relation is not necessary, then argues that the correlationist must either (a) deny the facticity of the relation and become an idealist or (b) go through "absolutizing facticity."[81] But while this may all be true, what is the warrant to say, just sentences and the next page after this—when he basically says onto-theology is dead—"we do not maintain that a determinate entity exists, but that it is absolutely necessary that *every entity* might not exist."[82] If there is no necessary being, this does not mean all things are as absolutely contingent as the relation of subject and world—for example, those structures that Nolt discusses as making his own arguments possible. There is no warrant Meillassoux provides for moving from "*the only veritable*" absolute (note the singular) to "*everything*" (note the universal), even if we take this absolute contingency to be part of what "*everything*" would be. In other words, as far as we can tell, he only proves what the correlationist has already known: that thinking did not need to be and that, yes, it is absolutely true. This only changes things if one depicts the correlationists as denying all reality as such, even the reality of the correlation, which was not the case, as we've seen in the last chapter. But let's allow Meillassoux himself to summarize his own argument from a lecture given the year after *After Finitude*'s publication:

> The correlationist must claim, against the idealist, that we can conceive the contingency of the correlation, that is: its possible disappearance, for example, with the extinction of humanity. . . . In this way, the correlationist must admit we can positively think of a possibility which is independent of the correlation, since this is precisely the possibility of the non-being of the correlation. . . .

> [T]hen it is a notion we can think as absolute: the absolute lack of reason of any reality; or, in other words, the effective ability of every determined entity—event, thing, or law of subjectivity—*to appear or disappear* with no reason for its being or non-being. Unreason becomes the attribute of an absolute time able to destroy and create any determined entity—event, thing, or law—without any reason for thus creating and destroying.[83]

This "necessity of contingency" is what Meillassoux dubs "*factualité*," translated by Brassier as "factiality"[84]: the fact of the contingency of everything. This is not merely about our facticity as thrown beings in a contingent world where we can never know the future. Nor does it concern the fact that, given the laws of nature, many physical types of being, including our own bodies, may come to be and just as haphazardly pass away. In later publications, Meillassoux provides an easier terminology: the virtual is what he calls "factiality" in *After Finitude*, while the possible is what he calls contingent there. The claim about virtuality or factiality is crucial: Meillassoux is ultimately saying not just that our universe provides us with a number of possible conditions, but that the universe itself can change at any time: it is not, as we shall see, a set of possibilities, but a hyper chaos in which *virtually* anything is always possible:

> Through the principle of factiality, I maintain that I can attain a speculative materialism which clearly refutes correlationism. I can think an X independent of any thinking and I know this, thanks to the correlationist himself and his fight against the absolute. The principle of factiality unveils the ontological truth hidden beneath the radical skepticism of modern philosophy: to be is not to be a correlate, but to be a fact: to be is to be factual—and *this* is a not a fact.[85]

Meillassoux's speculative realism is thus founded on the principle that the in-itself has an *independent* existence and our knowledge of it extends to knowing it "could actually be anything whatsoever"—thus meeting the traditional double-sided test of realism. This fact of contingency is at once minimal and breathtaking: we know that "everything can be otherwise," and this known fact of contingency is *factualité*, the non-facticity of facticity. Here we have Meillassoux's *absolute*, which is not a necessary thing from which all else derives its being. Rather, the only "eternal principle" is the factuality of contingency.[86] Following Meillassoux this far, we come upon three major consequences of his thought: (1) there is no necessary being (here, we have, in sum, a proof for the inexistence of any God); (2) the in-itself is freed, because of its eternal contingency, from the principle of sufficient reason, since no cause can be said to have a particular effect, a point covered in the next section; (3) the in-itself, as Kant argued, is non-contradictory, since any entity that is already otherwise would always be what it is, and thus non-changeable and hence non-contingent.[87] Meillassoux writes:

> Non-contradiction is therefore an eternal truth because it states that if something is, it is determined, and that being determined means being actual as a reality among other equally possible realities. Nothing can be what it is not, because nothing can exhaust, as long as it exists, the universe of possibility.[88]

Meillassoux calls these consequences "figures," which are derived from the principle of factiality, and his speculative materialism is meant to work out additional figures from this principle.

Irrational exuberance

The undoing of Leibniz's theorem that *nihil est sine ratione*, that everything happens for a reason, which has for centuries provided the grounds for thinking both causality and the divine *causa sui*, is for most an astonishing aspect of Meillassoux's work. "There is," he writes, "no reason for anything to be or to remain thus and so rather than otherwise, and this applies as much to the laws that govern the world as to the things of the world."[89] Pause for a moment to consider this approach, namely that any law would itself be up for grabs in this factiality, including gravity and so on. In philosophy of science, the question of what a "law" is and how science confronts it is, of course, a vexing question. But the usual view is that the universe, when it came into being, also came with a certain set of unbreakable laws, for example, the speed of light in Einstein's special relativity. This lays the groundwork for scientific theorizing since discovering the laws of nature is what we have come to expect at least since Newton.

But Meillassoux is not alone in seeing the laws of the universe as less than eternal facts ascertainable by science. The cosmologist Lee Smolin, in his recent *Time Reborn: From the Crisis in Physics to the Future of the Universe*, argues that if we are to think time as real, and not merely epiphenomenal, we must also think the laws of the universe as "evolving"[90] though this also raises the question of whether there is a "meta-law" of physical laws that makes such "evolution" possible. At the least, there would seem to be a link between one stage of this evolution and the next, just as we can see *homo sapiens* as relatable to early creatures such as the mollusk. Meillassoux argues, instead, against such evolutionary thinking. But Meillassoux has also taken many twentieth-century Continental philosophy discussions of the event and contingency to their ultimate conclusion: if there is an event that would produce the wholly new, as his mentor Alain Badiou argues, then it must not only upend the political state of things but also all laws that rule over the world. Here we see the end of the "structure" that provided the starting point for Nolt's realist arguments. Meillassoux argues, "time is not governed by the physical laws," which are the province of the sciences, "because it is the laws themselves which are governed by a mad time," found through his rationalism.[91]

Moving in closer to his argument, Meillassoux posits that he has found "a reason emancipated from the principle of reason."[92] What we have, then, is a "hyper-chaos," since, as Meillassoux points out, without the principle of sufficient reason, not just everything is contingent, but so is every law. (It's "hyper chaos" since even chaos theory begins with law-like principles.) Factiality stipulates that every intra-worldly law is itself contingent and thus possible of being otherwise. For those looking to Meillassoux's return to rationalism as a means for grounding the laws obtained in scientific analysis, Meillassoux's rational principle of "unreason" will surely disappoint. A modern-day Voltaire, Meillassoux is not content to mock the pretensions of Leibniz's assumptions about the best of all possible worlds, but to detach all thinking from the principle of sufficient reason. Cause and effect, indeed every axiom derived from the principle of sufficient reason, is itself contingent within a factial universe. Hume, as we noted in the introduction, argued that there was no epistemological certainty between any cause and any effect. Meillassoux makes this an ontological principle. Radicalizing Hume, Meillassoux argues that given this speculative absolute, it is not just that chance is involved in each roll of the die. The die itself, given the "eternal and lawless possible becoming of every law,"[93] is open to mutability between each toss.

Taking this example, Meillassoux argues that we rightly suspect that it would be infinitely improbable for a pair of die to come up constantly as a pair of deuces, just as we continually deduce that it would be infinitely improbable that the laws of our universe come out the way they do without some prior cause.[94] In other words, if rationally we know, on Meillassoux account, that the laws can be upended from moment to moment, why does the physical universe appear so stable? For Meillassoux, the model we are using is all wrong, since it would leave us to assume that the universe is a "whole" composed of possible laws that would be constantly changing, and thus it would be nearly impossible and unthinkable that our laws keep turning out the way they do each time they are measured. Hence, we assume that the stable laws we experience provide ample evidence for necessary laws governing the universe. "This probabilistic reasoning," Meillassoux points out, "is only valid on condition that what is *a priori* possible be thinkable in terms of *numerical totality*."[95] It is here that we move from the logical absolute of the principle of un-reason to a mathematically inflected absolute, which takes up the Zermelo-Fraenkel axiomatic of set theory in mathematics.[96] What Meillassoux must explain is not why there is something rather than nothing, but rather why what there is appears stable and amenable to physical laws from one moment to the next. (Without this stability, Meillassoux's can have no recourse to the ancestral, since one could posit a physical relativism that makes any stipulation of such facts the hostage of ever-changing laws.) Meillassoux warns us not to use aleatory reasoning to explain away this stability and, by extension, the hyper chaos of the in-itself he describes.

Meillassoux argues that contingency is not chance, since the latter depends on two assumptions called into question by Cantorian set theory: (1) one can logically totalize all the possible outcomes of the universe, in which case the likelihood of a stable universe would be so low as to be all but impossible; (2) and that one can talk about probability not only within the world, but also about the world itself, as one does when discussing the chances of this world being stable. These both mark what Meillassoux dubs the "frequentialist implication."[97] Hence Meillassoux argues there is a difference between chance, which is built out of a totalizable set of possibilities, and the contingency of the set that gives rise to the chance in one set in the first place. In order to make any critique of Meillassoux by pointing out the unlikelihood of the apparent universe, we would need to be able to calculate a set of all possible worlds, and then determine based upon that figure the chances of constancy among them. From there, we could deduce the probability of our own stable world. But chance itself would put order on this hyper chaos, giving this chaotic in-itself a boundary of given possibilities, and the chaos Meillassoux is discussing is one of unbounded possibilities. Or, to put it another way, the idea of chance, which is being used to prove inductively the necessity of physical laws, depends itself on a *set* of physical laws.[98] This bears quick explanation. Probability relies on the conception that there is a *sum total* of possibilities. The probability of a coin flip is derived from the total of all possibilities: heads and tails. Even lotteries, with slim odds, have a total number of possibilities: one's chances are one in several million. Meillassoux's argument relies on Russell's paradox, which means there is no *all*. If a whole, that is to say, a set of all sets, existed, it would have to be a member of itself. If this wasn't the case, then there would an outside of this whole, which then would make it, well, not-Whole. But there are many sets that do not have themselves as members: the set of all water bottles is not itself a water bottle. In this way, the whole would include sets that are members of themselves and sets which aren't.[99] But Russell's paradox means you can't have a set of all sets that are not members of themselves (since the set would itself be a Whole and non-Whole at the same time). This means, simply put, that set theory has had to figure a way out of assuming a set of all sets. Thus, there cannot be a Whole or total of all possibilities, otherwise we have that logical paradox. For Alain Badiou, this is why being is "pure multiplicity." Paul Livingston writes, citing Meillassoux,

> The axioms of post-Cantorian set theory provide "the resources for thinking that the possible is untotalizable." That is, given the fact of the non-existence of the one-all, there is no single, total set of possible worlds or scenarios. This, in turn, allows the disqualification of the "necessitarian inference," which deduces the necessity of physical laws from their apparent stability by reference to a supposed totality of possibilities accessible to *a priori* reasoning, and thus helps to support Meillassoux's own thesis of an overarching absolute and necessary contingency.[100]

Secondly, Meillassoux echoes Heidegger's call, for quite different reasons, to move beyond "calculatory reason," since in "factial ontology" no such calculations of possibilities can be made. For Georg Cantor, who relies on the non-Whole above, there can be no totalization of the possible, since the transfinite stipulates that the "(qualifiable) totality of the thinkable is unthinkable."[101] In the end, "what the set-theoretical axiomatic demonstrates is at the very least a fundamental uncertainty regarding the totalizability of the possible," and thus "we should restrict the claims of aleatory reasoning solely to objects of experience" and "to the very laws of our universe, as if we knew that the latter necessarily belongs to some greater Whole."[102] Thus, we can "detotalize the possible" and still think the "stability of the laws," which is in contrast to those pressing the position that the physical laws are necessary, who are unable to show why "these laws are necessary and why it is these laws, rather than others, that exist."[103] Meillassoux argues that three figures or "archi-facts" derive from factuality: (1) the absolute exists; (2) as we noted, the absolute is non-contradictory; (3) mathematics provides access to the absolute.

This is where Meillassoux leaves science behind, since it is not empirical work that provides an insight into what is, but mathematical "intuition" into the real. What Meillassoux doesn't yet describe is this: the physical world is not a set as in set theory, which are *unchanging* (and thus sets). But the physical world has things that come and go; such is the stuff that makes history and the world go round. This is not to say that the world is a configurable whole, a point at the heart of Heidegger's critique of previous ontologies, but one can't just, as in Badiou, leap from the order of ontology (set theory) to the order of appearing (stable), and expect that the universe is simply the Set of all sets in the mathematical meaning of the term. (Or to put it otherwise: isn't the world of set theory but one set among others?) That is to say, Meillassoux returns to Platonism to argue for an atemporal place from which to think the realm of becoming in a line of dependence. Or at least, isn't this another Cartesian dualism that sees an absolute distinction between the world as it appears and as it is in itself? In any case, if one follows Meillassoux, one can see Einstein was right in saying that God does not play dice with the universe, but for the wrong reasons: there is no God and the universe is not on the model of a pair of dice with a finite set of outcomes. We must be prepared to think after finitude. And when that occurs, then we must be open to the fact that anything can happen. That is what awaits us in the next chapter.

CHAPTER 3
BEYOND BELIEF: DIVINE INEXISTENCE AND THE NEW ETHICS

"Philosophy's concern," for Meillassoux, "is not being [*l'être*], but the perhaps [*le peut-être*]."[1] This dictum forms the basis for Meillassoux's speculative approach. Meillassoux, as we've seen, does not believe it is the task of philosophy to simply repeat the truths of science, or indeed to ground the principle of sufficient reason that underlies scientific practice. What would science even mean if investigators were not looking for the causes of events? Rather, in numerous essays written since *After Finitude*, Meillassoux speculates on what is deducible from the fact of the hyper chaos. This leads Meillassoux to conceiving a "possible God" as well as an ethics and politics that follow from this "divine inexistence." Meillassoux's discussion of this—there's no way around saying it—is where he likely loses many readers, even those who were willing to follow him to the edge of the hyper chaos.[2] His audacious claims may remind some of a graduate student locked away too long who grabs some colleague in the hallway to hold forth on how some error of Einstein means we can undo all of relativity theory, or how quantum mechanics offers a proof for the existence of God. Or how the CIA is involved in massive schemes to simply kill scores of people with robot planes—and no one's doing anything about it. Well, that *last one*. . . . Admittedly, the line between the audacious and the ridiculous is never clear, and as Thomas Kuhn's work on scientific revolutions should remind us, every new kind of knowledge has to negotiate its way from being considered the latter to the former. Adam Kotsko, who has written much on the contemporary Continental philosophy and is a perspicuous commentator on Meillassoux, has gotten off the best set of lines on this aspect of his work:

> My experience of reading Meillassoux:
> While reading: "Wow, this is really seductively counter-intuitive—could he have actually stumbled upon The Answer?"
> A little while after reading: "Wait, no—that's completely insane."[3]

We begin this way to prepare the reader for the chapter to follow, not to disparage Meillassoux's work, which is, without a doubt, quite important. If there is a madness to Meillassoux's claims, it is one for which there is a definite method, one that is not far afield imaginatively from Nietzsche's thinking of eternal return of the same (the view that given an infinite time, we will repeat *this life* eternally) and which follows up on his principle of hyper chaos.

Before proceeding, let us summarize quickly the distinctions from the previous chapter:

1. Contingency or the Possible: Every being in *this* empirical universe could exist, might not have existed, or may change. The timing of our mortality, for example, follows from certain physical laws, but its timing is contingent and thus ever-possible.
2. Facts: Meillassoux uses this word to point to entities that are, well, a fact, but are open to change and could have been otherwise. That you exist is one such fact as you read this book; another fact is the laws of the universe as they stand now.
3. Archi-facts or figures: these are facts that *cannot* be otherwise. First, there is the unchangeable fact that there is something rather than nothing. Another for Meillassoux, along with Kant, is that what exists is without contradiction. As we noted, for him, if there were a contradictory being, it would be necessary, since it is already what it is not, and thus immutable.
4. Factiality or virtuality: This is another archi-fact for Meillassoux, namely that the universe and all its laws can change. Thus, while possibility marks what can happen *within* a given universe, virtuality or factiality is the fact that, from one moment to the next, the whole universe of possibilities is open to change.

This fourth principle means that, for Meillassoux, there can be, from one moment to the next, creation *ex nihilo*. The doctrine of "creation *ex nihilo*" goes back, at least within the Judeo-Christian tradition, to Philo of Alexandria (c. 20 BCE–40 CE). Philo, who was interpreting Plato's notion of creation in the *Timaeus*, was attempting to answer whether or not God created the universe *out of nothing* or from some pre-existing matter. For him, God "created the whole universe out of things that had no previous existence."[4] Moreover, this God is outside of time and yet creates time as well. Hence God, for Philo, did not begin to create the world at a certain moment, but he is "eternally applying himself to its creation."[5] God, as *outside* time, as the eternal creator of time, is a necessary being who grounds the world at each moment. Now, for Meillassoux, there is no necessary being, yet there is a hyper chaos that is "eternal" and beyond the dictates of physical time: "Time is not governed by the physical laws because it is the laws themselves which are governed by a mad time."[6] For Meillassoux, then, this is a "time without becoming," since it is both what creates the possibility of (physical) time and what can make time or the flow of becoming stop. This is why, despite his view of hyper chaos, Meillassoux does not depict being as an inexorable process of becoming, since "the hyperchaotic time is able to create and destroy even becoming, producing without reason fixidity or movement."[7] Formally, at least, Meillassoux, whose dissertation worked through various philosophical conceptions of divinity, comes close to this Neo-Platonic conception of time. First, for Philo, as with the other Neo-Platonists, God created the world through the *Logos*, that is, the ultimate rational principle, and God was not Himself partaking in the matter to be formed. In addition, creation was not, as in Aristotle, simply at the beginning point of the cosmos, but *occurs at each moment*. The mathematical intuition that Meillassoux utilizes is precisely a form of *logos* and *ratio* (reason) that describes the movement from hyper chaos to the created. Secondly, God, as pure form, is not contaminated, according to Philo, by matter. And while Meillassoux has taken on the term "speculative materialism"[8] for his project, we'll see that, however difficult it is to perceive what is meant by a "before" and "after" in this eternity of hyper chaos—one finds this conundrum in Philo when he describes creation by an eternal being forever in the present—Meillassoux is clear that matter was created *ex nihilo*, and thus would always be second to a non-material, "non-corporeal," we could say, Time before time of this materiality. Hence as we've seen, for Meillassoux there is no inexorable structure, as in Nolt, nor is there an evolutionism found in Lee Smolin, or Charles Sanders Peirce, from whom he borrows the idea.[9]

But is this really a return to Platonism? Meillassoux argues that hyper chaos, as non-grounded, as non-necessary, provides an "anarchic" principle unrecognizable to the Neo-Platonists: "If laws themselves are temporal, then the advent of what *is* ultimately obeys no law—no *archē* where it would already be present before its advent."[10] And thus, he could argue, his principle of divine inexistence is one that has not been attempted or foreseen in metaphysics or ontotheology. Moreover, where the Neo-Platonists argue for a Good beyond being, that is, transcendence, Meillassoux stipulates that his work is to demonstrate the immanent principle by which such radical change occurs.[11] Immanence itself has a long philosophical trajectory, bringing in such figures as Spinoza, Bergson, and Deleuze. Few have understood the full stakes of its meaning, even as this term gets thrown around quite often by philosophical commentators. Giorgio Agamben, beyond those thinkers above, is one of the few to touch on just why Deleuze called "immanence . . . the very vertigo of philosophy."[12] He notes that in figures like Spinoza, if we take their immanence seriously, it is not only the case that we must take on the rather superficial conception that there is no "world beyond" this one, but it's also the case that our very concepts arrived in no other space than created being. For Spinoza, for example, there were no transcendent rights in politics; only the movement of power in given societies. The task, then, is to work out conceptions of nature, politics, and ethics while in some sense recognizing that reason *itself* is formed in and through the becoming of existence. There is, as such, no mental step back from creation, and thus we end up in a dizzying vertigo where we must give up our common-place notions, not least those views that look to "transcendent modes" of existence from which to value our own, whether it's the eternal God forever creating our fallen universe, or the rights we believe ourselves to have inalienably, but are utterly useless when power doesn't move our way. For the immanentist, there can be no metaphysical dualisms, as in Descartes, or the transcendental schematism found in Kant. Speaking of Spinoza, Hasana Sharp sets out the ethical stakes of these immanentisms:

> Action within a plane of immanence opposes any notion of activity that depends upon transcendence of one's situation, impulse, or causal environment. Action becomes an endeavor to cultivate a sensuous receptivity, in order better to determine the relations of composition that most enable one to think and thrive. Since one can exist only by virtue of the affects that circulate in one's environment, [immanentist] ethics entails the development of mutually beneficial affective compositions.[13]

Another comparison, just as in the last chapter, with Spinoza would be useful, not least since his power ontology will ground other thinkers we cover later in this book. First, Spinoza held that societal values were created in and through the movement of power in a given society. This often got him accused of ethical nihilism (no ethics exist as such), but the larger point was humans could *not* transcend in any particular way their given situation, and thus we must empower ourselves while recognizing our bodies are caught in a chain of cause and effect. In other words, Spinoza's immanentism adhered to the principle of sufficient reason, which in both Spinoza and Leibniz meant that all that occurs must necessarily happen. In fact, this prison-house of natural causality was one that many feared forever denuded humanity of freedom, since one could do no better than reflect upon one's position in a nexus of causal relations. This is the lacuna of determinism. But for Meillassoux, there is no principle of sufficient reason, no iron law of cause-and-effect, and thus he can say "we see that the world"—pace one form of reading Spinozism—"is by no means the prisoner of whatever arises within it."[14] He goes further to stipulate that there is always "more in the effect than in the cause," and without a God, we can still be astonished at the "staggering power of novelty in *our own* world."[15] In short, we can have Godless miracles, something Spinoza had worked to refute in his *Ethics* even for God.

For Meillassoux, rather than a mystification of being—all is "without-why" and we must throw up our hands and say it just happens—we can rationally *know* there is and has been creation *ex nihilo*. But there is also another attack on this line of Spinozism we will see: Meillassoux argues that our life as it is *now* is faced with the absurdity Albert Camus suggested—in contrast to the affirmation of this life found in Spinoza's and Deleuze's immanentisms. After the horrors of the twentieth century, we would be right to see this life as often accorded no value, and at times doomed to a politics that is nothing but the worst. Nothing could be further from thinkers such as Deleuze and Spinoza, however, who argue for affirming being. Meillassoux does not join this immanentist affirmation society, since meaning is not to be found from the vantage point of our current context—Lord knows, in our darkest moments, it's hard to argue with him—but in the rational knowledge that another World, literally, is possible. This World to come marks a time when justice reigns, not just for those then living, but for those murdered in the horrors of history, those who will be redeemed by rebirth through the power of a future God. Justice is never to be found in the here and now, but is always to come, an advent that may not happen, but is the only hope for us in this unjust world.

From nothing, everything

We have seen in the last chapter that Meillassoux's account of the virtual or "factial" is an indirect proof for the inexistence of the divine. That is, if there is no necessary being, then there is *nothing* subtending the world. And we have seen, too, that his rejection of the principle of sufficient reason means that he has arrived at an "irreligious" conception of creation, not just of the world, but of events taking place within *this* world: "Advent [*surgissement*] *ex nihilo* thus presents itself as the concept *par excellence* of a world without God, and for that very reason it allows us to produce *an irreligious notion of the origin of pure novelty*."[16] For Meillassoux, then, we have for too long allowed "creation" to be taken over by the fideists who shrug their shoulders at the mystery of creation and make "God" the stop-gap for what the faithful believe cannot be rationally explained.

> The origin of novelty is supposed to be unthinkable for a purely human understanding; it is pure nonsense, because it is transcendent; it is a divine act. Such statements are the inaugural declaration of faith, whose victory over human minds is now so complete that even the most intransigent atheists seem to pay homage to it.[17]

But Meillassoux argues that the idea of creation *ex nihilo* is a rational principle and is thus beyond belief—perhaps in both senses for some readers—since it can be known. Even atheists, who otherwise might describe the origin of the world as beyond some epistemic limit and hence "ineffable," can now have a rational basis for their *current* atheism. As will become clear, Meillassoux is not himself an atheist; his "philosophical irreligion is not a form of atheism, but rather the condition for an authentic access to the divine."[18]

Now, if there is nothing subtending the world and, indeed, there is no meta-universe that provides the laws for what happens *in this universe*, except the mighty hyper chaos, and if there are no external "laws" that tell us why *this* universe was created, Meillassoux pushes us still further: hyper chaos, indeed, has intervened in this world. This marks his antinaturalism. Here, we come upon another set of distinctions:

1. World (*Monde*) (with a capital letter), for Meillassoux, is a given universe of particular laws, which he also calls "orders" (*ordres*). These Worlds were created *ex nihilo* given the vicissitudes of hyper chaos and, for Meillassoux, they occur *without reason*, that is, each World comes about as an "effect" unexplainable from a given previous World.
2. The "intra-Worldly [*intra-Mondaine*]": what occurs and is possible within a determinant World. For example, in a World in which life

exists, evolution of new species can occur; in a World where thought is available, we can witness "creative invention."[19]

3. Finally, Meillassoux will use the word "world" (*monde*) (lower-case "w") to designate the "non-Whole" of what is. He's a bit unclear on what this means: "Worlds arise suddenly from the world, and if these have a right to a majestic capital letter for the first time, it is because there is more in the World than in the world, since there is more in what ensues than there is in the origin (more in the 'effect' than in the 'cause')."[20] This suggests that Meillassoux thinks of the "world" as the "factial" or the "virtual," the hyper chaos that gives rise to new Worlds.[21]

In *Divine Inexistence*, Meillassoux provides an account of three Worlds arising out the world of chaos. Let's discuss each, before turning to the possible God and the immortality to come that will be the focus of the rest of this chapter.

1. Matter

In both the published extracts in Graham Harman's *Quentin Meillassoux: Philosophy in the Making* and his 1997 dissertation *L'Inexistence divine*, Meillassoux has puzzlingly little to say about the appearance of this first World, namely the World of matter, out of the world of chaos, nor does he discuss this in several essays clearly building on the relevant sections of that work, such as his "The Immanence of the World Beyond."[22] Perhaps this is because it would make clear the limits of his own supposed materialism. Here is where he mentions, however, that the material World was one clearly not presaged by a previous World—and thus the World of matter appeared *ex nihilo*:

> [L]aws have no reason to be constant, and nothing entails that they will not contain new constants in the future. Such cases of advent [*surgissement*] . . . can be divided into three *orders* [that is, Worlds] that mark the essential ruptures of becoming: *matter*, *life*, and *thought*. *Each* of these three *appears* [my emphasis] as a Universe that cannot be *qualitatively* reduced to *anything* [my emphasis] that preceded it.[23]

We will turn soon enough to his accounts of these other Worlds, but it's interesting that he makes no mention of the advent of matter any further in his examples. In any case, it's clear for him that matter—in a manner analogical to the big bang physical theories—"appeared" not from proto-matter, as in the view of Divine *Logos* of Philo, but was created out of *nothing*, that is, out of non-materiality via the eternal chaos he describes.

2. Life

Meillassoux's argument is convoluted regarding this World—basically the point is that qualitative leaps cannot be explained by gathering more quantitative evidence—but his method is *not* to delve into the scientific literature, which is vast, concerning how organic creatures appeared out of the inorganic matter that first made up this world. Meillassoux is clear, though, that life could not be presaged by the causal relations of the World of matter, but rather is a qualitative leap irreducible to materiality:

> As long as reason is identified with thinking the constancy of laws, it remains impossible to think rationally about the advent of life in matter, because it cannot be understand [*sic*] how the lifeless can produce a qualitative multiplicity of affects and perceptions from a certain "molecular geometry."[24]

This World is a "universe of cases that were *in no way* contained in the universe previously."[25] In other words, against those materialists who argue that, in fact, matter provides the necessary and sufficient conditions for the creation of the organic, Meillassoux argues, "The configurations of life would break the laws of chance, because they would not at all be the possible cases *of* matter, but rather the correlate *within* matter of the appearance *ex nihilo* of vital contents."[26] Here, Meillassoux is walking a fine line between (1) wanting to describe the advent of life, which requires a limit to scientific, empirical investigations of the matter, and (2) not ceding any ground to those fideists who would use God to fill in the gaps. Meillassoux, though, repeats arguments made by fideists who want, too, to show that life is a creation impossible given the make-up of the previous World of the inorganic. Both groups, then, sidestep an entire literature that describes the causal reasons for the appearance of organic life from inorganic matter. No doubt, just defining the distinction between the organic and the inorganic is a vexing problem, filling volumes of excellent works on the topic. However, abiogenesis, the production of life out of the original matter pervading the Earth some 3.5 billion years ago, is not something that simply happened *then*, in the ancestral, as we might say, but has been reproduced in laboratories going back to the Miller–Urey experiments in the early 1950s; thus there would seem to be room for robust scientific explanations for the rise of organic from inorganic manner not needing a thinking of creation *ex nihilo*. Now, it could be that Meillassoux could say that, yes, *after the ex nihilo* event some billions of years ago, the laws of this World *now* make such lab experiments possible and thus explain his contentions. Indeed, he makes this exact claim:

> [T]his vital multiplicity *is added to* (and *inserted into*) the matter-Universe, *retroactively* [my emphasis] modifying the latter by its advent [*surgissement*] in the mist of it. For the advent of life is not the necessary effect of a material configuration (such claims *have never made sense* [my emphasis]). Instead, it is the contingent and conjoint creation of a Universe of qualities *and* material conditions that were both inexistent until then.[27]

But would this not make him the very philosopher whose caveats undercut the ancestral-type statements so important to his critique of correlationism? This is perhaps where the creation *ex nihilo* threatens the ultimate skepticism. For example, Bertrand Russell once provided a hypothesis that philosophers couldn't convincingly argue against the fact that the world was created 5 minutes ago, complete with the requisite fossil evidence and historical memories.[28] If an event *ex post facto* creates the emergence of its own physical causes, then one seemingly no longer can stand on the "literality" of the ancestral statements. In other words, Meillassoux's claims for a hyper chaos would threaten any claims for ancestrality that stages his critique of correlationism.

But he would also be joining common cause with the very fideists he chastises.[29] Instead of a God, though, he argues that what we have is the "contingent advent of a law" providing for life "without there being a law for the advent of laws," that is, procedures for foreseeing when this creation *ex nihilo* is to occur. We cannot begin to enter the *aporiai* of attempting to think the past based upon this view of hyper chaos, since it could be the case that whatever claims we make of the past will only be retrojections based upon the *new* laws created within a given world. It would seem to leave any account of the past relativized to the present: at this point, given the laws *now*, it is the case that we can carbon date these organisms and ascertain the date of the universe as such and such.

3. Thought

Here Meillassoux touches on another of the most written-about topics in recent philosophy: how did thought appear out of what was seemingly non-conscious materiality? That is, as he puts it, how did "the radical excess" that is "the travails of life or consciousness" appear?[30] Again, he suggests scientists are uninterested in the problem, which is demonstrably untrue, or perhaps he is just lead to sidestep all scientific assertions on the matter as beside the point. No doubt, simply defining the specific quality that marks so-called "thought" from forms of recursivity in the human raises interminable questions—perhaps the oldest in philosophy. Also, it's unclear if Meillassoux considers thought to be extra-material, that is, non-reductive to physical processes in the brain. In this contention, he would not be alone, but various neuroscientists and those working on the philosophy of mind have not simply thrown up their hands at the problem of how consciousness arose through material, causal relations.

Another point is important: thought, for Meillassoux, has a specific meaning, namely the ability of the human being, as opposed to other forms of organic life, to think the contingency of the laws of nature: "All quality as quality is without why, since none of its content refers to anything other than the advent *ex nihilo* of its being."[31] In this way, the human is radically different from other living beings, since it has the ability to reason and thus come to grips with the creation of Worlds: "Humans are in fact defined by their access to truth, understood as the eternal contingency of that which is."[32] (Of course, as of this moment, Meillasoux may be the only human to be acceding to this.) To be, for the existentialist, was to be condemned to be free; for Meillassoux, to exist is to be burdened with the fact that all that exists is free to be otherwise.

The God who may be

Concerning the fourth World, the World of justice, he is perhaps on steadier ground. While the previous Worlds of life and thought could arguably be explained by the intra-worldly forces, there is simply no physical force that could give rise to the Future God he argues for; there's no way to get from our vast, if finite universe, to an omniscient, omnipotent, infinite being; this is the premise of Anselm-type proofs for the existence of God. We have seen that Meillassoux has already argued that *there is no God*, but his fourth World requires, out of the world (lower case) a creation *ex nihilo* of a future God who answers human beings' greatest aspirations.

I borrow the title for this section from Richard Kearney's 2001 *The God Who May Be: A Hermeneutics of Religion*. By discussing Kearney's work, we can, as with Nolt in the last chapter, accent the difference in approach by Meillassoux. Kearney is interested in thinking neither a God that *is* nor a God that *isn't*, since both define God onto-theologically, that is, as a Being that subtends all of being. He also thinks metaphysics has a "tendency to reify God by reducing Him to a being—albeit the highest, first, and most indeterminate of all beings."[33] We will soon see Meillassoux's own reasons for rejecting this choice as well. Kearney is interested in reversing the schema of thinking of God as pure actuality, as found in Aristotle and Aquinas, among others. The thinking goes, if God were in any way "possible," that is, incomplete, then God would be an imperfect being and therefore not God. But Kearney inverts this gesture by arguing for thinking hermeneutically a "possible God" that "neither *is* nor *is not* but *may be*."[34] Meillassoux uses exactly the same wording. Kearney, like Meillassoux, does not believe that God is a necessary being. If this were the case, he argues, it would come at the cost of thinking of God as unfree and also face Heidegger's critique of onto-theology. This God would also be responsible for all the evil in the World, since it would be the transcendental cause of all that is—the good, the bad, and the ugly. Kearney proposes his own hermeneutic eschatology that thinks God not as what *is*, but as a promise *for us*. The hermeneutic aspect of this reading—we are moving quickly here—comes from reinterpreting Exodus 3:14. There God answers Moses at the burning bush, in Hebrew, *'ehyeh 'aser 'ehyeh*, typically translated as "I AM WHO AM." This is the translation of the Greek "*ego eimi ho on*," that is, "I am the one who is." For Kearney, without going into too much linguistic detail, this Greek translation misses the "dynamism" of the Hebrew, which he renders as "*I am as I shall show myself*"—a translation that is less an ontological statement than an *ethical* promise made in the face of Moses, who returns to Egypt to declare "a message of emancipation to his people."[35] Put otherwise, God is revealed as a promise, as a "God who may be," and therefore—we will see the ultimate correlationist move here—is revealed to be not "an essence *in se* [in itself]," but as an "I-Self *for us*."[36]

> Exodus 3 is the proclamation that God has invested the *whole of Himself* in his emissary's history [that is, without remnant beyond that history]. . . . [T]he Exodic act of divine self-disclosure signals

> an *inextricable* communion between God and humans . . . a *shared* history of becoming. . . . God may henceforth be recognized as someone who *becomes with us* [his emphasis], someone as *dependent* on us as we are on him. . . . Faced with the burning bush one doesn't merely *speculate*; one runs, or if one holds one's ground, one praises, dances, acts.[37]

The retranslation of Exodus 3:14 as "I-AM-WHO-MAY-BE" reveals a God less as *esse* (being) than as *posse* (possibility), and thus reveals a "promise" of a "a kingdom of justice and love." Meillassoux repeats this eschatological promise, in quite another register. As Kearney nicely summarizes, "the Exodic God obviates the extremes of atheistic and theistic dogmatism in the name of a still small voice that whispers and cries in the wilderness: *perhaps*."[38]

Again, God neither *is* nor *isn't*, but is the radical "perhaps" to come. Yet we can already begin to see the dividing line from Meillassoux's "God who may be," given that Meillassoux would see no need for these passages in Exodus, since his thinking is the result of speculation on the pure contingency of being. Nevertheless, as with Kearney's approach, what drives Meillassoux's "eschatological" speculation is very much ethical and political. Recall from the last chapter that the correlationist, according to Meillassoux, has left open the field for all kinds of theism. Once we "limit" the "cognitive claims of reason" concerning the absolute, he argues, "we generate a vacuum in which belief can find its niche."[39] We have also seen that the necessity of contingency is also his proof for God's inexistence. But Meillassoux is no atheist, since he thinks the metaphysical tradition has given us a false choice, using words that mirror Kearney's claims in *The God Who May Be*: "either God exists, or God doesn't" forecloses thinking that "God is possible . . . that God can really come into being in the future."[40] This is not formed given the background of a particular Biblical passage, as in Kearney's correlational view of God's place in our history, but through a deduction from Meillassoux's speculative pivot: if the correlationist must admit the absolute fact of the contingency of the relation, then the real is *absolutely* contingent, that is, factial or virtual. In this way, nothing can be ruled out of bounds; the only impossibility is that there could be a contradictory or a necessary being. But everything is possible, there's nothing to rule out, even the event of a future God: "God does not exist, *but there is no reason that this should remain so*, that his non-existence should *always* remain so."[41]

For Meillassoux, this does not mean that it must happen that a future God will come to be, nevertheless there remains an eternal hope for "an essentially uncontrollable event—for a man and for a God—which cannot be rendered improbable, since it concerns the emergence of physical constants and not of facts subordinated to those constants."[42] To use his terminology from above, out of the world of the virtual or the superchaotic may arrive a fourth World beyond matter, life, and thought: "For only this [W]orld[43] could introduce into the future an irreducibility and a novelty as radical as that of life in relationship to matter, or thought in relationship to life," or indeed the matter from whatever existed before it.[44]

But what forms the basis for Meillassoux's hope is not simply the outcome of an abstract set of arguments one expects from the writer of *After Finitude*. This fourth World he dubs "justice," and thus he provides an eschatology where, created *ex nihilo*, the God once promised in Exodus will mark our own exodus from enslavement to tyranny and death in this World. Indeed, he argues not only that this thinking of the possible God marks a future just world, but should have effects upon us in *this* one.

> Our intention then is to make the fourth [W]orld a possibility which can enhance, *in our own world*, the subjectivity of human beings living in our day by profoundly transforming the private lives of those who take seriously such a hypothesis. . . . I think that the *most important for philosophy—its final challenge—is not being, but "may-be [peut-être]*," For the may-be unites within itself the true heart of every ontology (the absoluteness of factial possibility) and the deepest aspirations of ethics (the universal fulfillment of justice).[45]

These considerations should produce not a "theoretical" consideration of the virtual God, but a "dense possibility," one that has effects on one's actions in the here-and-now mirroring Heidegger's own privileging of the practical over the theoretical.[46] This is his "spectral dilemma."

The departed

"We must revive the extreme hope of eschatology in order," Meillassoux writes, "to act—and right away—in view of an unconditional equality for all people, whose ultimate realization no longer depends *on us* [my emphasis] but on an omnipotent God who guarantees 'the soundness of our folly.'"[47] For Meillassoux, the atheism/theism debate presents not just a false choice ontologically but introduces a "spectral dilemma," which, in some sense, demonstrates a need to believe.

On the one hand, the theist, in her better moments, does not wish for immortality for her own sake, but rather for the sake of the other whose loss she cannot begin to express. A belief in God is necessary, not to give her life meaning but to contemplate the redemption of humanity after all the horrors of our history. For this reason, Meillassoux presents us with the "essential specter," whose death deepens us "into a destructive, because obsessive, memory of the disappeared."[48] The essential specter, he writes, cannot be properly mourned since it results from a "death that bears no meaning, no completion, no fulfillment: just an atrocious interruption of life, such that it would be simply obscene to think that it was not experienced as such by those who suffered it."[49]

There is no getting around the central affective role death and immortality play in Meillassoux's work, from his argument from death in *After Finitude*, covered in the last chapter, to his assertion that the only proper response to this finitude is an "essential grief," which "would mean to live with essential specters, and *no longer die with them* [my emphasis]."[50] The dividing line is unclear concerning essential and non-essential specters—for numerous reasons, he probably wouldn't wish to suggest there are deaths less mournable than others—but we should pause to think through the relation to death Meillassoux is espousing, not least since he argues that lives interrupted in such ways would need a "completion" or "fulfillment."[51]

In essence, he is arguing that the "work of mourning" for essential specters—he lists the deaths of children and those who died in mass slaughters—is but a "morbid" dying *with* the dead, and his task is to end the work of mourning through an eschatology that ends the despair over these specters.

> How can we accept the appalling injustice done to some, which renders impossible a grief capable of making sense of our relation to the departed? The problem of immortality should not be conceived in terms of personal salvation, but in terms of collective justice, of possible reparation of an extreme wrong. . . . I do know that some lives are entitled to begin again so as to overcome the atrocious end inflicted upon them.[52]

For Freud, the "work of mourning" meant the effort to evince a "libidinal withdrawal" or displacement from one object to another, which would mark a "successful mourning." Without this displacement, there is only interminable melancholia; for Meillassoux, this is precisely our mortal condition without God. The most eloquent writer on mourning in recent memory has been Jacques Derrida, who writes, for very different reasons than Meillassoux, that the work of mourning is impossible: "Whoever thus works *at* the work of mourning learns the impossible—and that mourning is interminable. Inconsolable. Irreconcilable."[53] There is a double injunction in mourning, one that those who have had a parent, sibling, or friend die will instantly recognize, even if, as Derrida argues, the work of mourning structures all our relations from the very beginning. (As a friend, we may always have to bear witness to the death of the Other.) To mourn means an unconditional witnessing to the singularity of the Other, a testimony that could go on without end: each death is just this once, the end of the world, because each will have lived just this once, and one's own uniqueness is how one testifies while mourning all those who have passed. There is always more than "one world," Derrida writes, and a God, he argues, could only ever guarantee a succession across worlds, but never a world as it is lost in the impossible mourning.

> The death of the other, not only but more so if one loves the other, does not announce an absence, a disappearance, the end of this or that life, that is to say, of a world as it would *appear to a given living being*. Death signifies each time the end of the world in totality, the end of every possible world, and each time the end of the world in its total uniqueness, thus *irreplaceable* and infinite. As if the repetition of an infinite whole were once more possible: of the end of the world as such, of *the only world which is*, each time.[54]

Each time the end of the world, not as it's given "for us," but each time, all over again. There is no rule or law for when one stops the testimony to this death. When to end mourning formally? When to retire the black clothing? If truly it were the end of the world, how could this not go on without end? When would your return to "normalcy" not be a betrayal? And yet, would not this endless mourning also evince a crucial narcissism, given that one's mourning for the other, endlessly, would only have the effect of always speaking *for* them—so caught in grief *are you*? And would not all this mourning risk replacing you *for* the Other? Each work of mourning is conditioned by this impossible *aporia*; there thus can be no law of mourning—the regularized spectacles around death barely conceal this fact.

Central to Derrida's account—despite his many criticisms of Heidegger, he never diverted from this point—is the Heideggerian conception that our lives are lived in our being-towards-death, our being towards our future impossibility—and not just ours, but that of our friends and indeed the whole of the world. Existence itself is just this once, singular and unique, always in the shadow of the end of the world. Post-Heideggerian ethics in Continental philosophy starts with the premise of our finitude and Meillassoux reverses this, since a life without God would be "absurd" and intrinsically unjust.[55] As the atheist would point out, in Meillassoux's depiction, a belief in an existing God would be as absurd as a World without God, since this would be a God who provides for a "moral hell" in which such "essential spectres" come to be.[56] Here is Meillassoux's summation of this "spectral dilemma":

> The religious position maintains that grief is possible only if one is able to hope for something other than their death on behalf of the dead. Spectres join their side only on the day when we are able to hope to see them join our own. For the atheist position, the existence of God is an unsurmountable obstacle to the working out of such a hope, because it is unthinkable for the atheist that a just God could allow horrendous deaths.[57]

The only ethical relation to the dead, he believes, is to wish for their resurrection, to wish for immortality on their behalf. "The sole possible novelty surpassing humans just as humans surpass life would be the recommencement of the human . . . it is only the World of the rebirth of humans that makes universal justice possible, by *erasing* even the injustice of shattered lives."[58] Before arriving at Meillassoux's "solution," we should emphasize again how overcoming death structures his work—to the point that it is something we can hope is forever put under "erasure." One of Borges' most insightful stories, "The Immortal," concerns a Roman soldier who, after a battle, escapes through the desert only to come upon a city of byzantine structures. The people of that city do not die, though this is not a place of joy, but infinite tedium: all has been done before as it will be done again—sorrows and joys, the quotidian and the extraordinary. Some fall and writhe in pain, but no help is forthcoming, since even pain has lost its meaning. In the darkness of the night, who doesn't wish to negotiate away the deaths of our loved ones and ourselves? But Heidegger's account of being-towards-death argues that this ontological finitude is what impels us to act here and now, perhaps for a more just world (though not, it should be said, necessarily in Heidegger's own case), or perhaps for more quotidian, if still important acts. The fact of death would not, then, lead to simple nihilism, but to the event of meaning and value in the first place. That is, on Heidegger's account, our finitude is the source, speaking loosely, of our will to act, not just to stare myopically into the dead of the night. This marks Derrida's affirmation of life as well.

Meillassoux's answer to the spectral dilemma is that we neither choose *for* or *against* God's existence, as the theists and atheists do, but follow the proposition that "God does not *yet* exist." This is his irreligious doctrine of "divine inexistence." If God does not exist *now*, then the atheist cannot condemn God for the evil of this World. And yet, that this God *may* exist brings hope for the resurrection of the dead. This God will thus be "innocent of the disasters of the world and in whom one could hope for the power to grant to specters something besides death."[59] Accordingly, the event of God is "really possible," though not necessary, and is therefore "eternally contingent, forever uncontrollable and completely improbablizable"—just as improbablizable, he thinks, as the *ex nihilo* advents of matter, life, and thought.[60] Moreover, "this eternal possible *frees me* from suffering over the appalling misfortune of those who have experienced atrocious deaths, allows me to escape being paralyzed by an impossible mourning"[61]—in short, it provides a rationalistic therapy for impossible mourning. Where many twentieth-century French philosophers put the fact of death at the center of their philosophical work, Meillassoux's French philosophy of the twenty-first offers the hope for superseding our mortal coil, a hope for the day, if we can call it that, when death is itself given its last rites, or rather, put on life support for the time being, since, of course, given hyper chaos, one cannot rule out another World of death to come, a point that would seem to obviate much of the analysis in the first place.

Come, again?

But, certainly, many have passed away already, and so Meillassoux argues that the immortality to come, if it is to equal the dignity of a God, requires the resurrection of the dead. "The rebirth of bodies is not illogical" and "it must also be possible": it would "occur suddenly in the very fashion in which a new Universe of cases suddenly appears in the midst of the non-Whole."[62] As such, "Rebirth can thus be assimilated to the improbablizable advent of a new constancy."[63] This hope is ethical in nature. If we believe in true equality, then we will see no difference among different races, creeds, and even life status. For Meillassoux, the great crimes of the Soviet Union and other totalitarian regimes resulted from a sacrificial politics that put the dead in the service of the living. He argues that if those who died did not matter to the politics of the present, then so many would have to die in the present for the sake of those to come. This nihilist politics is thus premised on an inequality of the living and the dead. But if justice is due to "every human without exception," it would engage the living and the dead, the young and the old, and so on.[64]

The importance of his solution to the spectral dilemma, he says, is not just that it provides hope. Rather, he argues that the rational subject that comes to grips with the possible God will experience a "transformation of subjectivity." "Unchained" from the "sickness of spiritual misfortune" of an unjust the world this subject will neither be without God nor with a God that exists but allows all sorts of calamities. Meillassoux calls this "transformed" being the "vectorial subject," who is "neither religious nor atheist but philosophical."[65] This subject is "liberated" from what is now eroding it, namely "disillusionment" and "despair."[66] Against the Kantian version of practical reason that is "finite," Meillassoux argues for a new ethics based on the "illimitation of the capacities of reason."[67] Now, on this point he is imprecise, since one can see the "illimitation" of a certain theoretical reason, but it's not straightforward why this "illimitation" should lead to a different praxis by the subject. That is, is this a theoretical understanding of this hope, or a change in praxis in this World? Moreover, Meillassoux's tact is highly rationalist, not simply in terms of this illimitable reason, but, more specifically, given that he deduces from the dilemma itself a certain "despair" eating away at the subject—a theoretical claim trumping a sociological claim: *a priori* it is the case that you should be desolute over the current World. But surely even after Nietzsche's "death of God," it's not a given that these beings he discusses see the choices as starkly as Meillassoux portrays them.

In any event, Meillassoux argues that this "transversal subject" will not just need to cross from the despair of the choice of either an unjust, but existing God or a non-existing God, but also traverse a secondary moment he calls "nihilism." Once this subject realizes the possibility of a future God, only this subject can be a true nihilist, since the subject may not want the World of justice to come *once it has arrived.* According to Meillassoux, the vectorial subject, formed wholly by hope of a new World, would then lose meaning in the face of that World's arrival; there is nothing to hope *for*, since God has come and equality prevails. Meillassoux suggests that his vectorial subject will face the predicament of Borges's story: "What will we do when we will have become forever what the Middle Ages calls a traveler—a *viator*—a man of the earth and not the blessed in heaven?" This "*viator*" would be "forever condemned to his living condition, a kind of prosaic immortal without any transcendence or struggle to give meaning to the undefined pursuit of his being."[68] In other words, we would finally have, following Marx, a life "without politics" and with universal equality. All that is left would be to live "an existence dedicated to its own proper experience."[69]

This has been central to Meillassoux's work from his dissertation to his most recently published works. Inevitable questions arise and we should not be shy about them. Meillassoux's claim is that there is a transition from this World to the next that is not of our own making, since it "proceeds from an ontological uprising that is independent of our action."[70] He quickly notes that the vectorial subject will not simply await, passively, the coming World, but it's not at all clear why this would be the case, if, again, all this is "independent of our action."[71] He may have solved the spectral dilemma, but his work is still haunted by the specter of political quietism. What is more Meillassoux's claims that despair comes from the divorce of ethics from being, that is, we literally can't live our values in this World. This provides him with an immanentist theory of ethics, since unlike in Kant, for example, values do not transcend being itself, though of course it's unclear why equality would spring from hyper chaos—how is it immanently inscribed in being, except as a future possibility, among many others? In any case, "the goal of every philosophy must be the immanent inscription of values in being."[72] But Meillassoux has yet to explain why his set of values (a world of equality) trumps all others, or would automatically do so for the future God. All thinkers of immanence have had to face the problem of the link between their ontology and their ethics. Certainly, they have ways to answer this question: if there is only this plane of existence, this movement of power, from where does one derive ethics except the authorities in place? How does this not end in might makes right? We've seen Sharp define this ethics as "action within a plane of immanence" that "opposes any notion of activity that depends upon transcendence of one's situation, impulse, or causal environment. Action becomes an endeavor to cultivate a sensuous receptivity." Meillassoux has yet to explicate an ethics of *this* world, except by attempting to represent this *future* World in the here and now. We should all praise a world of absolute equality, though he's not clear what is "equal" beyond adequate material sustenance for all. But in a World without equality, demonstrably *without* an inscription of the values he seeks, where does his assertion of values come from, if not a transcendental use of reason that most thinkers of immanence decry, one that can step back, so to speak, from the historical ethics of the here and now? How can he claim a "radical immanence" and then declare, from within *this* given World, the ability to leap ahead to think a future worthy of the name? In Derrida's work, for example, we get a thinking of the "to-come," the future "worthy of the name." But in Derrida's work, this future is never *wholly* new; it is unforeseeable but is not a total detachment from history. For example, his notion of "democracy to come" is an unconditional claim on us here and now, and one can never have the assurance that this legacy—this promise from the past—has ever arrived. Thus politics is interminable for him—as it is from thinkers ranging from Arendt to Žižek in the alphabet of philosophers over the last century. But Meillassoux's literal World "to come" is a foreseeable World that is wholly new, yet one might suggest Meillassoux mines Western political philosophy and its history for precisely what is to come: material equality and so on. And if Meillassoux is right that the true immanentist affirms this life—this is in line with immanentists such as Deleuze and Spinoza—then the irony is that Meillassoux is precisely not doing this: he is saying the *only* life we can affirm is, in fact, not *this* human life: one that faces injustice and the infirmities of age, a life of politics and a life of difference from one to the other. This all must be "erased" such that then we can live this life forever, and it would be *that* life that he would *then* affirm. Finally, it's not clear why this outcome would come over any other: why not a life born by a Demiurge who resurrects us only to provide us with greater evils? To paraphrase Dostoyevsky, when God is possible, all is permitted. To conclude, then, Meillassoux has brought us to the limits of thought in the form of an audacious argument not for a belief in God but for a rationalist ethics that proceeds from his speculative realism.

CHAPTER 4
OBJECT-ORIENTED ONTOLOGY

> We then have to go beyond the phenomenology that reduces things to the structures that govern and are revealed in the succession of sensible appearances. Things are as real as we are, and just as our bodily reality is not reducible to a succession of visual and audible patterns, so things are not reducible to what we perceive or can perceive of them. As substances they are not simply solids that hold together of themselves; they maintain crystal or arboreal or organic forms, and to see them is to see what is achieved by them.[1]
>
> Alphonso Lingis

Coming to the end of our last chapter, we found that Meillassoux gives us less a realism of things than a hyper chaos, since his radical "perhaps" tells us less about *what is* than *what may be*. In this chapter, we arrive at the realism of Graham Harman, whose vibrant work in short order has become widely discussed by theoreticians and artists, architects and literary critics, and whose version of speculative realism is in many ways an inverted form of Meillassoux's. Rather than proceed chronologically through his writings—from his earliest *Tool Being: Heidegger and the Metaphysics of Objects* (2002) to *Quadruple Object* (2011) and beyond—I will treat his work systematically in terms of his theory of objects. As we will have but one chapter to do so, we could be said to leave much of Harman's work aside, but given that his thinking is clear and schematic, it won't take long for the reader to understand the stakes of his work as well as why it's struck a chord with so many disillusioned with contemporary philosophy. In Chapter 2, we discussed the phenomenologies of Husserl and Heidegger, in part to prepare ourselves for Harman's own readings of them. But a better passkey to his work is through the writings of Levinas, who in *Totality and Infinity* calls for an end to "ontological imperialism" that is but another word for what Meillassoux dubs "correlationism." This is not to say Harmans's account is not original, but instead to show contiguities not normally discussed concerning his writing. Another way to put this is that Harman himself has often told of his own development in terms of Husserl and Heidegger in eminently readable prose, and thus a different way into his work will help elaborate crucial issues that come up later in the chapter. The plan here is to proceed from Levinas's thinking into a full engagement with Harman's ontology.[2]

In *Totality and Infinity*, Levinas presents us with his claim that ethics precedes ontology. Levinas calls us to an ethics both beyond and prior to ontology and what he calls philosophies of the Same. Levinas famously argues Western ontology has reduced the ethical to the epistemological, for example, as found in Husserl's noetico-noematic correlation between thinking and its object. The regimes of representation are "violent" in that they attempt to capture the Other in terms reducible to the same, that is, the self's own categories. Aristotle provides a simple example: you judge a friend by how similar they are to you. For Aristotle, this would be for the virtuous person and so he has eminent reasons for this argument but nevertheless, "I like you, you're like me!" doesn't exactly evince daring in the face of otherness. The ontology par excellence, for Levinas, is the political. "For the philosophical tradition, the conflicts between the same and the other are resolved by theory whereby the other is reduced to the same."[3] For Levinas, this "correlationism," to use Meillassoux's term, is essentially an "idealism," since the self never gets beyond Berkeley's reduction of what is represented to concepts in the mind.[4]

Less discussed than his ethics of alterity, however, is Levinas's critique of Heidegger and Husserl in terms of their phenomenologies of things. When Levinas goes "beyond phenomenology," as Lingis puts it, it's not simply to testify to the Other who is "older than I," but also to delineate at least three ways in which the things of the world have been reduced to order of the Same: (1) First, as that which is represented to thought. This is the work of epistemology in general, for Levinas, but is also fundamental to Husserl's phenomenological account. He critiques any "realist import" to Husserl's distinction between the "object of representation," that is, the correlate of the intentional relation, and the "act of representation," intentionality itself, which, he says, is always "hastily given."[5] (2) As that which is handy (*zuhanden*) in Heidegger. For Levinas, as for Harman, the circumspective concern by which we "ontologically" approach tools and equipment does not exhaust what he dubs the "element," which Harman calls the "object in withdrawal." While for Heidegger, our practical engagement with the things of the world is prior to any theoretical knowledge of them, Levinas argues that the element gives but "one side" of itself in this relation. (3) Levinas adds that that there is a "sensuous" relation to things missed by Heidegger. Through enjoyment and "living from . . . ," such as in the case of foods, things of the world "take on the signification of fuel in the economic machinery."[6] All three approaches miss, in a clunky phrasing that is nevertheless important, that "what is the 'other side' of what offers us one side does not arise in the relation maintained in the element." Rather, "the sky, the earth, the sea, the wind—suffice to themselves."[7] Otherwise put, beyond these three types of relation to the elemental, there is for Levinas, as John Sallis notes, "the recession of the elemental, its *withdrawal into fathomless depth*, a withdrawal that is neither simply revelation nor concealment."[8] Levinas provides no way for the elemental itself to unveil or "reveal" itself: his metaphors are always of exteriority or depth. That is, objects, as Harman will call them, have a sensuous relation, while also having qualities in themselves hidden beneath this or that side of itself.[9]

Harman has repeatedly noted that his thinking of objects comes from two sources. On the one hand, he argues that Husserl provides the distinction between objects and their qualities—between the tree as it appears to us as a single thing and its different adumbrations or qualities. However, both are the result of an "intentional" structure, such that outside of the relation to human consciousness—Harman repeatedly says "within the mind," though in fact, it is correlational in the truest sense—no sensuality can be given. For his part, Heidegger provides a world of things, either present-to-hand (broken tools, objects of theory, and so on) or handy equipment that is the pre-cognitive backdrop for our being-in-the-world, the "world in itself . . . made of realities withdrawing from all conscious access."[10] This part is well known. But Harman argues that things withdraw from our practical engagements as well, not just the theoretical glance: "Our use of the floor as 'equipment for standing' makes no contact with the abundance of extra qualities that dogs or mosquitoes might be able to detect. In short both theory *and* practice are equally guilty of reducing things to presence-at-hand."[11]

But, though the term is all but missing from his work, thinking the notion of objects in terms of an inexorable "alterity"—that is, its reality is not simply an epistemological problem, but ontologically concealed—helps us to highlight the "sensuousness" and "sincerity" that derive in part from Levinas's move beyond phenomenology, since they are key terms for both thinkers. Levinas's central insight is that the elemental, like the Other, has aspects that are relatable through sensuousness, but in its depths, it is a *relata* without relation. This is the core argument of object-oriented ontology.[12] As Harman writes:

> It is surprising that so little attention has been paid to the concept of substance in Levinas. . . . Enjoyment . . . is always the *surface*

> configuration of some individual substance. The same is true for exteriority, also known as alterity. If things cannot exist without being permeated by Infinity, the same holds true in reverse—after all, Levinas claims that the Infinite is not a preexistent monolith or *apeiron*, but instead can only be produced in some *specific manifestation*.[13]

That is, as a specific object. As is the case with what is "present-to-hand" and "ready-to-hand," what is enjoyed also are only these sensuous qualities: "things are manifested in enjoyment, but never reducible to it."[14] In this way, "Levinas tells us that the *alterity of a thing* is not exhausted in its visible form."[15] This "alterity" is specifically what Harman means by "withdrawn objects," since they are irreducible to any relation, just as the Other is irreducible to the face in Levinas, and just as the elemental stirs beneath the winds of change in our sensuous activity.

Altered substances

The salutary aspect of "object-oriented philosophy," as Harman calls his specific branch of speculative realism, would seem to be that it explains our common-sense realism, and that it doesn't ensnare us in discussions of otherness, thought by some to belong to the worst forms of 1990s "postmodernism." After all, what could be more everyday, less *other*, than the objects that surround us: chairs, tables, vintage posters, and water bottles whose carcinogens are yet another object. Indeed, this sense of familiarity is what led Heidegger to describe things in terms of their "homeliness," since we are so used to them that we simply take their existence for granted. Before turning to Harman's account of objects, it's important we first differentiate the strategies he argues have dismissed the study of objects.

Undermining

This is the view that objects are a "mere surface effect of some deeper force."[16] He lists several schools of thought, including (1) the pre-Socratic monists, who argued that the basis of the world was a particular element, such as water or fire. Undermining is also a symptom of (2) Democritus's atomism in the ancient world and scientific naturalism in the contemporary one: "the object is regarded as *nothing more than* either final microphysical facts, or as an empty figment reducible to such fact."[17] Also undermining objects is (3) empiricism, in particular David Hume, who argued that objects are but "bundles of qualities" that we attach to given ideas by habit. Since Harman often critiques empiricism in particular, it's worth quoting Hume on this:

> When we gradually follow an object in its successive changes, the smooth progress of the thought makes us ascribe an identity to the succession; because 'tis by a similar act of the mind we consider an unchangeable object. When we compare its situation after a considerable change the progress of the thought is broke; and consequently we are presented with the idea of diversity: In order to reconcile which contradictions the imagination is apt to feign something unknown and invisible, which it supposes to continue the same under all these variations; and this unintelligible something it calls a substance, or original and first matter.[18]

The linguistic version of this, for Harman, is that we apply these aggregates of sense data to linguistic substantives or nouns and thus suggest "objects" are just words derived from cultural ways of thinking. (4) contemporary monisms such as the early work of Levinas, whose *Existence and Existents* revealed a "formless *il y a* (or 'there is') that only human consciousness can hypostatize into individual objects."[19] This is also found, he claims, in the work of Jean-Luc Nancy, where being is a shapeless "whatever."[20] For these thinkers, "the object is *nothing more than* a byproduct of a deeper primordial reality."[21] (5) Harman also describes thinkers such as Gilbert Simondon and Manuel Delanda as undermining objects. While, according to Harman, these theories don't view objects as monists do, they think nevertheless that "the object is still *nothing more than* the derivative actualization of a deeper reality—one that is more diverse than a lump, but also more continuous than specific horses, rocks, armies, and trees."[22] Close to these theories, Harman argues, are (6) the theorists of flux, from Heraclitus to Bergson to Deleuze, in which objects "merely crystallize becoming in an abstract state, deprived of its inner dynamism."[23] For them, objects are but a "process."[24] Akin to this, one presumes, is what Harman calls the (7) "genealogical approach," in which an object is "*nothing more than* its history,"[25] that is, any object must be thought within a given historical milieu. He doesn't name anyone, but presumably he's thinking of Foucault's apparatuses of power.

Overmining

We need not list all the types of overmining, since Harman's view is that "correlationism," as discussed in Chapter 2 in its many varieties, is one such "overmining," and thus we have covered most at length. Harman argues that relationism (not just correlationism), which argues that *all things* relate to one another in a manner similar to the human-object doublet, overmines objects as well.[26] For the relationists, "objects are important insofar as they are manifested in the mind, or are part of some concrete event that affects other objects as well."[27] The first type he mentions is the relationism of Bruno Latour,[28] whose work Harman has claimed as important to his own, as witnessed in his book on Latour, *Prince of Networks*.[29] Latour's fundamental claim is that each thing, as such, is but a "black box" that is to be broken into by the theorist in order to tease out the relations that tie each given thing to a whole range of other things. In his *Laboratory Life: The Construction of Scientific Fast* (1986) and *The Pasteurization of France* (1988), Latour argued for thinking the reality of scientific facts in terms of the network of alliances made among the various objects of the laboratory, the scientists undertaking given studies, and the facts that arise out of these interactions. Latour claims that there is no scientific set of facts that is not borne from "trials of strength" made among actants, including the apparatuses and materials of the scientific profession. This is where the charge of anti-realism enters the scene, since Latour argues that bacteria, for example, did not pre-exist Pasteur's discoveries, since their "reality" is only thinkable through the set of relations brought about by Pasteur's discovery. Harman's claims Latour as a realist ally in *Prince of Networks*, however, one who is unwilling to grant theories of knowledge, including science, privilege over ontology and the assemblage of relations. For Latour, epistemic facts are but another actant among others, and he argues, Harman says, that "all entities are on the same ontological footing."[30] Thus, Pasteur's bacteria are not real until they enter into alliances, though presumably Latour would have to argue more precisely that the bacteria were previously "real" as actants in relation to other organisms before becoming another fact of human knowledge. "Against the traditional gesture of isolating the real from all its distorting associations," Harman writes, "Latour holds that a thing becomes increasingly real the more associations it has."[31] Human beings confront things, translate them (describe them to others), and reduce them to one level of reality (you drive your car, not use it as a rather large coaster), and this, too, is what actants do to one another: fire burns cotton, to cite Harman's favored example, while other levels of the cotton and other things interact in ways no less real. To trace any x, one must work out its "hybrid existence" as a set of relations within ever-widening networks: "to follow a quasi-object," Latour writes in *We have Never Been Modern*, "is to trace a network."[32] All the difference between Latour and Harman will be on that "quasi-" in the above formulation.

This leads to Latour's key idea of "irreductionism," an "actualism" that grants reality only to the shifting relations of the world and not to hidden forces (even potentiality) that don't relate to the things of existence. As Harman describes it, Latour is committed to thinking actants as "events," in which each takes place in a "single place and time," and thus he "is committed to entities with only a momentary existence."[33] But this "actualism" means that his descriptions of any given moment is always from the present, and thus he treats the past and the future as being outside any particular "trial of strength." Thus they are but shadows in the face of what is in relation. The question that Harman asks in *Prince of Networks* is whether such actualism can account for change: if all is actual, why is there not an eternal repetition of the same?[34] For Harman, Latour's irreductionist account must be supplemented with a thinking of the "interiority" of objects, which is what he calls the "something more" of things beneath their relations. Harman thus departs from Latour to argue that there are "things" beyond sets of relations: "an actor must already exist if other actors are to exist in the first place."[35] In this way, for example, the microbes of the type discovered by Pasteur have existence before their discovery, even if this "latent substance hidden from public view beneath an actor's overt performance" is indescribable, since it has not yet made such alliances that allow for publicity.

Harman thus argues that "a thing is real beyond its conditions of accessibility," even if this "access" is not made by human beings, but other things as well. "Things," he writes, "must be partially separated from their mutual articulations. If this were not the case, they would never be able to enter new propositions."[36] Latour thus overmines objects in a web of relations, according to Harman. Nevertheless, as we approach the next section, we will see how close they are:

> All relations are of fundamentally the same variety, in flat contradiction of the correlationist view. Nonetheless, both positions share the notion that a thing's existence consists solely in its relation with other things. An object is exhausted by its presence for another, with not intrinsic reality held cryptically in reserve.[37]

Materialism

The general default, even among the most formalist thinkers of recent years, is to proclaim oneself a materialist. Harman is one of the few to attack it openly: we need only quote the title of his 2010 *Society and Space* article, "I am also of the opinion that materialism must be destroyed."[38] According to Harman, materialism practices both overmining and undermining at once.[39] For Harman, scientific materialism "jeers" objects from below, while a "German Idealist" "dialectical materialism" "jeers" from above. He first quotes from Trotsky: "These relations among 'all things and phenomena in continuous change' are not withdrawn into some dusky underworld of things in themselves, but are concealed from us only by 'ideology,' which will eventually be eliminated."[40] Hence, he views Marxism as not denying the importance of objects, but as thinking they can be wholly unveiled: "there is no need for a material stratum deeper than all access, since access itself *is* the material stratum; the rest is mystification."[41] Thus objects, he argues, are both treated as ultimate elements and as "actually nothing but sets of qualities."[42] In the end, he argues all philosophies that undermine have to account for overmining, that is, relations to human beings, and end up doing both. In the case of materialism, Harman posits that it has difficulties explaining nations, or the European Union, which are irreducible to matter and yet are still objects for him.[43] Heidegger himself thought materialism to be a form of "onto-theology," that is, a philosophy that reduces Being to one set of entities (matter)—in short, an idealism. Materialism, following Heidegger, would be, in Harman's phrasing, an "idealism with a realist alibi."[44]

Tepid realisms

While Harman at some point will identify Meillassoux, for example, as a "materialist," we have discussed how this is less than clear.[45] For Harman, the mathematical knowledge that discerns the absolute still puts human beings at the center of Meillassoux's "realism":

> For speculative materialism . . . humans remain at the center of philosophy, though their knowledge is no longer finite. Humans are capable of the absolute; any qualities that can be mathematized are primary qualities that can be known absolutely, with no dark residue lying behind them.[46]

If the real is only mathematizable, then, Harman asks, is this not another "form of idealism," that is, a focus on the concepts through which the real is said to be available?[47] But Harman is also dubious about other realisms, such as Kantian-inflected realisms (e.g., Nolt in Chapter 2; Sellars, discussed in Chapter 6, is another) who maintain a certain "reality" beyond human experience:

> [M]any philosophers claim to be realists despite upholding the Kantian duopoly of human and world. They think that to posit some unarticulated reality beyond experience is enough to escape idealism. Perhaps they are right; perhaps they do deserve the name of realists. But if that is the case, then there is little reason to be excited about realism. Against such claims, we should always observe the following litmus test: no philosophy does justice to the world unless it treats all relations as equally relations, which means as equally translations or distortions.[48]

As with correlationist undermining, these realisms still privilege the relation of human and world, while denying relations among objects as having import. In this manner, Harman shares much with Latour, who helps to "restore the flat ontology that treats humans no differently from candles, armies, and stars."[49] But it's also the case that these types of realisms, including Latour's, fail to pay heed to the irreducibility of the object.

> What I have tried to show is that if we define an object through its role in a system of interrelations, objects are thereby undermined, reduced to the caricatured image they present to all other things. The only way to do justice to objects is to consider that their reality is free of all relation.[50]

Hence Harman cannot accept Meillassoux's claims about the dignity of the human, which relies on the human ability to know the absolute and thus have hope for a World beyond this one. He also finds Meillassoux too credulous of the correlational circle, which is "a terrible argument from the start."[51] As he notes, analytic philosopher David Stove once held a contest for the worst argument in the world. (He awarded the prize to himself.)[52] Here is how one writer tidily sums up "Stove's Gem":

We can know things only

- as they are related to us
- under our forms of perception and understanding
- insofar as they fall under our conceptual schemes,
- etc.

So,

- we cannot know things as they are in themselves.[53]

Stove argues this thinking is tautologous, since all it says is that thinking of things is a form of *thinking* things, and logically no tautology can lead to a non-tautologous conclusion. Meillassoux takes correlationism to task for not recognizing its own foundation, the *real* facticity of the relation of human and world. But Harman also critiques Meillassoux's adherence to immanence, which Harman dubs "a catastrophe."[54] Harman, for his part, is devoted to the "alterity of things," that is, the "transcendence of objects,"[55] which are anything but "immanent."

Withdrawal symptoms

What should philosophy's thinking of objects be after it has gotten over the shakes of its addiction to reductionism? Recall that through Levinas and Husserl, Harman discovers the distinction in phenomenology between the phenomenal or sensual object and its specific sensual qualities. This is but one aspect of the object. For Husserl, one does not come upon "bundles of qualities," but upon a preformed object in one's phenomenological experience. One doesn't bundle together colors and light and solidity to make a tree, but one simply experiences a tree. This experience is the sensuous object. In Levinas, we saw that our approach to objects can come in three ways: as a representation in the noetico-noematic relation, that is, "objects" as bereft of their autonomy, but as taken up in intentionality; as a tool, that is, as something implicitly ready-to-hand and forming the very home in which we take on our being-in-the-world, "objects" as a relation within a matrix of equipment; and lastly, as discussed by Levinas, objects as "lived from . . ." or as "enjoyed," that is, sensuous objects in the fullest sense of the term. These are but three ways of relating to objects, but the object in-itself exists in none of them. For Harman, just as you can't simply piece together qualities or add up the specific adumbrations to make an intentional object, so too, you can't simply add up these three types of relations to produce a real object. Since we've come this far in the chapter without mentioning Spinoza, another analogy: Spinoza held that human beings have but two modes through which they experience nature: through ideas and through bodily extension. Let's leave aside how close or not this fits the first two categories above. Spinoza's point is that there is no reason there wouldn't be infinite modes or means of accessing the things of this world. Harman's depiction of sensuous objects is similar: there may be indeed many ways objects, animals, and so on, have of relating or accessing the objects of this world beyond the three noted above. His irreductionism looks beyond the reduction of possible modes of relations to the human-world correlation.

The "sensuous object" is one way in which we come upon an object. But "sensuous objects" have various qualities: my coffee is a milky brown, the leaves outside this window are turning reddish yellow in the Australian fall, and so on. None of these qualities, as Husserl argued well, are seen *as such*. There is no "red" outside it being a quality of some *thing* (red cars, red sauces, and so on). For Harman, this will mean objects only relate to each other through the intentional or sensual object, not through sensual qualities. There are many such qualities and, of course, over time, they shift: the tree remains the same sensual object even as its leaves redden and fall to the ground in the crisp autumn air.

These sensuous qualities, Harman argues, are in "tension" or "strife" with the sensual objects. The qualities we view of objects may change variously as we move about a room, or engage it in the three ways discussed above. As such each quality is but a "caricature" of the sensuous object.[56] Here is Harman's example:

> The geological survey of a mountain and the climbing of that mountain have a very different structure, but what both have in common is their failure to exhaust the mountain in its very being. The geologist must always leave many of its features unnoticed, while the climber also fails to grasp aspects of the mountain that are relevant for birds, ants, snow leopards, or yeti.[57]

Let's turn to another example of a mountain in recent philosophy. As Merleau-Ponty demonstrates in his "Cézanne's Doubt," this inexhaustibility and multitude of sensuous qualities is what led Cézanne to repaint his beloved Mont Ste Victoire endlessly. As Merleau-Ponty notes, Cézanne wrote just one month before this death, "Will I arrive at the goal, so intensely sought and so long pursued? I am working from nature, and it seems to me I am making slow progress." Cézanne was caught in the very tension between the sensuous object and its sensuous qualities. Here is Merleau-Ponty, from one of the finest essays on the craft of painting:

> Cézanne did not think he had to choose between feeling and thought, as if he were deciding between chaos and order. He did not want to separate *the stable things which we see* [the sensuous object] and *the shifting way in which they appear* [the sensuous qualities]. He wanted to depict matter as it takes on form, the birth of order through spontaneous organization. . . . Cézanne wanted to paint this primordial world, and his pictures therefore seem to show nature pure, while photographs of the same landscapes suggest man's works, conveniences, and imminent presence. . . . He wanted to put intelligence, ideas, sciences, perspective, and tradition back in touch with the world of nature which they were intended to comprehend. He wished, as he said, to confront the sciences with the nature "from which they came."[58]

But just as for Cézanne, so too for all of us, and indeed for all objects in their relations with one another, according to Harman. One picture or another, he argues, just won't capture it. As such, it is not a human failure or mark of our finitude, but is endemic to the things themselves:

> A raindrop does not make contact with the full reality of the mountain, and neither does a snowflake, a gust of wind, or a helicopter crashing into its face. All of these objects encounter the mountain-object only in some translated, distorted, over-simplified form.[59]

Put another way, just as the Other in Levinas is irreducible to the qualities we give it, the "alterity of the thing," as Harman puts it, is irreducible to its representations or, indeed, any of the modes through which humans, animals, or anything else encounters it. Thus, again, for Harman, as in Levinas's relation to the Other, the contact between real objects is "asymmetrical," that is, a real object only broaches the other through the "sensual object," with the other object forever "transcending" the space between them.[60] According to Harman, beneath these sensuous qualities and the sensuous object lies the "object in withdrawal," which has its own real qualities. The withdrawal symptoms, if you will, come in four ways:

Space

This is the "relation" *within* the object between the object-in-itself and its sensuous qualities. Harman holds that there isn't any "isomorphic resemblance" between these sensuous qualities and the withdrawn object, just as we should not confuse the Face in Levinas for the singularity of the Other. Levinas, too, held space to be both relation and non-relation,[61] or, as Harman puts it, "Things make contact in space, but space also has distinct regions in which things can hide from each other."[62] There can be purely "sensuous objects"—the works of imagination—that do not take place in space, given that they are only on the side of the sensuous and therefore do not have this "tension" between the reality of the object and its sensuous qualities. Thus they are not objects in the full "quadruple" sense he means.

Eidos

This word has a long philosophical history, but for Harman it is the "tension" between "real qualities" and the "sensual object." The "eidos" marks the relation between the unified object as it appears and the disparate qualities it has. Just like the thing in itself, we have no access to these disparate qualities, only "allusions" left through its relations. In other words, the "real qualities" produce or are connected to the idea one has of the real object.

Essence

This is the "tension" between the "real object and its real qualities."[63] Of course, there is a long argument about whether the essence of a thing, its *ousia*, is universal. Aristotle himself discussed primary substances (particular things) and secondary substances (the class of things).[64] In this way, you may have the primary substance of this book before you, with all of its particular qualities and attributes, but you also know it as a substance in the secondary sense, that is, as a thing belonging to the class of all books. Harman disavows that any substance or *ousia* could mark such a universal: "qualities according to the present book are shaped by the object to which they belong, just as the moons of Jupiter are molded by their planetary lord."[65] This makes sense only in terms of his "alterity of the thing"; such a universal would make the object in its essence knowable, a move Harman from the beginning disavows, though it forms the basis for Aristotle's *Metaphysics*. This is also why Levinas described his work as going "beyond essence," though Harman retains the word.

Time

For Harman, this names the "tension between sensual objects and their sensual qualities." In other words, Harman follows Husserl in this regard, not Levinas, for whom time is the very relation between the self and the Other, or analogically here, the relation between one object and the other. In his lectures from 1905 to 1911, Husserl attempted to work out what he called "inner time consciousness," that is, the way in which the "transcendental ego" "constitutes" time as a flux that moves through the living present ("*die lebendige Gegenwart*"), while implicitly lit by the past (retentions) and the glimmer of the future (protentions). The transcendental ego is *outside* of time as *constituting time*, since, for Husserl, there is no such thing in intentionality as a static entity. Our protentions and retentions are what deliver to us, through the flux of time, not a single picture of this adumbration or that side of the object, but rather the "immanent object." These retentions and protentions—Harman, to his loss, makes little use of Husserl's discussions of time, though they bear directly on the discussion of adumbrations in all of Husserl's texts—are central to thinking intentionality. While Husserl was interested in understanding how we could intend an "object" (*Objekte*) such as music, time was also crucial to the constitution of *any* object, since only with protentions and retentions as a unified horizon anchored in the present could Husserl account for an "immanent object." Otherwise, all we'd get is a frozen moment attached to one adumbration or another. (Incidentally, for Husserl, an object can always hold a surprise for us, since our protentions can fail to be matched by the intended object, such as reaching for a glass of water in the desert that turns out to be a mirage.) Thus while space itself adheres to the object-in-itself, for Harman, just as in Husserl, time does not touch what is outside intentionality, or, in Harman's terms, outside the sensuous relation. That is to say, there is *no* timeliness to the transcendent object, just as the transcendent ego, in Husserl, is *outside* or *beyond time*, forever in the living present. The transcendental ego—and this is the mark of Husserl's idealism—*cannot change*, since it must retain the intentional structure (intentionality constituted through retentions and protentions in the living present), lest *that too* give itself over to the chaos of the flux of time we find in the flow of consciousness. The transcendental ego is the pure form of our psychological egos and is without content; it is literally *nothing*, as Sartre describes in his *Transcendence of the Ego* (1936) and later in *Being and Nothingness* (1943). Put another way, if Harman is to give *content* to objects, which our discussions above certainly show he wants, there is the risk of an idealism worse than anything he critiques. If time is but the sensuous, it cannot touch the reality of the thing itself, and he himself notes there is no correspondence between the thing itself and its sensuous objecthood or qualities. Time would be, in the strictest sense, "illusory":

> According to the object-oriented model *only the present exists*: only objects with their qualities, *locked into* whatever their duels of the moment might be. In that sense, times seems to be illusory, though not for the usual reason that time is just a fourth spatial dimension always already present from the start. *Instead time does not exist simply because only the present ever exists.* Nonetheless, time as a lived experience [that is, within the sensuous; here he follows Husserl to the letter] cannot be denied. We do not encounter a static frame of reality, but *seem* to *feel* a passage of time. It is not pure chaos shifting wildly from one second to the next, since there is chance with *apparent* endurance. Sensual objects endure despite swirling oscillations in their surface adumbrations, and this is precisely what is meant by the experience of *time*. Time can be defined as the tension between sensual objects and their sensual qualities.[66]

This is precisely what Heidegger and Derrida critique as the "metaphysics of presence"—the view that there is an eternal present beyond or behind the appearance of things, whether the forms in Plato, the *cogito* in Descartes, the transcendental ego in Husserl, or indeed, the non-material, transcendental objects in Harman.[67] In the eternal present, the "real" object cannot change, cannot give itself over to the passage of time, and all we get is what "seems to be" an "illusory" or "apparent" change of time never happening in the reality of things. Or put differently, it may go round and round, but underneath it all, as an object, there's literally nothing new under the sun.

Recall from Chapter 2 that Heidegger argues for the reality of time implicit and prior to any correlation of *Dasein* and *Sein*, humans and world; it is the condition of possibility for our "thrownness" towards the future itself. Harman, in his most polemical moments in *Quadruple Object* and elsewhere, dismisses this fundamental part of Heidegger, who he says "actually has nothing whatsoever to tell us about time,"[68] since he "merely alerts us to the ambiguities found in any given instant, and has nothing to do with time in the usual sense of the term."[69] It's true that Heidegger was not interested in "time in the usual sense of the term," which he dubbed "vulgar clock time." His interest instead was in the aporetic but nevertheless real time to which we accede; this is precisely his move in his lectures after *Being and Time* from *Dasein*'s time (*Zeitlichkeit*) to the time of Being (*Temporalität*).[70] In this way, as we'll show later in this book, there is still much to learn from Heidegger and Derrida, who I am arguing put the reality of time at the center of their works and speak to a certain absolute, even if Harman's view of them as correlationists would mean they haven't stood the test of time.

Recovering objects

Let's quickly sum up the above. Real objects relate "asymmetrically" to their others through sensuous qualities, and this is just as true for the coffee grinds and a filter as it is for the human relation of knowledge to things themselves: "A real object meets only the shadow of another, thereby allowing effects to proceed asymmetrically in one direction alone."[71] In this way, the inner aspect of the object—we should be wary of this metaphor, since technically there is no *inside*, given that spatiality is a relation *within* the object and its manifestations—is forever withdrawn from the sensuous domain. What is unclear, though, is how to think the "space" between and among different objects, since "space" is an "internal" relation of the object itself. Otherwise put, another object only ever comes upon the "sensuous object," and hence object-to-object relations are asymmetrical. As Levi Bryant puts it, "objects are characterized by withdrawal such that they never directly encounter one another."[72] Therefore, one can never come upon the "tension" *between*, for example, the real thing and its manifestation (space), or the relation *between* its real qualities and the sensual object (*eidos*), let alone *between* the "real object" and its "real qualities" (essence). These "tensions" or "strifes" are, by definition, forever hidden from view. Here is perhaps a hermeneutic lesson: each philosopher has a depiction of the absolute, or a method that begins with a given starting point. For example, the absolute in Schelling is indeterminacy; for Hegel, is it the dialectic itself. Methodologically,

Dummett begins with language; a materialist philosopher of mind might think our concepts are rooted in the brain, and so on. Harman's claim is not methodological, but is a depiction of the real or absolute. The problem is, once it is put out of view as *other*, then it is difficult to see why it shouldn't be pure indeterminacy as in Schelling, or number as in the Pythagoreans, or firstness or *prius* as in Peirce, and so on, given all the absolutes that metaphysicians have made their starting point. That is, if one thing can literally not relate to these "relations" or "tensions," it's unclear how things come into contact at all—though it's suggested that contact is not spatially or temporally mediated. And if object-oriented ontologists can't relate to them, then what method is used to warrant one absolute over another? This was a constant question put to Levinas: how does he account for the infinity of the Other through the sensuousness of the face? But Levinas had a method, which was to take phenomenology to its limits, as he lays out in *Totality and Infinity* and *Otherwise than Being*. For critics, this otherness still amounts to a mystification, but at the least Levinas uses a well-known method to show where that method would fail, namely in trying to make the Other correlate back to the ego of transcendental phenomenology. The question is how to account for an interiority that is closed off: is it one thing behind all objects? All different objects in themselves? Processes of becoming that throw up appearances of objects? Are they but *monads* unrelated to one another through time and space?[73] Timothy Morton seems to argue that they are while detailing something of a method used:

> Each object is like one of Leibniz's monads, in that each one contains a potentially *infinite* regress of other objects . . . . Objects don't sit in a box of space or time [a view dismissed by Heidegger and Derrida as well]. It's the other way around: space and time emanate from objects. How does this happen? [Object-Oriented Ontology] *tries to produce an explanation from objects themselves*. Indeed the *ideal situation* would be to rely on just one single object. Otherwise we are stuck with a reality in which objects require other entities to function, which would result in some kind of undermining or overmining.[74]

But why *ideally*? If having multiple objects would only lead to the confusions of overmining and undermining and if there is, in fact, always more than one object on the scene, then how in a less than ideal situation does one find a movement from the object rather than multiple objects? Let's let these questions linger, since two further words need to be defined before we continue: "allure" and "sincerity." For Levinas, sincerity is what names the inexorable response of the self to the call of the (human) Other. Harman's sincerity is the "relation" of "immediate contact" between an "experiencer as a real object" and the sensual object; it occurs in all asymmetrical relations. In other words, intentionality, now endemic to all things, is "sincerity" for Harman. Allure, Harman argues, on the other hand, occurs when the thing in itself is "severed" from its qualities in some way.[75] It is a play in its essence, something akin, one presumes, to what Husserl meant by eidetic variation (the allowable change in adumbrations before an object becomes something wholly other—for example how much milk would I have to put in my coffee before it becomes something else?). The fact that there are always more sensuous aspects to a thing than necessary is what he dubs "encrustation," while "submergence" is the withdrawing of the "real qualities of the sensual object," which "can only be inferred indirectly rather than witnessed."[76]

Having now defined the key terms of his system, we can focus on this crucial term "tension," which is doing much of the conceptual heavy lifting in Harman's accounts. For him, a tension "implies simultaneous closeness and separation,"[77] which again we would have to take metaphorically, since these tensions are not an "internal space," since that is *but one* of the tensions themselves. This word is the key term in his work—it accounts for space, time, essence, and *eidos*—yet this is as far we get: tension brings together (fusion) and it drives apart (fission) the object *within* itself. This takes us to Harman's discussion of causation. Let us follow him through his example:

> Consider the skyline of a giant city, filled with countless spires and towers. Insofar as these are all merely sensual objects, they obviously cannot make contact except through the deputy or mediator who experiences them. And insofar as they are real objects I cannot come into contact with them, for the simple reason that real objects always recede from one another. . . . If contact in the realm of the real is utterly impossible, but contact in the sensual realm is an absolute requirement, then obviously the sensual realm of experience must be where all causation is triggered.[78]

Pausing for moment in this account, we are in danger of another Platonism. Recall that the vulgarized Plato posits a two-world theory—Harman argues his is not "two worlds," but "two faces" of objects[79]—in which there was the world of becoming where time takes place, and an eternal realm in which the "form" of things is accessible only to thought. Now here, Harman differs in the sense that the reality of the things in themselves is never open to thought; this is his fundamental disagreement with Meillassoux, who thinks the absolute can be the subject of knowledge. Furthermore, all change for Plato can only take place in the world of becoming, not in the world of the forms, which mirrors Harman's own claims that temporality is but a "tension" in the sensual world, and Harman, as does Meillassoux, adheres to the Platonic distinction between being and appearance. In addition, the whole problem of Platonic dualism has always been the way in which one world "participates" or "shares" in the world of becoming.[80] How can it do so and remain a unitary form? In what way is it participating in this world? And in particular, how can Platonism *find* that there are *multiple forms* if the forms are always hidden behind the world of becoming? Could it not just be one form? The whole ripe history of Neo-Platonism revolves around just these questions. How do *new* things come into being? If one object never touches upon another, how does it, in itself, in its very reality, come to be, or come to differ, that is, pass away? The early Platonists are still our contemporaries on this and many other issues. This is all the more notable because Harman claims that objects include not just cities and armies, but also quarks, electrons, and "The Arab Street,"[81] and so on. This risks a literal nominalism in which words create things, yet those things are not subject to change or mutability, given that the essence is always secreted away in the withdrawal of things—away from time. More to the point, how does change come about to the real thing, which, as we've noted, "endures" and is outside the play of time at the sensuous level?[82] Let's continue along the same passage from Harman:

> The real objects that withdraw from all contact must *somehow* be translated into the sensual caricatures of themselves, and these exaggerated profiles are *what must* serve as fuel for the causal relations *that are impossible* between concealed real things. *Somehow*, the events that occur in the sensual sphere *must be capable* of a retroactive effect on the reality that lies outside all experience.[83]

The earlier citation on time was not a one-off from Harman. Here he is in a 2012 interview:

> Time in my model is *nothing but* the tension between sensual objects and their sensual qualities. What gives us the *sensation* of time passing is the fact that the same sensual objects endure for a certain period even though there is a constant shimmering of qualities along their

> surface. . . . From this model it should become clear why time is always reversible but space never is, or never perfectly so. Time concerns *nothing but the superficial drama of surface qualities* swirling atop a sensual object that is somewhat durable *but ultimately unreal.*[84]

Let us pause again. Harman has already noted that he no longer has available the type of "vicarious causality" from an essay he published in 2007.[85] Here, he proposes a "rough answer" for the problem of causality, but nothing more than a "must" or a "somehow" is figured in this "rough answer" above for what was to be our literal object lesson. In "The Road to Objects" (2011), Harman mentions that "between real objects only *indirect causation*" involving an "intermediary" would be possible, at which point the discussion in that essay ends, but these writings only accent the problem, since if there is no "mediation" between and among objects, then no object can act as an "intermediary" of any other.[86] There are two more citations in *Quadruple Object* on the topic of causation. The first mention is to note that "direct causal relation[s] between entities is impossible"[87] He then notes two pages later: "[T]he real, hidden, and essential do very much exist, but communicate only by way of the *unreal* [my emphasis], apparent, and inessential."[88] Note that, as with the discussion of time above, he equates the "apparent" and the "unreal." He continues, "It would be as if mushrooms communicated with their own qualities, not directly or through rhizomatic networks, but via radio waves. A real object is real and has a definite character, but its essence is first produced *from the outside* through causal interactions."[89] However, this doesn't appear to be the case, given that the "essence" names the "tension" between the "real object" and its "real qualities," which Harman had already argued out of bounds for any such contact, since it is *always withdrawn*—they are the unrelatable as such—from the world of appearances, and one object can only ever reach the level of another's outward "sensuous object."

This comes to the foreground in terms of the principle of sufficient reason, which he calls the foundation of philosophy: "For Meillassoux, the principle of sufficient reason must be abolished; for me, it is the basis of all ontology."[90] Harman does mention the "indirect causality" of Ash'arites, but their occasionalism was subtended by God, just as Leibniz's *Monadology*, which Harman often cites in important ways, required the divine for all "indirect communication" between and among monads. This Harman takes up analogically in terms of the "unreal" "radio waves" between and among mushrooms—a metaphor I take he's using to mark the "unreal" set of relations impossible for such things. He calls his view about causality above "a strange result" that "would take too long to argue," but it seems "strange" only in light of his views on time and regional contact. His use of "somehow" and "must" covers over an argument for causality, and previous antecedents in the history of philosophy using occasionalism could only offer mysticism in place of explanation. The theme of causality never returns in this book, even as its aim, announced in the first pages, was a "new metaphysics able to speak of all objects and the perceptual and *causal relations* in which they become involved."[91] Those amenable to Harman's position could point to his statement on causality in a 2010 essay, whose subtitle is "The New Causality." The essay is mostly a recitation of his ontology of the four parts of objects we've touched on. Near the end of the essay, we come to two paragraphs on his view of causality. Here is the second paragraph (which, in order not to tire the reader, contains a summation of the previous one in any case):

> [T]he primary meaning of "cause" is to create a *new* object. Only secondarily does it mean that an object has an effect on others or retroactive impact on its own parts. If we see one thing influence another, this is merely a retroactive effect of a joint object that unites the two, or once did so. What I want to suggest is that this gives us a new way of reflecting on the principle of sufficient reason. For according to the model just sketched [his view of objects taken from Husserl and Heidegger, as well as the fact that objects can have parts, which are themselves objects], sufficient reason is *less a matter of knowing that the fire necessarily burned the cotton* than of knowing that certain pieces *arranged in a certain way* necessarily resulted in the existence of cotton [but not its demise in the face of the fire]. If this *could be* shown [my emphasis, since the discussion is dropped from here, suggesting a true impasse[92]], then the rules *would be* the same when fire and cotton combine to produce a joint entity called "burning cotton ball." But if the fire might not burn the cotton the next time under the same circumstances, as Hume holds, then it *should* also be true that the real components of the cotton arranged in a certain way *might* give rise next time not to cotton, but to steel or a rabid bat, or a miniature angel dancing in flame. A "mereological" view of causation—objects as parts always generating new objects as wholes.[93]

This view is evidently abandoned by the next year's publication of *Quadruple Object*, since mereology doesn't appear in it precisely at those places where one would expect.[94] His suggestion, which follows from Morton's quotation above, is that any causality "must occur" within (and only within) the object. But I'm skeptical there can be a mereology of objects in Harman, for the simple fact that objects (even great and smaller ones, even "parts" and wholes) only get as far as the *sensuous*, that is, can't be a part of anything. (What would it mean to think a part that is not *really*, but only "sensuously" a part of something?) And if the "interior" of one object is the "sensuous" of another—the obvious way out of this whole maze—then the "interior" is not in the depths but surfing along the surface, which means it was never interior in the first place. In other words, if I say the interior of the house is never seen, and you tell me, yeah but its interior is made up of other objects whose sensuousness can be seen, like doors and walls, then it wasn't an interior in Harman's sense at all. Ian Bogost tries his own response:

> The thing that needs to be remembered here is that Harman's sensual object only exists in the experience of another object in the first place; it's not some persistent abstraction. . . . [W]e must remind ourselves that objects have different senses of presence, both in themselves and in relation to other units. Time is on the inside of objects.[95]

But this is not Harman's model, and in any case this inverts the problem: if time is on the *inside* of an object, then the sensuous part would be forever frozen in the present, which at least to this object that I am appears not to be the case—things in the world appear very much to be in motion and changing, which is generally taken to be an index of time.

To come from another angle, where Levinas describes the relation—yes, perhaps all too human—between self and Other as the duration (*durée*) of time itself, and where Harman takes much from this model, Harman nevertheless puts time merely on the appearing level of the object, not as related to another object, and certainly not anywhere in its depths. As such, in its "infinite withdrawal," the essence outside of time of objects cannot change, either whole or in part. Finally if time is only at the layer of the sensuous, even for its parts, there can be no change, since they are "ever in the present"—the true dictum of Harman's view of objects. Object-oriented ontology—including the version in Levi Bryant and the recent work by Timothy Morton, which adhere to this central principle—has hit an impasse, which is why I will argue we must, if temporarily, strategically privilege the reality of time as this book comes to a close. If the real is outside or withdrawn from time, there is only stasis and lack of affection either in or out of its inner depths. We should recall that Husserl began his examinations on time because he needed to account for objects such as music, which require a horizon of protentions and retentions, with him realizing that these were necessary for *all objects*, since if they were simply frozen in the present, there would be no way to move from adumbrations to the "immanent object" (and back again). Critically, then, Husserl's return "to the things themselves" was precipitated through an investigation of time. To be more precise, if the real object and its qualities do not "have" time, then how could something like music be an object? More to the point: Husserl realized *all* objects require time. In this way, he begins a long consideration, contemporaneous with Bergson, of orienting twentieth-century Continental philosophy to the question of time. Without a thinking of "time *and* the other" that Levinas himself develops, there is a worry that Harman's "alterity of things" would be unalterable. His work has tirelessly and quite importantly reminded us to pay attention to the carts and chairs, houses and mugs around us, *as they are*, not as we think or wish them to be.[96] He has, in a word, endeavored to shred the last vestiges of human sovereignty.[97] However, his "real objects," ever in present, could never be something musical—recall for him "only the present ever exists"—and until time is *realized* in his work, it'll be more difficult to sing its praises.

CHAPTER 5
THE POWER OF THINGS AND THE NATURE OF POLITICS

> Thing-Power: *the curious ability of inanimate things to animate, to act, to produce effects dramatic and subtle.*[1]
>
> Jane Bennett

Those writing on speculative realism, especially in the work of Timothy Morton, often discuss its relationship to questions of ecology during the Anthropocene. What may appear to be abstract metaphysical discussions of objects are for many readers anything but. In this chapter we will take up the politics of nature and its link to the power of things in three important recent thinkers. But first, there has been an irony at the heart of our discussions of correlationism: it has been precisely during the last 10 years, when these critiques of correlationism arose in speculative realism, when climatologists, geologists, and theorists of various sorts have argued that it has been during this "era of correlationism" (the last 200 years, as marked out by Harman and Meillassoux) when we have, at least since the end of the eighteenth century, been in the era of the "Anthropocene." This marks a new geological time, one in which the real things in and around us are effectively a hostage of "human" artifice, witnessed by the ecological catastrophes first set in motion at the dawn of the industrial revolution. Paul Crutzen, the Nobel-winning chemist who argued that we had left the era of the Holocene, which had been with us since the receding of the glaciers, puts it thus:

> Because human activities have also grown to become significant geological forces, for instance through land use changes, deforestation and fossil fuel burning, it is justified to assign the term "anthropocene" to the current geological epoch. This epoch may be defined to have started about two centuries ago, coinciding with James Watt's design of the steam engine in 1784.[2]

This is but one year after Kant's publication of the *Critique of Pure Reason* (1783), which Meillassoux and Harman believe introduced us to the era of the correlation. Of course this fact itself is one of correlation, not causation. Yet it helps us to point out the ways in which speculative realism has been in dialogue with ecological materialists, at least insofar as both call for an end to anthropocentrism, whether normatively or ontologically, and to an end of any neat divides between what counts as human and what counts as "nature." The task of this chapter is to move to new conceptions of the real by thinkers who have discussed the need to think the existence of the "real beyond the human's consciousness and control"[3]: Iain Hamilton Grant, Jane Bennett, and Elizabeth Grosz. What links these writers is an attunement to the strange power of things at the heart of the real. They also, especially the latter two, comment on the ecological stakes of de-anthropocentrism, and work to undo "fantasies of human mastery."[4] Grant and Grosz argue against thinking the absolute in terms of objects as affirmed by Harman (and thus would be described by him as undermining objects). Instead they depict the absolute in terms of activities that produce all such objects. As Grosz notes, her task is think "matter in terms of events and processes rather than in terms of things and objects."[5] But before coming to these important points, there is another question that might be lingering for readers: since at least 2000, when P. J. Crutzen defined the "Anthropocene," we have been all-too-aware—surely before that time as well—about the effect of human activities on what we dub nature. To describe, then, the power of things at precisely *this* time could have the feel of an alibi for the human responsibility in the ecological strife in and around us—like an only child suddenly talking about the powers of an invisible friend when caught with a mess. With regard to the Earth, we have been but petty tyrants remaking the world in our image—an ecological correlationism where indeed the real has become an effect of anthropocentric thinking. Be that as it may, these realist thinkers propose undoing the sovereignty we take ourselves to have over nature, especially as climate-change-related storms increase and Earth's inhabitants, notably those least responsible for carbon-based emissions, reap the whirlwind.

Now, turning to the philosophical encounters in this chapter, I've noted a key hermeneutic in any philosophy is discerning its first principle or starting point, the absolute that it must take for granted and then build a system defending. In post-structuralism, this came to be known as the "transcendental signified," the starting point that must be put out of bounds by a given system of thought. In Harman's work, as we've seen, that starting point or absolute is substance. In Kant, it is knowledge itself, or rather, the relation of understanding to that which can be known. But at least since the work of Deleuze and Foucault in the 1960s–70s, there has been the return of Spinozistic power ontologies. This brings us to Iain Hamilton Grant, whose work on Schelling and German idealism does not make for easy reading, but which are in line with other philosophies of nature taken up below. Though they write in different styles, they share important considerations of nature as having forces of its own beyond and through the human, though these authors are all mindful of not thinking "nature" as but the flip side of human being or its cultural acts. This is in line with Morton, who has argued for an "ecological thought" that would stop using the word "nature":

> "Nature" fails to serve ecology well. . . . Ecology can do without a concept of a something, a thing of some kind, "over yonder," called Nature. Yet thinking . . . has set up "Nature" as a reified thing in the distance, under the sidewalk, on the other side where the grass is always greener, preferably in the mountains, in the wild.[6]

On this point, Morton is joined by Bennett, who posits that we need to think "human and nonhuman actants on a less vertical plane."[7] Each agrees with Bruno Latour, who finds that the concept of "nature" is untenable, since we need to think horizontal relations among actants or things within, beyond, and alongside the human. As such, any use of the word "nature" here is meant as not simply the binary opposite of the human or its culture.

In the first part of this chapter, we will look at Grant's work on Schelling, whose thinking of the absolute leads Grant straight into loggerheads with Graham Harman's object-oriented ontology. Having described Grant's elucidation of nature and his thinking that "powers . . . *are* natural history,"[8] we will then show how his work, at least in broad outlines, falls in line with a certain Spinozism that is the under-discussed side of modern philosophy, not least because Spinoza is crucial for important thinkers such as Deleuze and Bennett. It's somewhat of a scandal that Spinoza is positively misunderstood by a majority of philosophers. Yet his place in history is crucial, since long before Nietzsche, he provided a power ontology whose account of nature presaged the death of God and aimed at bringing down to Earth any transcendent Being as well as all transcendental structures of thought. With this in view, we can then turn to the "thing power" found in the work of Jane Bennett, whose 2010 *Vibrant Matter: A Political Ecology of Things* is among the most cited books in the humanities of the last several years. This conception of "power" was something that Deleuze had developed in part from Spinoza, and his influence on Grosz's work is notable. Grosz, for her part, mirrors many of Grant's claims about the real, and offers, through her accounts of Deleuze, Darwin, Bergson and, Nietzsche, a thinking of the real that speaks to the dynamism of the world as it is. That Grosz has done so while both (a) offering a realism, (b) critiquing social constructivism, and (c) advancing feminist and other political concerns demonstrates, at least for her thought, a need not to separate ontological and political considerations.

Iain Hamilton Grant and the power of Schelling

It is not merely a quirk that I began with a quick discussion of the geological Anthropocene, since it is Grant's stated claim to return philosophy to thinking itself within the purview of a "geology" of "natural history."[9] Grant's "geology" will not reveal a nature with humdrum mechanisms, but rather, as Joseph Lawrence interprets him, to "understand nature as always more subject than object, the ground and condition of human subjectivity rather than simply the object of human reflection."[10] We can thus see why Grant fits among the speculative realists. Grant's work derives from his reinterpretation of F. W. J. Schelling, arguing that the nineteenth-century German philosopher was a speculative realist *avant la lettre*.[11] At the heart of Schelling's work was his belief that "the whole of modern European philosophy since its inception (through Descartes) has this common deficiency—that nature does not exist for it."[12] In this way, Schelling was "capable of an expansively non-anthropocentric conception of nature."[13]

For Schelling, we must have a "speculative physics" that would give us nature's own history, rather than seeing nature as *opposed* or *outside of* human history, or as something that remains ever what it is.[14] This history would focus on processes that deeply "unthings" or, to make the difference from Harman sharper, "de-objectifies" existence.[15] As Grant puts it, "If the actual involves genesis, then at no point do presently actual objects exhaust the universe."[16] In other words, his principal argument against Harman is that the productivity of nature is *prior to* any particular objects. For him, the "philosophical pertinence of natural history consists . . . in the demonstration of the constancy of production, of powers *always at work*, always *intrinsic* to the formative process."[17] Here is how he puts it:

> In the present context, "the mark of all being is power." Powers are inseparable from their products; if not products, then there were no powers, but not the reverse. It is neither the case that things ground powers, nor the converse; rather powers *unground* the ultimacy attributed to substantial being and necessitate, therefore, rather than eliminate, the becoming of objects.[18]

This "ungrounding" is the most important word in Grant's work. For Schelling, the "*prius*" or absolute prior to substances or things is not a ground or ultimate substance, as in onto-theology, where one substance subtends all others, but rather a dynamism that can never be thought, since thought itself is a product of that power and thus could only provide a schema that cannot do justice to this *prius*. The ultimate "ground," then, is a certain becoming that is less a ground than the shifting sands of reality. Here is how Schelling puts it in his *First Outline for a System of Nature* (1799):

> The analysis cannot be permitted to stop at any one thing that is a product; it can only cease with the *purely productive*. But this absolutely productive character (which no longer has a *substrate*, but is rather the *cause of every substrate*) is that which absolutely blocks all analysis; precisely for that reason, it is the point at which our analysis (experience) can never arrive. It must be simply posited into Nature, and it is the first postulate of all philosophy of nature.—It must be that which is insurmountable in Nature (mechanically and chemically); such a thing is thought to be nothing other than the cause of all original quality.[19]

In other words, the absolute is thinkable, but cannot be apprehended directly through the things of the world. But just as importantly, Schelling also rejects the "alibi of vitalism" that Grant believes to still be a part of post-Kantian correlationism, especially in the life philosophies of Nietzsche, Bergson, and Deleuze—and by extension, then, the work of Bennett and Grosz.[20] He shares this critique of vitalism with Harman and Meillassoux, who see it as correlationist. His take is that matter can be anything and vitalism

> maintains the *isolation* of organic from inorganic matter. To the extent that any naturephilosophy retains a *particular* kind of physical organization—any body whatsoever—as its "primal type," it remains [Kantian]. Schelling gives the implications of this particularization... in the form of the "test of life," which has retained enormous value from Nietzsche to Bergson, from existentialism to Deleuze: such naturephilosophies, that is, have invariably given the vital instance as the particular physical organization, or contingent physical product, from which philosophy may ascend to action and consciousness *independent of the motions of matter in general.*[21]

In addition, while Grant jettisons vitalism for speaking to the absolute, he is certainly not allergic to the title of "idealism," arguing for a form of Platonism very different than the one usually described. If the "*prius*" is always "prior to things" and "unthings" them, and if it is thus *unconditioned*, then it follows that the Infinite Idea in Plato, at least through Schelling, cannot be *conditioned*, that is, put in a box on the flip side of materiality, since that would make it a finite thing.[22] As Markus Gabriel puts it, Schelling gives us "an ontology of incompleteness,"[23] or as Schelling himself notes, "one can never say of the unconditioned that it '*is*.' For it is BEING ITSELF, and as such, it does not exhibit itself entirely in any finite product, and every individual is, as it were, a particular expression of it."[24] As Devin Shaw correctly suggests, though Schelling shifts views concerning Spinoza at different points in his career, he finds the latter's importance "in correctly interpreting nature as both producing (*natura naturans*) and product (*natura naturata*)."[25] By differentiating between nature as productive (power) and nature as product (specific events and processes), and by emphasizing the primacy of the productive power, *natura naturans*, Schelling provides a dynamic account of nature-philosophy that avoids fatalism and mechanism; contingency, not mechanical cause and effect as in Spinoza, is inherent to nature. Freedom thus falls on both sides of the "correlation" of human and world.[26]

But why does Grant choose Plato's notion of the Idea to name *natura naturans*?[27] The error of Western philosophy, for Grant, was to separate physics from metaphysics, and this happens, he argues, in Aristotle, who presupposed substances as at the heart of being, which, are given over to a correlational *logos* or rational way of speaking about things. In this way, the form of substances and their essences become the focus of metaphysics, and matter ceases to have its "primacy."[28] But isn't Platonism supposed to give us non-productive Forms beyond being and denigrate anything material? As always in the history of Western philosophy, to know a philosopher is to also ask his or her thoughts on Plato. Grant argues that the Plato of the *Philebus* and *Timaeus* gives us a physics, in which the *prius* or absolute cannot be given in the sensible world of becoming, "because it is the production of sensible nature that is itself not sensible."[29] Thus, this "*natura naturans*" or "productive Being" is only available to intellection, and in that way, is also, ironically "unprethinkable." That is, the productive element is Being itself, producing those beings who attempt to think this Idea, that is, the source of Being. But these beings, *Dasein* or humans, can only ever do so by way of the world of the sensible, by nature as "*natura naturata*," that is, those things and objects around us. For Plato, according to Grant, ideas are supra-sensible, not because he denies becoming, but because the fact of the "becoming of being [*genesis eis ousian*]" is itself not sensible.[30] For Grant, Schelling picks up this side of Plato and "his physics is non-phenomenal not in order to segregate it from the dross of experience, but because *productivity is non-phenomenal*, while products are phenomena"[31]—we see things, not processes. Thus, as non-sensual, the Idea is the form of the movement of this natural history itself, one that is indirectly intelligible, analogous to the manner that you indirectly feel the power of the sun, though you should not look at it directly. But this power also makes possible the fact that one can have ideas about it in the first place. After all, for any realism, it must be the case that the real *itself* provides those with intellect the ability to access it, otherwise we wouldn't be having these debates about reality in the first place. This knowledge is not separable from existence; it, too, is a very real thing.[32] As such, against correlationism, Grant's form of Idealism attempts to think the "Unground" (*Abgrund*) or "dethingifying" (*das Unbedingte*) ground[33] that produces *both* subjects *and* objects in the first place. With all this in mind, we can now sharpen the divergence between Grant's Idealism and Harman's object-oriented ontology:

> The difference [between Harman and I] lies between two conceptions of actuality, one of which I will call the depth model, and which consists either of objects all the way down or of a single ground from which all emerge [Harman][34]; and the other, the genetic model, which makes depth regional with respect to anteriority.[35]

We have seen that Grant argues that productivity is prior to products, but here he goes further, essentially marking Harman's work as another onto-theology, one that puts one form of substance before all others, namely objects. But this would be a vertical model of being that Harman himself suggests he's critiquing in his "flatter" ontology, by putting all objects on the same playing field, so to speak. However, just as we suggested that Harman's objects, as ever existing in the present in their reality, cannot account for time, Grant is arguing that his Idealism, contrary to the normal uses of that term, concerns horizontal formations of powers that would both produce and undo any particular being, and thus, unlike Harman, is fully temporal. One cannot discuss any given object without discussing its history and its becoming. This is what links all forms of Spinozism from (early) Schelling to Deleuze.

But Grant implicitly, I think, is making another suggestion: it is Harman who is a reductionist in his object-oriented ontology, reducing being from its utter contingency and creativity to an order of given objects. And this is, given Harman's rhetoric on undermining and overmining, a proper question to ask of his work, especially since his critiques of "overmining" and "undermining" have been taken as an "anti-reductionism." Why would it be the case that simply choosing the "middle path," as Harman calls it, in terms of objects between over and undermining not *also* be reductive? Why is talking about matter and time and crowds, and so on, "irreductive," in terms of objects, but not in terms of all the types of over and undermining? In other words, Harman suggests we somehow fall into idealism or some form of correlationism if we discuss reality in terms of matter or history or what have you, but how does the depiction of the absolute wholly in terms of "objects" avoid this fate?

Let's pause on that question and circle back to the beginning, going back down into the mines of eighteenth-century Britain, where geologists first plied their trade in the service of incipient mining industries seeking to ascertain what these digs had uncovered.[36] This early geology literally dug the ground for the anthropocentric correlationism to come. At perhaps the end of the era of philosophical correlationism, if not, alas, the Anthropocene, Grant argues for a "geology" that digs through to our natural history, not simply for those objects whose fuels endanger the world, but for a power that makes the world possible in the first place. These are precisely the "mining conditions" that are the absolute power at the heart of Grant's speculative realism, one that mines different depths in the cave of Plato's allegory, finding not inert Forms but the real ideas that are productive of being.

Jane Bennett and her political ecology of things

I borrow this subheading from Jane Bennett's subtitle to *Vibrant Matter* to highlight the coming discussion of the political import of speculative realism, at least at it is realized in its fellow travelers, Bennett and Grosz. If we have been discussing power, then we are not just on ontological, but also on political ground. But first two different notes of caution need to be signed before we move onto this political landscape. On the one hand, thinkers of power following Spinoza need to be able to describe how a politics other than simple "might is right" follows from their thinking. If values are produced by power, how do we produce values other than the simple status quo? This is a perennial question for thinkers of immanence—and the answer is usually inscribed in the heart of their systems. Secondly, there is often the critique that flat ontologies in some speculative realists lead to a normative flattening of the difference between humans and objects. The critique goes something like this: if (a) everything is an object and (b) these objects have what was supposed to be human qualities, then (c) one would think it impossible to make any normative distinctions. That is, if we talk about the "alterity" of rocks and soil, not just the alterity of the Other, as in Harman, then the grounds for any norms seem altered as well. Grant, for his part, repeatedly admonishes against the ethical turn in recent Continental thought as too "correlationist."[37] Another example, as we saw in the last chapter, occurs when Graham Harman critiques Meillassoux for adhering to a form of "correlationism" for designating a special dignity to the human being. Critics of flat (or in Harman's case, flatter) ontologies often accuse such philosophies of putting human claims for values on an equal plane with rocks and couches, stores and calendars. Meillassoux's argument for human distinction may be in error—there are no shortages in the philosophical stores for critiques of Kantian-type ethics that locate our dignity in the ability to reason—but it is a normative claim, not an ontological one. By critiquing this strand of Meillassoux's thought as against the spirit of anti-correlationism, Harman risks falling into the very critique he has time and again called "nonsensical" as a view of his work. For example, dealing with a reader who thought that a critique of militarism should be built into thinking "armies" as an object, Harman writes, "I can't say that I see any 'ethical considerations' at all as concerns calling an army an object. Whether or not an army counts as a unified object is a metaphysical question, not an ethical one."[38] While this might be philosophically inarguable—and should be for his would-be critics—his discussion of Meillassoux walks precisely into the trap the reader believes Harman has set for himself. This is all the more the case given that Harman often argues for "doing justice to objects,"[39] which is a locution that cannot be thought without a normative valence. Finally, it is not just Harman in terms of his "alterity of things," but also Morton who has borrowed from Levinas's ethics his discussion of the "strange stranger" of things and used it to discuss the ontology of object. In his *The Ecological Thought*, Morton argues for thinking ecology as a "mesh" of entities co-existing. In this way, he argues, no entity exists "alone," but always in relation to others. In that text, he saves his notion of the "strange stranger"—essentially the Levinasian notion of the Other—for humans and animals. Recently, however, he has extended that to thinking the depths of objects:

> What we now see is that nonhumans *are also* filled with infinite inner space. Some of us are ready to grant this inner infinity to certain kinds of sentient being. . . . Some are willing to grant it to all life forms (this was my position in *The Ecological Thought*). And some still further out are willing to grant it to all nonhumans whatsoever, no questions asked. These are the object-oriented ontologists, in whose number I now find myself. I see no inherent reason why what I called the strange stranger in *The Ecological Thought* should not apply to any entity whatsoever: fireplaces, the Oort Cloud at the edge of the Solar System, flamingos and slices of pork rotting in a garbage can. Since lifeforms are made of nonlife, and since what counts as a lifeform is very much a performative act down to the DNA level, I see no big reason not to extend the concept of the strange stranger to cover *all* entities. . . . The more we know, the more objects, and the more the objectness of objects, rise up to meet what and how we know. . . . Emmanuel Levinas's line about cosmic space is appropriate here: how when I look at the stars, I realize that I am sought out by inhabitants of the intersidereal spaces.[40]

To discuss the human or animal Other is one thing; to export that otherness to objects risks producing a "democracy of objects," as Levi Bryant calls it, where we use the language of alterity and justice for things in a manner called upon for cultural and racial difference. Here is how Bryant discusses this "democracy":

> Such a democracy, however, does not entail the exclusion of the human. Rather, what we get is a redrawing of distinctions and a decentering of the human. The point is not that we should think objects rather than humans. Such a formulation is based on the premise that humans constitute some special category that is other than objects, that objects are a pole opposed to humans, and therefore the formulation is based on the premise that objects are correlates or poles opposing or standing-before humans. No, within the framework of onticology—my name for the ontology that follows—there is only one type of being: objects. As a consequence, *humans are not excluded, but are rather objects among the various types of objects that exist or populate the world*, each with their own specific powers and capacities.[41]

To be a bit pithy, this risks an object-oriented political correctness, where difference accorded to human and animal others is dismissed normatively on ontological grounds. To paraphrase Arendt's dictum from a very different context, namely that where all are responsible—she was attacking collective notions of responsibility—none are: where every*thing* is due justice and respect, then nothing is. A different line of critique comes from Alexander Galloway. Galloway argues that this attunement to objects and things is "political retrograde," as "there is," he writes, "little to differentiate the new philosophical realism from the most austere forms of capitalist realism."[42] In short, his main critique is that one cannot claim, as Harman in particular seems to do, that "one simply can do metaphysics over here, while doing politics over there."[43] Ultimately the problem is that Meillassoux has a "naive trust in mathematical reasoning" and that object-oriented ontologies ignore the "material history of mankind."[44] In this way, this Marxian-type critique finds these "flatter" ontologies as ultimately making the things of the world meaningless in a way similar to capitalism—where anything can be bought and sold and the alterity of things has its price. Galloway's article, it should be said, is a textbook case of argument by analogy: that capitalism has x or y operations, and there's something similar in the new realisms, therefore one is the ideological correlate of the other. This kind of Ideology analysis can often provide important results, and certainly ontologies that claim to be apolitical are often anything but. Nevertheless, at this superficial level, all kinds of similar claims can be made for any philosophical system, and Galloway would be better to look at the specific political logics employed by the new realists, including Meillassoux, Bryant, and Latour. The reader can think this through for him or herself, as it is a worry voiced often in online discussions of object-oriented ontology and speculative realism. This question arises not least because we live in the shadows of a critical tradition that precisely wished to move away from thinking of certain humans as living, as Frantz Fanon once put it, "in crushing objecthood."[45] It's also notable, then, that Elizabeth Grosz argues that objects are what humans bring to the flux and flow of the world as it is—and thus we would only be respecting and doing justice, on her account, to our own creations.

Bennett, for her part, charts a middle course, between thinking of objects as wholly correlated to human practices and thinking of them as having inherent depths beyond the flux and flow of the world. Bennett is clear that the political stakes come precisely from getting a better description of human activities:

> The starting point of ethics is . . . the recognition of human participation in a shared, vital materiality. We *are* vital materiality and we are surrounded by it, though we do not always see it that way. The ethical task at hand here is to cultivate the ability to discern nonhuman vitality.[46]

In this way, she seeks to "articulate a vibrant materiality that runs alongside and inside the human to see how analyses of political events might change if we gave the force of things more due."[47] What Bennett thus offers is a "vital materialism" that, like Grant, attempts to think of the entities of the world as not simply mechanically determined, though she is not shy about using the word "vitalism" for discussing the power of things. But what does this "power" of things mean? Here, she is borrowing from the notion of the *conatus* in Spinoza, which is the way in which things, that is, different "modes," seek to persist in their being. For Spinoza, all beings are but modes of a common substance, which he calls God, but which is the expressive power of existence as such. In this way, he finds superstitious any belief in the human as being separable from nature as a "kingdom within a kingdom."[48] But, as with Bennett and Grant, Spinoza argues against thinking of nature as having a given end towards which it tends, which he calls "the widespread belief among men that all things in Nature are like themselves in acting with an end in view. Indeed, they hold it as certain . . . that God made everything for man's sake." Spinoza's ontology thus calls for anti-anthropomorphism, an insight needed wherever humans think of existence as being an object for itself: "For the perfection of things should be measured solely from their own nature and power; nor are things more or less perfect to the extent that they please or offend human senses, serve or oppose human interests."[49] Hasana Sharp, who cites Bennett at several important points in her recent study of Spinoza's legacy, notes well:

> Avowing humanity as part of nature entails understanding individuals with complex histories, exposed to many diverse bodies and minds, and ever open to forming new compositions with ambient forces. Nature on Spinoza's model is not opposed to history.... History is not a progressive spiritualization of nature, where humans, working together, come to master ... "external" elements of our existence.... Spinoza's nature affirms the variability intrinsic to relational existence. To be a relational being is to undergo a history of constitutive affections and transformations in response to encounters with other beings, human and nonhuman.[50]

This "relational" ontology, of course, recalls Morton's thinking of the "mesh" as co-existence in *The Ecological Thought*, which Morton in recent work downplays, given that he now agrees with Harman's claim that objects, in their interiority, have a hidden non-relational existence. Morton writes in *Realist Magic*:

> *All the things by which we specify the object are not the object.* By we I mean humans, lavatory brushes, quasars and durum wheat, and the object in question itself. We have a very strange situation then, in which there are objects, and there are qualities and relations between these objects and other objects. There is a *chōrismos*, an irreducible gap. Qualities and relations are much the same thing, since they are born in interactions between the object and 1+n other things.... Think about a zero-degree dark object, some object that may or may not be behind a red curtain. It strictly has no qualities for us, yet this very lack of relationship is itself a kind of relationship, as if the dark object radiated some kind of energy that passed through us.[51]

But where Spinoza takes us, as both Sharp and Bennett emphasize, is a thinking of the relations of things, where the power to persevere is not as a lonely entity, but rather always in concert in and through other things (that we ourselves are). Each thing is singular and unique, on their accounts, as part of a web of relations.[52] That is, each thing is itself a "mosaic" or "assemblage," as Bennett puts it, maintaining movement and rest among its parts as part of its overall *conatus*[53]: "conative substance turns itself into confederate bodies, that is, complex bodies that in turn congregate with each other in the pursuit of the enhancement of their power . . . bodies enhance their power *in* or *as a heterogeneous assemblage*."[54] In this way, Bennett therefore will use Spinoza to describe vibrant networks of change operating beyond and within human beings, without providing a purposiveness to the separable matter of nature, either coming from human beings (anthropocentrism) or some divinity (ontotheology).

Borrowing Bruno Latour's term "actants," Bennett sets out to describe the quasi-agency of non-human materials, which in turn are nothing but the stuff of what matters (in all senses) to humans. The philosophical position that Bennett critiques is a post-Cartesian description of nature in modernity as mechanistic and lifeless. The subject of modernity under this view lives off the materials of the world and, in contradistinction to the inorganic materials around it, has a freedom and agency that transcends its natural environment. Once we question this opposition between subjects and things, as she puts it, a number of traditional "ontotheological binaries," such as organic/inorganic, human/animal, will/determination, and so on, begin to "dissipate."[55] Thus, Bennett is not just questioning subjective idealisms or correlationism, but also supposed materialisms, such as some variants of naturalism that provide mechanistic views of nature better left to the era of Newton than to the enchanting, post-Freudian and post-Einsteinian universe to which we accede. Bennett's previous work in *Thoreau's Nature*, for example, explored what the latter meant by the "wild," a term that captures something of what is happening everywhere beyond the Concord woods.[56] Environmentalism, for Bennett, is the wrong term for thinking ecologically, since the "wild" is untameable as a concept that would leave it off to one side of the natural world, in a manner similar to Morton's rejection of the word "nature." There is, as such, a certain "thing-power" at work in the wild, an agency that marks the "curious ability of inanimate things to animate, to act, to produce effects dramatic and subtle."[57]

The key term for thinking through this aspect of Bennett's work is the notion of "assemblage," borrowed from Deleuze and Guattari, which is a concept of "distributive agency" that is horizontal across a number of domains. For Deleuze and Guattari, assemblages are admixtures of things, expressions, and the qualities of those things that gather and function in new and different ways than previously. Like the Spinozistic *conatus*, Deleuze and Guattari label "desire" as the force producing these transitory connections, and these assemblages, for Deleuze and Guattari, become productive "machines" such as the state, an individual, and the very places in which these assemblages operate. These assemblages face the twin forces of territorialization and deterritorialization that make them possible; this web of relations, for Deleuze and Guattari, by producing different connections, immanently creates the "new" in the spaces of the world.[58] Following Spinoza as well as Deleuze and Guattari, Bennett is attuned to describing the vitality of systems not driven by a given principle or vertical power *over* things, since assemblages are horizontal formations that change through interrelations in and among other assemblages:

> Assemblages are *ad hoc* groupings of diverse elements, of vibrant materials of all sorts. Assemblages are living, throbbing confederations that are able to function despite the persistent presence of energies that confound them from within. . . . Assemblages are not governed by any central head: no one materiality or type of material has sufficient competence to determine consistently the trajectory or impact of the group. The effects generated by an assemblage are, rather, emergent properties, emergent in their ability to make something happen.[59]

This agency is at work, Bennett claims, on our airfields, in the wild, in the rush of a blackout, and all around and within us: our bodies are nothing but organic and inorganic assemblages. Bennett takes the *deus ex machina* of our typical explanations of the world, namely the quasi-divine, sovereign human being standing over mechanistic nature, and mocks the presumption of this emperor. As she argues, human agency, as assemblage, "remains something of a mystery" in the "face of every analysis,"[60] a fiction that grants sovereignty over nature even as human material bodies suggest otherwise. Bennett grants that her work risks a "touch of anthropocentrism"[61] but she argues that without this risk of exporting what was previously considered human onto a supposedly mechanized nature, we can never pull off descriptions that render animals and things not merely as "behaving," but rather as acting.[62] In this way, she attempts to avoid the kind of critique provided by Meillassoux and Grant that any hint of vitalism is but another subjectivism exporting human powers onto the world.

What then is the politics of this material ecology? In the everyday sense, this attention to non-human assemblages would seem to leave us bereft of any politics worthy of the name. The reader may worry Bennett has brought us either to the edge of some pan-psychic New Age philosophy, or worse, a nihilism that renders meaningless all human actions by an attention to the things of the world. With each decentering of the human being, either in terms of structures or the play of language in the philosophies of the last century, there has been less a philosophical answer to these vital questions than a normative disgust that human beings have been cast from their throne. That may well be, but merely decrying this result does nothing to question, for example, Bennett's new materialism, with its focus on more-than-human assemblages—or indeed the neuroscientific research central to our last three chapters. Such a reader is invited to follow Bennett's discussions of political praxis, the molding and unmolding of more-than-human assemblages, and see how her analyses bear fruit for rethinking crucial concepts of democracy and political change. For her to do politics without talking about more-than-human assemblages means not only being too limited in our definition of politics, but also failing to describe forces that have very political effects for human and other beings, in her view.

Ultimately, Bennett argues, vibrant assemblages offer the germinating seeds of change, since nature on her account is a "process of morphing, of formation and deformations, . . . of the becoming otherwise of things as they enter into strange conjunctions with one another."[63] This is a thinking of change without a given teleology, just as in Grant and Grosz, since nature is a vital force tempted but never fully lured in any given direction. And it takes human sovereignty along with it, which is indelibly the goal of many speculative realists: "one can note . . . how agency is always an assemblage of microbes, animals, plants, chemicals, word-sounds, and the like—indeed, that insofar as anything 'acts' at all, it has already entered an agentic assemblage."[64] This is not to say that human beings are wholly determined from the outside, since such a conception is too mechanistic (neither nature nor culture on her account is an engineered machine) for the vitalism Bennett describes both in and around human beings. We cannot turn a philosophical blind eye to these assemblages, and certainly Bennett is right that in her narratives many such non-human agencies "chasten . . . fantasies of human mastery."[65]

The politics she offers, then, is not a Marxist materialism, since, for her, any Marxian analysis "is confined to human relationships."[66] In this way,

Bennett's political ecology takes note of the power of things in and around us: garbage dumps, blackouts, and all manner of material assemblages. For Bennett, it's not enough to perform ideology critique, which gives us her answer for the type of critique provided by Galloway above. She writes:

> [D]emystification, that most popular of practices in critical theory, should be used with caution and sparingly, because demystification presumes that at the heart of any event or process lies a *human* agency that has illicitly been projected into things. This hermeneutics of suspicion calls for theorists to be on high alert for signs of the secret truth (a human will to power) below the false appearance of nonhuman agency. . . . Demystification tends to screen from view the vitality of matter and to reduce *political* agency to *human* agency.[67]

The question one might introduce, then, is whether these Latour, Spinoza, and Deleuze-inspired forms of analysis offer anything other than a "naive" empiricism, one that reports narratives on the things of the world, without the complex work the German idealists and Meillassoux, for example, use to recognize the implacability of thought as part of any ontological set of descriptions.[68] This is also a question asked of Act-Network-Theory (ANT) forms of study, which are also influenced by Latour and Deleuzian notions of assemblage, which often risk replacing ontology with a narratology of things, that is, providing descriptions of blackouts and garbage dumps, while denying the implications of language, conceptual schemes, societal apparatuses, modes of access to those things, or even delving into the substantial questions of what it means to exist in the first place, the latter of which Bennett begins to develop in her discussions of Spinoza and Deleuze. Otherwise put, no one has ever doubted the determinative aspect of the things of the world on human beings: there would be no architecture, no medicine, and indeed no applied science of any sort without an age-old attunement to the power of things. Architects recognize that the spatiality of our existence is also determinative of our very being-in-the-world. Even the antiquated notion of "humors" within our body showed how we are afflicted by a "nature" within us. The task, then, has been less to create a "new" materialism than to remind us that the human sovereignty often taken for granted has always been drowned in the shifting waters of material assemblages. This is the politics whose assembly has begun in Bennett's work.

Elizabeth Grosz and the reality of chaos

As I noted in the introduction, it is not enough to circumscribe speculative realism within a pre-given canon of four or five supposed "speculative realists," especially when writers such as Elizabeth Grosz are plowing many of the same depths. Her work, especially in the past two decades, has joined with speculative realism to denounce a previous generation's emphasis on the "constructedness of the real":

> It is perhaps time to reconsider the problem that has faced philosophy from its inception, the problem that may be what first forced us to think at all: the problem of matter, the problem that the existence of a real beyond the human's consciousness and control has posed for the human. . . . I would like to return to the question of the real, the question of ontology, the questioning that the privileging of subjectivity and representation has tended to foreclose.[69]

As with the other thinkers we cover, we can't touch on all of Grosz work, but we will first describe her ontological commitments as in line with those of Iain Hamilton Grant and the Spinozism of Jane Bennett. Moreover, we'll show how these commitments lead to specific interventions in feminism and identity politics, before finally turning to what Sara Brill has called her "ecology of the future."[70]

For Grosz, the "denaturalizing" moves of Continental philosophy have had unfortunate political consequences. As Bennett's discussion of Marxist materialism also argues, Grosz finds there is a critical need for denaturalizing pernicious concepts in political philosophy; she's not throwing the denaturalizing critiques out with the post-structuralist bathwater. As Rousseau noted long ago in his *Second Discourse*, those with power tend to export onto nature political conceptions in order to demonstrate the implacability of these ideas. The task, then, has been to "denaturalize" conceptions of women, racialized others, and heteronormative structures in order to critique the play of power underlying them. This is precisely what Fanon meant by "crushing objecthood." If women are not by nature "irrational," if depictions of African Americans depend on animalistic metaphors, if we somehow deem heterosexual marriage as "natural," then the denaturalizing move would be to explicate the societal structures founded on patriarchy, racialisms, and heteronormativity, which are anything but natural.

The problem, as Grosz sees it, is that theorists have rendered *all* discussions of nature as implicating forms of societal power. "We have, by now, been denaturalized as much as we need to be," she noted in an interview. "What I'm much more interested in [is] renaturalizing that which was taken away, redynamizing a certain kind of nature."[71] In this way, Grosz will be opposed to conceptions of nature as inert, as "non-lively." But it also gives us a politics of renaturalization, which, Hasana Sharp notes, "decenters human reality by acknowledging its production within a force field of powers and counterpowers indifferent to human flourishing."[72]

To understand these claims, we must recognize that for Grosz what is "real"—that is, independent of human machinations—is utter chaos. This chaotic "beginning" is not simply temporally prior, but like Spinoza's *natura naturans* (power), is productive of things and events. It is in light of this "chaotic" real that she calls for a "renaturalization" of philosophy. She reads Darwin for how his insights on nature can help us rethink politics, though she does not simply make philosophy a handmaiden to scientific endeavors. But she is not a "materialist," since for her the productivity of matter is what results *from* chaos: "the real, chaos, is a larger category, of which the philosophical concept of the material is one component."[73] Thus, this "chaos" is the condition of possibility for any order in the first place, which means, in a manner close to Meillassoux's hyper chaos, that the future is always an open possibility:

> The chaotic indeterminacy of the real, its impulses to ceaseless variation, gives rise to the creation of networks, planes, zones of cohesion, which do not map this chaos so much as draw strength, force, material from it for a provisional and open-ended cohesion, temporary modes of ordering, slowing, filtering.[74]

This is why, for Grosz, the sciences miss this chaotic "becoming," since they "focus on closed systems and isolatable terms."[75] She thus argues, "chaos is the universe before and independent of how it is organized through conceptual categories and bodily habits, before it is capable of being lived."[76] This flatter ontology is one where even artistic practice is not simply human:

> The very forces and energies of the earth and all that populates it are summoned up and become sensation. Even the most elementary forms of life, plants, for example, make of their situation, their territory, their

> climate, and milieu a contraction, a making of something more—colors and perfumes that motivate and provide materials for art. Everything—territory, events, animals, man—are produced equally, without hierarchy, on the flat plane of canvas or board.[77]

We can now turn to her reading of Darwin's work. She deems Darwin central to critiquing the independent existence of objects; it is the chaotic that is the in-itself for her, not substance. In Darwin's work, she argues, "being" is transformed into "becoming," as he imparts an open system of "material organization" that is nothing other than "the dynamism of time."[78] Darwin, like Spinoza before him, denies that nature has a given teleology, since there is always the random element that opens living beings to further complexity, providing "the generation of *endless* variation, *endless* openness to the accidental, the random, the unexpected."[79] In this way, the future is not determined by the past, but the latter is merely the "ground from which divergence and difference[s] erupt."[80] By providing an account of the material "evolution" of complexity that is non-mechanistic, Darwin "brings the concept of the event to the sciences."[81] But Darwin's work consists not in the survival of "species," which are delineated as a "species" *ex post facto* by scientists themselves, but rather in singular transformations, which unpredictably may or may not lead to changes at aggregated levels:

> Darwin develops an account of the real that is an open and generative force of self-organization and growing complexity, a dynamic real that has features of its own, rather than simply exhibit stasis, a fixed essence or unchanging characteristics, are more readily understood in terms of active vectors of change.[82]

Hence she finds in Darwin a radical openness to nature that Grant finds in Schelling, and she takes evolutionary theory to be what Grant called "power . . . as natural history." The question, though, is if there can be such a radical "chaotic" openness in Darwin's work. After all, as Grosz points out, there are only certain conditions under which life can grow and thrive, which would seem to tame the forces of chaos she finds: "Life is not possible without the prior emergence of the material, chemical, and spatiotemporal conditionals that support it and enable it to evolve. There must be something of the spark of life's indeterminacy in the operations of pre-living matter."[83] (One can see, too, that she would deny Meillassoux's claim of a leap from a World of the inorganic to the World of life discussed in Chapter 3.) As Dorothea Olkowski points out, "it is important to recognize that it would be difficult for life to emerge and survive in a structurally unstable world, where no situation and no pattern could be counted on to repeat itself with any regularity."[84] But as Olkowski also notes, no particular system is fully determinable; we can never count all the possibilities in any given situation, especially when it comes to innovations produced under evolutionary processes, which are in Grosz's writings "assemblages," or what Bennett called "the wild." There is a political upshot to this. First, against the post-structuralists, on her account, nature is not to be treated as some inert clay that gets molded by discourse.[85] Secondly, while Darwin produced a work called *The Origin of Species*, origin for him is a "nominal question": "what constitutes a species depends on what we *call* a species, where we (arbitrarily or with particular purposes in mind) decide to draw the line between one group and another that resembles it, pre-exists it, or abides in close proximity to it."[86] Where the post-structuralists for her viewed any origin as presupposed and yet produced by specific structures of thought, Grosz argues we can renaturalize philosophy—in ways amenable to arguing against all forms of essentialisms—without rendering nature as inseparable from who we are. Thus the politics of Grosz's work is to provide an account of culture that grows from the seeds of the same "chaos" that produces "nature," while also demonstrating that nature's becoming means our politics must be open to a future worthy of the name, one unpredictable from the present, since "real chaos" produces change we can indeed not just believe in, but know will come. "Darwin shows that the human is both that which is in the process of necessarily transforming itself and that which can never know itself to the point of predictability."[87] Politics, then, as in Bennett, is not something that happens beyond or without nature, but is embedded in the chaos of the real, which, yes, may make our "projects endless" (since chaos can always interrupt them) and perhaps "unattainable," but also makes politics the outcome of "ongoing experiments rather than solutions."[88] Politics and matter are "not opposites . . . but implicated in each other, different degrees of one and the same force."[89]

But there is a third set of political reconsiderations derived from the above. While we have to move quickly, Grosz finds appealing a new realism after constructivisms of various sorts as a means for reorienting feminist discourses once allergic for many good reasons to naturalizing philosophy. In *Time Travels*, she lays out distinct ways in which Darwinian theory reorients feminist and political practices[90]:

1. First, feminist discourse should not circle around getting a given culture to "recognize" women as fully human. This, she believes, is self-defeating. Rather, "politics is an attempt to mobilize . . . possibilities of self-overcoming in individuals and groups."[91] Like Spinoza, she argues that of "rights" that need to be recognized puts one in a weak position:

> Instead of regarding feminist politics as a struggle around the rights and needs of female and racialized subjects . . . subjugated by male subjects, who require a more adequate and respectful recognition by male subjects [which she says is found in liberal feminism, identity politics, and Judith Butler's notion of performativity aligned to Hegelian theories of recognition], feminist and other forms of political struggle may more ably function as a mode of rendering the subject the backdrop to a play of forces which are themselves what constitute the ever shifting and uncontrollable terrain of politics and identities. . . . It is the struggle to render more mobile, fluid, and transformable the means by which the female subject is produced and represented.[92]

She finds this thinking of fluidity in Darwin, who articulates for her something like a Spinozistic politics: all forms of domination are not inexorable but are open to "resistance and alignment by virtue of the very forms of distribution of patterning that power itself takes."[93] This is precisely Spinoza's argument about the masses in his *Political Treatise*, where the "common" can move from "passive emotions" of fear to producing the state of things in which it exists. It does not need the permission of "recognition" for this revolutionary act and, indeed, by asking permission, one merely reinstantiates the power dynamics of a given social milieu. There is all the difference between asking and demanding. Grosz summarizes this view quite well: Darwin gives us a "theory of how transformation and change remains in principle open because of the position of the subordinated, because domination remains precariously dependent on what occurs not only 'above' but also 'below.'"[94] For Sharp, following Grosz, this gives us a politics that is not foreign to supposedly "human" concerns, but as in Bennett's work, redescribes the very ways that human and politics are defined:

> As renaturalists, we do not aim primarily to be understood and valued by our fellows. We pursue strength, affinities with other vital forces, and alternative futures. . . . We depend upon and affect innumerable forces, human and nonhuman. The measure of our agency that is determined by other's perceptions may be significant, but it is hardly the totality of our power and freedom. [We look to] siphon enabling energy and power where it happens to find it. It infects and enjoins whichever beings and forces might aid in the construction of a joyful insurgency against patriarchy, misanthropy, imperialism, and yes, "crippling self-hatred."[95]

2. For Grosz, evolution is not just distributed spatially, but also indexes a real time. Clearly this will have import for us in the final chapter of this book. Beings are open to the chaos we have discussed, and thus philosophy requires an attunement for "a future" for which we "cannot prepare" and where our "bodies and capacities will be open to recontextualization and reevaluation."[96] Efforts to combat pernicious essentialisms must recognize there is no "linear or progressive development" and that politics is to be thought in terms of "movements rather than goals, processes rather than ends."[97] In this way, the future, she argues, may arrive as a "productive monstrosity" to "prevailing models and norms."[98] This is not to say that political activists will not have goals—"come join us, we stand for nothing but the process itself!"—but that these goals themselves are revisable in the movement of political situations. Slavoj Žižek announces something like this logic in a 2013 article on the revolts in Egypt and Turkey:

> A political movement begins with an idea, something to strive for, but in time the idea undergoes a profound transformation—not just a tactical accommodation, but an essential redefinition—because the idea itself becomes part of the process: it becomes overdetermined. Say a revolt starts with a demand for justice, perhaps in the form of a call for a particular law to be repealed. Once people get deeply engaged in it, they become aware that much more than meeting their initial demand would be needed to bring about true justice. The problem is to define what, precisely, the "much more" consists in.[99]

In this way, political praxis does not have a particular end goal and is not utopian, but an unending process in which one's demands are open to change.

3. Feminist theory should not, she argues, depict culture as that which overcomes nature, since nature and culture are not different in kind. In her view, "language, culture, intelligence, reason, imagination, memory," as well as the "natural," are "all equally effects of the same rigorous criteria of natural selection."[100] She says that each must provide "some kind of advantage to survival, some strategic value to those with access to them."[101] It is not clear if this admitted vitalism—that is, the force that produces life—is so easily amenable to sign systems, reason, and culture, the latter of which can be found in Richard Dawkins' rather reductive account of memes. But in any case, she is evincing a certain Spinozism: each thing—even language and intelligence—seeks its own perseverance, which is nothing other than its power to survive.

4. Darwin, she argues, depicts sexual difference not as a cultural phenomenon, but as an "ontological characteristic of life itself," an ineradicable productive force in the real.[102] The need for genetic material from two sexes provides the motor for the variety, combination, and exchange inherent to life. This puts her at odds with certain constructivist accounts of gender difference.

5. History does indeed, she argues, have constraints. What is biologically or culturally possible occurs within a given set of trajectories, though without the past or the present fully determining the future. Culture is one such reaction to the nature of chaos: "it is the selection and harnessing of some of the forces of natural differentiation in order to cohere and give itself form and to structure its practices in highly particular, learned ways."[103] As such, she believes, feminism need not find scientific practices anathema to its own work, nor colonize nature with discourse. Rather, by delineating what is real, she argues she doesn't reify or essentialize the reality of what exists now, since her work concerns the real chaos that means there is always something new coming around the bend.

Processes, not things

Grosz is clear, too, that the things themselves are accretions that humans cut into the world of chaos. We give the world form and structure, but these things, as Grant argues against Harman, are always open to change. It is less clear where Bennett falls in this equation: she shares a certain Spinozism to be found in both Grant and Grosz's work, yet her depiction of the "power of things" seems to split the difference, recognizing the discreteness of particular objects, while acknowledging their power of change in networks of relations with other things. For her part, Grosz argues that, like the "species" that are nominated by biologists out of evolution, so too "things" are cut into the world by human processes, which is to say, that to discuss the activity of things is to export human values and concepts onto the world as it is:

> We stabilize masses, particles large and small, out of vibrations, waves, intensities, so we can act upon and within them, rendering the mobile and the multiple provisionally unified and singular, framing the real through things as objects for us. We actively produce, make, objects in the world and in doing so we make the world amenable to our actions, but also render ourselves vulnerable to their reactions. This active making is part of our engagement in the world, the directive force of our perceptual and motor relations within the world. Our perception carves up the world, and divides it into things.[104]

In other words, things "produce life" and "we need to accommodate things more than they accommodate us,"[105] but things are nevertheless "*our way* of dealing with a world in which we are emmeshed."[106] Thus what we make of the world remakes us in turn. And by concentrating on things or objects, "we leave behind something untapped of the fluidity of the world," the "movements, vibrations, transformations that occur below the threshold of perception and calculation."[107] This, however, is not "some fault," but is in line with Darwinian adaptation: "we could not function . . . without some ability to skelatize [the real], to diagram or simplify it."[108] The things we produce, of course, nevertheless have consequences, and thus we can come back to the Anthropocene discussed at the opening of this chapter, which demonstrates that the things of this world are indeed remaking "us" and constricting the horizons of our possibilities. With ecological disasters in the offing, we have, as always, to be attuned to chaos "beyond our own control."[109] In the sense meant by Grosz as well as more literally, we do indeed need to think "ecologies of the future." The power of things is all too real, and we need to conceive this all-too-real future in which nature may just go on to evolve past what has long been dubbed the human. But this future is not yet written: perhaps there is as yet another untapped power, one that recognizes a "common" or political power acting against those who would avert their eyes from the products of our "mining conditions," a power that would turn the world away from the dangerous ecologies of the moment, all so that we can evolve past the Anthropocene, but not past our being-in-the-world itself.

CHAPTER 6
RAY BRASSIER'S TRANSCENDENTAL REALISM: NOTHING (ELSE) MATTERS

The discourse of science leaves no place for man.[1]

Jacques Lacan

"Over the past half century, scientific matter concerning neuroplasticity, mirror neurons, epigenetics, and newly proposed revisions to Darwinian depictions of evolution have destroyed," Adrian Johnston writes in *Self and Emotional Life* (2013), "the caricature of biological approaches to subjectivity upon which the ever more hollow excuses of a tired old antinaturalism rely."[2] As we saw in the last chapter, Elisabeth Grosz has challenged the often opposed relation between scientific knowledge and phenomenology, hermeneutics, discourse studies, and deconstruction. Continental philosophy's supposed longstanding, if quickly ending, antipathy to naturalism is well known. Heidegger's critique of technicity and "scientism" is often a starting point for Continental reflections on science, and numerous thinkers from the Continental tradition have linked scientific rationality to the worst forms of political violence. Such figures as Heidegger were not ignorant of the latest work in mathematics and science—indeed Heidegger often provided nice thumbnail sketches of many theories in his lectures—but few Continental philosophers would see science as a paradigm for how philosophical inquiry should be conducted or as having results that tested one's ontological suppositions. For example, while Husserl's phenomenology aimed to be a "science," he considered the facts discernable by the natural sciences reductive of our original being-in-the-world. The starting point for a phenomenological inquiry could be said to be Cartesian in the sense of beginning with that being that declares itself "I" (however rethought in the history of phenomenology), where science was but one way of describing the world, one that reduced the self-world relation to quantifiable sets of data. No doubt, long after phenomenology ceased being synonymous with Continental philosophy, it's still the case that major conferences in the area present few, if any, papers referencing scientific findings, and this long-standing antinaturalism can seem to form something of an ideological kernel for what gets called Continental philosophy. The treatment of science in Anglo-American philosophy has been directly the inverse, since questions of naturalism and scientific epistemology are at the heart of wide study. Part of this difference is historical, linked to the academic backgrounds of early and mid-twentieth-century thinkers, but also because the sciences of the late nineteenth century and early twentieth century, if not later, worked hand-in-glove with the institutions of political power, and Foucault's analysis of power/knowledge refused, as did many feminist and post-colonial thinkers, to see the scientific endeavor as "objective" or separable from the larger forces percolating in a given society—and for good reason.[3] Moreover, even if Continental thinkers were to find the scientific literature as valuable for thought as, say, Joyce's *Ulysses*, the *Social Text* scandal of the mid-1990s, where two anti-Continental thinkers were able to publish in a leading theory journal a faux-reading of quantum theory, certainly would quiet those who wished to do otherwise. Why risk, without full expertise, such opprobrium?

Nevertheless, the last 10 years have seen an end to this hesitancy: Badiou's work on set theory has come to prominence (his take may be esoteric, but no one questions his mathematical *bona fides*), Meillassoux's *After Finitude* begins by assaulting Continental correlationism for undermining the ancestral facts provided by physics, and Slavoj Žižek's work is rife with references to neuroscience and quantum mechanics. We could also cite thinkers influenced by Gilles Deleuze, François Laruelle, William Connolly, Ray Brassier, and Ian Hacking, as well as Shaun Gallagher and others researching neurophenomenology. As Brassier puts it in this spirit, "The idea of a purely *a priori*, armchair metaphysics, presuming to legislate about the structure of reality while blithely ignoring the findings of our best sciences, strikes me as indefensible."[4] The danger is that, as in some precincts of Anglo-American philosophy, the pendulum swings the other way, with philosophers mimicking science as an authority to end debates over, for example, metaphysics, materialism, or time. Moreover, it's a good rule of thumb that if your philosophical colleague is often led to use science as a cudgel in any debate, then his or her knowledge is likely to be perfunctory and not more advanced than the scientific knowledge of third-year undergraduate majors in biology, psychology, or physics. (The number of philosophers who cite pop books, not technical studies, for facts from physics or biology to teach others patronizingly is disturbing.) This is, of course, not the case with the best philosophers of science, who do not merely ape scientific findings, but open up new areas for inquiry by scientific theorists. Nevertheless, if philosophy sees itself as merely explaining experimental research, then it will parody itself as a kind of academic ventriloquist dummy—and deserve the same tepid claps one gives the lame puppet master. There is a much wider conversation to be had—and is happening—about the relation between philosophy and science, which has been interminable since Plato first explained Socrates' youthful interest in the science of his day, as well as between different modes of work in so-called Continental and Anglo-American philosophies.

In the next three chapters, I move into this discussion by looking into different philosophical reactions to the research in neurobiology and questions of realism and materialism by Ray Brassier, Adrian Johnston, and Catherine Malabou. I am aware that framing them in these terms risks reducing their work to a single facet: any summary risks a philosopher's summary execution. Nevertheless, despite their evident differences, there is an interesting congruency among them, namely that they think through the future of the subject after neuroscience and the death of a certain self, which in turn upends an entire tradition's considerations of meaning, value, and politics. In short, they share a view that, after the deconstruction of the histories of ontology and Nietzsche's invocation of the death of God, neuroscience is a practice that calls forth the true "end of man."

The manifest image and the ends of man

In order to introduce these themes, let me turn briefly to the Anglo-American philosopher Wilfrid Sellars, who must be understood as we bring Brassier's transcendental realism into focus. In his seminal "Philosophy and the Scientific Image of Man" (1962), Sellars paints two different portraits of the human being's place in the world. The first image presents the very notion of the "man-in-the-world,"[5] that is, an image of itself *as humanity* with concomitant mutual obligations and rational agency. As Sellars puts it, this "manifest image of man-in-the-world" provides the "framework in terms of which, to use an existentialist turn of phrase, man first encountered himself—which is, of course, when he came to be man."[6]

This "manifest" image is not the folk wisdom of the rube, but is the highly developed philosophical and cultural enterprises that are "discursive": using reason first to develop a picture of the human and its community, and then to develop a picture of the world that correlates with this community of thinkers. The manifest image is hence inherently anthropocentric and "correlational," not least since before its existence, there was no such thing as "man"; "he" is an invention of a particular biological species, not an essential and ineliminable fact about the world. For Sellars, the manifest image is proto-scientific in that it looks to explain the world and the human's fit within it, while aiming to correct previous views that no longer fit the world as it appears. To this image, Sellars counterposes the "scientific image of man-in-the-world," which provides models for explaining what is manifest and postulates theorems of what is unapparent (electrons, quarks, the speed of light), with the upshot that human beings are treated as wholly within physical systems.[7] Since the manifest image of man-in-the-world is self-correcting, it gives rise to the scientific image in modernity, since science, of course, is fallibilist. But the scientific image diverges radically from the manifest image and is not merely an addendum to it. In fact, as Sellars seems in places to fear, the scientific image may eventually supplant the manifest image altogether. But while both Sellars and Brassier, as Pete Wolfendale points out, argue for ontological univocity or monism, they don't offer an explanatory monism.[8] There is still a place in Sellars for the manifest image, namely the functional dimension of reason as providing agency. This is why Brassier differentiates the *subject*, which is the locus of conceptual norms, from the *self*, which is the manifest image of self-consciousness. The latter can go the way of the dodo, as well as other aspects of the manifest image undermined by science, such as mid-sized objects such as chairs, which are made up of sub-particles and so on. There is then, in both thinkers, a methodological dualism between the space of reasons and the physical spaces of causes in the material world. The task of science should be to show how the manifest image of the self came to be; this Brassier finds in the neuroscience of Thomas Metzinger. But he critiques Metzinger at just the point where he thinks he can collapse agency into the neuronal processes of the brain. This is because, following Sellars, epistemological statements arise within a "space of reasons," which is a set of interlinking concepts and propositions beyond which nothing can be judged true or false. This is juxtaposed with the "space of causes," the physical world and its chain of cause-and-effect relations. This is how Sellars can differentiate between sensations and perceptions, usually used interchangeably by other philosophers: the former is in the space of causes that produce effects on the human organism, though also for beings that do not have agency in Brassier's sense. Perception, though, requires the space of reasons and its conceptual framework.

This is all to say, one cannot collapse norms (conceptual or moral) into ontology, nor export them onto it: this is the price of his nihilism, which is another way of saying that Brassier adheres to a Kantianism that has become more apparent in his writings since *Nihil Unbound*. This is what makes his "realism" transcendental, without returning to the correlationism many read into Kant, since he believes we can access the noumenal through scientific inquiry.

The consequence of the manifest image is that it allowed humanity to see itself, to borrow Spinoza's phrase, as a "kingdom within a kingdom,"[9] which is upended by the scientific image that describes "what there really is"[10] in ways that provide no special place to the human being. Importantly, one aspect of the manifest image is that even a philosophy that rejects appearances (as in vulgar Platonism) still places a premium on how things are given to the thinker. Therefore Sellars sees the manifest image as inherently "correlational," in the speculative realist sense of the term, since it always attempts a relation of thought to what appears or is "given" to us. (The task for Sellars is to find a scientific explanation for sensations, that is, Kantian intuitions, and their causes, which continues his ontological monism.) In addition, as is well known—one need only read the opening pages of Descartes' *Meditations* to see the problem—the "manifest image's" reliance on appearances has led to skepticism, various anti-realisms, and ultimately the worries of solipsism, since the minds of others can never appear to a given subject. Or alternatively it has led to a turn inward to idealisms and rationalisms that provide the certainty appearances cannot. (We will see how Sellars reverses this move and turns concepts "outward," arguing that there is no reason without a community of speakers, and that this puts a normative constraint on the use of concepts.) Sellars ultimately calls for a scientific realism as accessing the in-itself and a notion of personhood as a normative and historical configuration, not as a supernatural substance lying beyond the forces of nature. As Sellars put it, "In the dimension of describing and explaining the world, science is the measure of all things, of what is that it is, and of what is not that it is not."[11]

The focus of the scientific image, as we noted, is to describe what is "manifest," even if ultimately it undoes much of what appeared previously. It provides theories of the non-given, whether concerning quarks or germs or black holes or the inter-neural connections within our brains. Consider the switch from Newtonian physics, which by and large fits our manifest image of the world, to relativity and quantum theories, which are anything but straightforward and require a specialist's knowledge of mathematics to understand. There is nothing apparent about quantum superposition or, for that matter, the latest string theory. Sure, many entities discovered by chemists or physicists can be made to appear through electron microscopes, telescopes, and the like, but their import and meaning can only be detailed through explanatory theories developed by scientists, who then test these theories through further models and empirical exploration.

Once science has advanced to a certain point, Sellars leaves us to wonder if one day the manifest image may be found to be an unnecessary appendage, a point the neurophilosopher Thomas Metzinger suggests. Like the closing image of the "death of man" in Foucault's *The Order of Things*, this notion could wash away like a stick figure drawn all-too-close to ocean waves coming ashore. As Sellars puts it, without this normative framework of the manifest image of the man-in-the-world, "man himself would not survive."[12] While Sellars is not interested in providing anything but a heuristic set of images, Foucault, for his part, locates them in the last discourses of modernity, a point worth revisiting. For Foucault, the past two centuries in the West have been governed by an *epistemé* dominated by the empirico-transcendental doublet, that is, a post-Kantian notion of subjectivity that Sellars elaborates as the manifest image of man-in-the-world.[13] For Foucault, man *as such* can only be thought in relation to an *epistemé*—in sum, discursive practices in which certain forms of knowledge are privileged and others marginalized. The modern *epistemé*, Foucault writes in *The Order of Things*, created much of what Sellars describes in these two images: the manifest image of the self-reflecting, self-aware human aware of its finitude and historicity, in short, its empirical existence. This "man," however, transcends the empirical in unifying the fields of discourse, and it is this "empirico-transcendental doublet" as "man" that centers a whole era's discursive practices. As implicit in the discussion by Sellars, this discourse of the "empirico-transcendental doublet" ("man") is inherently unstable: wholly conditioned by external factors it comes to know (historical, biological, and so on), the subject is also that which is supposed to have sovereignty over itself and thus to be the maker of history, not its result. In a word, the empirico-transcendental doublet is but a shaky correlationism through which humanity determines what counts as the empirical (as that which is "given" to itself), while the latter is the ground from which the transcendental gains its existence. Based on this instability, one can thus foresee the end of an *epistemé* with man at its center, and one is left to wonder just what would come after it. Foucault writes, famously:

> One thing in any case is certain: man is neither the oldest nor the most constant problem that has been posed for human knowledge. Taking a relatively short chronological sample within a restricted geographical area—European culture since the sixteenth century—one can be certain that man is a recent invention within it. It is not around him and his secrets that knowledge prowled for so long in the darkness. In fact, among all the mutations that have affected the knowledge of things and their order, the knowledge of identities, differences, characters, equivalences, words—in short, in the midst of all the episodes of that profound history of the Same—only one, that which began a century and a half ago and is now perhaps drawing to a close, has made it possible for the figure of man to appear. . . . As the archeology of our thought easily shows, man is an invention of recent date. And one perhaps nearing its end. . . . One can certainly wager that man would be erased, like a face drawn in sand at the edge of the sea.[14]

Looking forward to the end of humanity

Sellars' two images of man-in-the-world provide the opening for Brassier's *Nihil Unbound* (2007) and several of his later essays, but we now turn to that book's closing pages, where Brassier argues there is a cosmic reason that human knowledge is traumatized from the start over its own demise. Brassier, it should be mentioned, is a rare breed of philosopher equally fluent in Anglo-American and Continental philosophy, which often can make his claims misunderstood by thinkers in both traditions. It's also the case that those philosophers that influence him most, such as Laruelle and Sellars, are rarely the clearest stylists, and Brassier's writing is often dense in ways not helpful to the beginning reader. This derives from his involvement in subtle debates concerning realism, the philosophy of mind, and the relation of thought to reality, and the beginning reader can have the feeling of trying to figure out a vast detective story after skipping to the last pages of a novel.

At the heart of Brassier's work, as the title of his 2007 book makes clear, is an attempt to resuscitate nihilism on rationalist and scientific grounds, instead of the supposedly irrationalist nihilisms of the last century. (Think of your typical black-clothed first-year undergraduate: they know that nothing matters, though it's more a mood than a reasoned-out philosophical stance.)

For Brassier, nihilism is not a subjective view in the world to be overcome in some existentialist manner—the human creates its own meaning—but is the only derivable fact from the disenchantment caused by scientific modernity. The world is not there for us; there is no God looking after our existence; and all that awaits us is the death of the universe and long before it, the death of our sun, and thus any archive of all thought that will have been collected.[15] Philosophy's task, for him, has been one attempt after another to make the human important, even existentialism, which recognized the absurdity of human existence while offering that the human was irreducible to physical nature. Where Meillassoux provides something of a quasi-teleology of a God to come who would finally give meaning to existence, Brassier concludes that the continuing task of philosophy, after the disenchantment of nature, is only a further cutting away of any lingering anthropocentric views of reality and their "pathological" affirmations of life.[16] "Philosophy should be more than a sop," he writes in *Nihil Unbound*, "to the pathetic twinge of human self-esteem."[17] It's fair to say that all manner of realisms have this implicit kernel, given their talk about moving beyond what is given to the human and so on. One can see this in so many quotes in speculative realism, many provided already in this book, about the import of the human and the question of "flat" ontologies. At the least, there is an underlying motif concerning what is external and independent to the human, and thus would exist upon the death of all humanity. Brassier makes the link unambiguous:

> [Nihilism is] the unavoidable corollary of the realist conviction that there is a mind-independent reality, which, despite the presumptions of human narcissism, is indifferent to our existence and oblivious to the "values" and "meanings" which we would drape over it in order to make it more hospitable. Nature is not our or anyone's "home," nor a particularly beneficent progenitor. Philosophers would do well to desist from issuing any further injunctions about the need to re-establish the meaningfulness of existence, the purposefulness of life, or mend the shattered concord between man and nature.[18]

Where Nietzsche's nihilism, on Brassier's account, equated the will to truth with the will to falsity, Brassier argues that there is no doing away with the will to truth, since it is this that provides the disenchantment needed for nihilism. This focus on the death of the human, a view of the world without the human and its enterprises, comes to the fore when Brassier ends *Nihil Unbound* with a meditation on Lyotard's discussion in "Can Thought Go on without a Body?" (1988), an essay concerned with the end of the sun (and all possible thought with it) in 4.5 billion years. Depicting a dialogue between two characters, "he" and "she," the first person in Lyotard's essay directs a set of accusing questions at "you philosophers" who ask all manner of questions that can never be answered.[19] "Long live patience," the character says sardonically, turning to the foretold death of the sun. "It will explode in 4.5 billion years," "he" says, striking a worrisome tone for such a distance of time. This "is the sole serious question to face humanity."[20] Why go on if thought itself cannot endure? If no one will be left to remember human accomplishment? What is the purpose of the will to know if knowledge itself will have been but a speck against the entirety of cosmic history? Hence the tragic irony that this will to know is precisely what leads to the knowledge of this end of all knowledge in the solar apocalypse. There is no negotiating this reality away, which in the explosion to come will take the Earth and every last human archive and project with it—so much for our manifest image—presuming *we* haven't done ourselves in already, and we are mightily trying. Lyotard and, following him, Brassier, have a good touch for the absurdity of this solar mid-life crisis vented by "he." The philosophical question, one we fear to address, "he" argues, is the "true limit" belonging to thought, since with the "sun's death there won't be a thought to know that its death took place."[21] All that will be left is simply "matter taken as an arrangement of energy created, destroyed, and recreated over and over again, endlessly."[22]

Here we have a literalization of the title of Quentin Meillassoux's *After Finitude*: after the finitude of our own existence, there is still an *after*; there is still time (left). Indeed, Lyotard's essay offers an allegory—here we've even slipped, since it's an inexorable fact given to us by science, and calling it an allegory is a cosmic version of saying to someone, "*If* I die . . ."—for how, to quote from Meillassoux, "thought is able to think what there can be when there is no thought."[23] For Lyotard, this "trauma" is not just out ahead of us in the future, but is one that marks our relation to time. This is the possibility of our collective impossibility, to cite Heidegger's formulation of our being-towards-death, and in this way, Lyotard addresses this event as uncorrelatable back to any thinker: "with the disappearance of the Earth, thought will have stopped—leaving that disappearance absolutely *unthought of*."[24] Lyotard posits that this inevitable closure is the hidden event behind our mortal will to truth, which seeks at any cost to find a way past the time horizon of the last setting sun, or at least to find a means to escape this solar system when it does: our will to truth seeks not truth for its own sake, he suggests, but rather the science and technology to escape the very last setting sun. "He" notes:

> Now this event is ineluctable. So either you don't concern yourself with it—and remain in the life of the mind and in earthly phenomenality. Like Epicurus, you say "As long as it's not here, I am, and I continue philosophizing in the cozy lap of the complicity of man and nature." But still this glum afterthought: *après moi le deluge*. The deluge of matter. . . . Once we were able to converse with Nature. Matter asks no questions, expects no answers of us. It ignores us.[25]

As Brassier argues, this event is "real yet not empirical,"[26] since this extinction can never be experienced. Thus thought is ultimately without purpose, and this provides "a gain in intelligibility" once we understand this extinction. We are no longer deluded about human purpose and this scientific knowledge demonstrates a reality that cannot be manifest. There is hence, he posits, a trauma at the heart of the will to know, which is the knowledge of an image of the end of all such images and all such knowledge. Brassier writes:

> In becoming equal to it, philosophy achieves a binding of extinction, through which the will to know is finally rendered commensurate with the in-itself. This binding coincides with the objectification of thinking understood as the *adequation without correspondence* between the objective reality of extinction and the subjective knowledge of the trauma to which it gives rise. It is this adequation that constitutes the truth of extinction. But to acknowledge this truth, the subject of philosophy must also recognize that he or she is already dead, and that philosophy is *neither a medium of affirmation nor a source of justification*, but rather the organon of extinction.[27]

Much as in Heidegger's "being-towards-death," which is implicit in the life of each *Dasein*, this ultimate death, Brassier concludes, is implicit in our will to know and the lifeworld of the manifest image. However, Brassier argues this is not some "cosmological transcoding of Heideggerian finitude but its speculative sublation in the form of a new synthesis of thought and object, or subject and death—a dead subject."[28]

It's not clear, at least in *Nihil Unbound*, why this should render the will to knowledge so meaningless, given that such a being-towards-death subtends all manner of affirmations of life, including in Nietzsche, Heidegger, and Derrida. It's true that the grander *telos* of an ultimate purpose to the physical world is no longer available and our collective endeavors to escape the one end we do know about (extinction) render moot our grandest plans of cosmic escape. Such a lack of teleology has been thought in philosophy at least since Spinoza. But it *will not have* been the case that our tenuous communities didn't exist, that loves *will not have* been tendered, and meaningful events in both the politico-historical and everyday senses *will not have* occurred, in short, that affects *will not have* passed between and among those biological entities still quaintly called "human." Even if it is not a perfect future, it is not enough to deny these locutions made in the future perfect. Each death marks, just this once, the end of the world, as Derrida writes. And yes, the end of all possibilities of the world, of the worldhood of any meaningful world, is visible on the horizon as the end of all horizons with the death of the sun, but this still leaves open the question of meaning in the face of this annihilation, at least as it stands now in Brassier's work. To put it otherwise, it's notable that Brassier leaves aside all the research on affects and neurobiology, focusing instead, as we will see, on the normativity of rationality, a point that will return when we look at Adrian Johnston's transcendental materialism in the next chapter. Perhaps even Adorno didn't envision this coldest of rationalities. Yet, it's the case that Brassier shares with Meillassoux that *this world*—and for Brassier there is no other—is meaningless, and one must bring atheism to its proper conclusion by ridding any notion of spirit or purpose from the human being, beyond continuing the scientific adventure and its acknowledgment of our ultimate end.

The major point to be concluded, for Brassier, from the coming apocalypse is that we can think a reality, namely the extinction event, that transcends us, but is not immanent to our experience (and therefore not empirical). Hence we can think a transcendental realism that binds itself coherently around the thought of this extinction and thus also what is *unbound*, since it transcends what is empirically given or correlational and is nevertheless real.

At the heart of Brassier's nihilism is a consideration of the temporality of the "manifest image" that provides meaning in the first place. That is, once the manifest image, to quote from the title of part I of *Nihil Unbound*, is "destroy[ed]," then the very notion of "man" and "his" being-in-the-world will be wiped away, and a certain "self" with it. Unambiguous, as we've seen, in Sellars' essay is the finitude of this image: it was not inexorable that it would come to be and, given the vicissitudes of cultural and evolutionary history, it is untenable to think it will immortally hold sway. For Brassier, the final "death" for "man" is arriving in the form of recent neuroscientific endeavors, which he believes have rung the final death knell for the "self" that was the dominant pole in correlationist theories. For Brassier, the latest neuroscience is precisely anti-correlational and, for that matter, also calls into question the discourses Foucault mentions as empirico-transcendental:

> The injunction in question is that of the impossibility of continuing to conceive of the human as if it constituted the unobjectifiable exception in terms of which the ontological validity of what the empirical sciences define as objective nature is to be gauged. This is not quite as banal or easily admissible a requirement for contemporary philosophy as some may initially think. Although many will readily concede the inappropriateness of Man's ontological designation as a *zoon logon echon* or a *res cogitans*, few seem willing to admit that, after Darwin, it is no longer possible to continue to conceive of human being transcendentally, whether it be as *Subjekt*, *Geist*, or *Dasein*.[29]

For Brassier, scientific naturalism has liberated the human being from its pretences to cosmic (or *any*) importance, while also explaining those processes we had previously described under the *deus ex machina* of the *cogito*, the subject, and indeed, the phenomenal self, which seems the most self-evident of things. For that matter the test of evidence is nothing but the presence of some x to a given self, since this "presence to the self" is precisely the evidence of evidence. And in turn the evidence *of us*.[30]

At the heart of Brassier's project is to recognize the findings of science as the passkey to the in-itself, while also deliberating on the meaning of this for thought. Without accusing Brassier of underwriting in the least the pharmacological industry, at a simplified level, we can see that many are leaving behind the phenomenal self in the name of the scientific image: talk therapies that operate at the level of the phenomenal self (and at its substratum in the unconscious) dominated when Woody Allen was last funny, and most are likely to describe their moods in terms of biochemical processes, all to be adjusted by the introduction of chemicals that would balance out this computational system. We treat the "self" less often, it seems, in terms of what Heidegger discussed as "mineness" than in third-person descriptions: instead of *I* am depressed, it is rather that a given pharmacological intervention is needed in several neurological systems. Moreover, we have seen the end of Cartesian dualism not just in the sense that we no longer posit ourselves as two substances (the thinking thing [*cogito*] and the body), but also because we reject Descartes' dictum that the mind is more knowable than the body. It is through the body, that is, the brain's physiology, that we explain the seemingly free conscious moods that strike us as if from nowhere. Catherine Malabou provides her own gloss on this:

> If mind and body are two aspects of the same thing [she here is giving an updated Spinozism], if they mirror or reflect each other, then it is not even useful to use the terms *mind* and *body* any longer; it is not even useful to refer to their unity as a conscious subject. . . . Considering the neural patterns that constitute the biological basis of subjectivity, we can state that there is a process of heteroaffection in autoaffection [in short, a reference to outside of ourselves when looking inward, the latter being the mark of a supposed subjectivity] refers to itself in the third person. . . . Something remains nonconscious and nonreferable to an "I" or a first person.[31]

For now, we cannot enter in the wide thicket of debates in the philosophy of mind over the ontological status of mental events, since the more limited point is to show how Brassier's adherence to the scientific image dovetails with his nihilism and transcendental realism. The effect is that the neuroscientific "subject" is to be treated not as an "I," but as an "it" or third person. Here, Brassier differentiates his work from the existentialists:

> [E]xistentialists thought it was still possible for human consciousness to provide the meaning that was absent from nature: existence may be meaningless, but man's task is to provide it with a meaning. My contention is that this solution is no longer credible, because *a project is now underway* to understand and explain human consciousness in terms that are compatible with the natural sciences, such that the meanings generated by consciousness can themselves be understood and explained as the products of purposeless but perfectly intelligible processes, which are at once neurobiological and sociohistorical.[32]

That project "now underway" is best represented by Thomas Metzinger's *Being No One: The Self Model Theory of Subjectivity* (2003). In this work, one that Brassier clearly values, Metzinger argues for a naturalist account of consciousness, without relying on the folk psychology that is not just the common-sense view but also the stuff of Western philosophy since the latter takes the first-person subjective experience as indubitable:

> Folk psychology naively, successfully, and consequently operates from the first-person perspective: a mental state simply is what I subjectively experience as a mental state. Only later did it become apparent that not all mental, object-directed states are also conscious states in the sense of actual phenomenal experience. Only later did it become apparent how theoretical approaches to the mental, still intuitively rooted in folk psychology, have generated very little growth of knowledge in the last twenty-five centuries.[33]

In other words, the Sellarsian manifest image has not advanced since Plato, and Metzinger thinks he can naturalistically account for how this phenomenon arose. We will not pause over the pride of the idea that *now* we are lucky to live in such a time that, in a mere few years, we have been able to dispense with thousands of years of thought; lucky, apparently, are we few in human history. In any case, while the self-present subject—the being that transparently represents itself to itself—has been the target in Continental philosophy for a century (and farther back in Hume and Kant), Metzinger provides a neuroscientific basis for his critique. His writings are an assault on the manifest image of the man-in-the-world, providing the last funeral ritual after the death of God: having lost not just God in Nietzsche's sense, but any overarching system for giving meaning to reality, we now stand ready to kill the last witness to this death. As such, we are moving, according to Metzinger, with Brassier following him in important ways, from an anthropocentric age to a "nemocentric" one, when, from the Greek, no one centers anything. But while Metzinger provides the basis for an assault on the notion of the "self," this does not mean we can throw away the notion of the "subject," which in Brassier's telling is the locus of rational agency. He is critical of the eliminative materialism of Paul and Patricia Churchland in *Nihil Unbound* for similar reasons. One side of Brassier's critique is that these accounts import into brain science questions of meaning, which his nihilism finds is not a proper subject of knowledge. Moreover, they attach "superempirical virtues" to physical processes unwarranted by the science; they thus fall to the very idealism of human values, such as unity of purpose for the mind and so on, that these materialisms were meant to critique.

Again, I think it is important to emphasize that Brassier's chapter on the Churchlands diagnoses the incoherence of their eliminativist program. That is, despite pervasive references in summaries of speculative realism online and elsewhere of Brassier as a reductive materialist, he argues for the autonomy of the space of reasons and an epistemology attached to it that at once attempts to go further than he believes the Churchlands do—by not exporting any norms onto the workings of the brain—and stepping back from the precipice of dissolving the Kantian space of reasons.

While Foucault subtends his depiction of this end of "man" in terms of an archeology of the modern "*epistemé*," Metzinger grounds his narrative in an evolutionary account, as is fitting a philosopher looking to supplant the manifest image.[34] For Metzinger, at a given moment in evolutionary history, the (proto-)human organism activated within itself a "phenomenal self-model" (PSM), at which point it developed its manifest image of the man-in-the-world by way of self-consciousness. For Metzinger, the self as we understand it is an after-shadow of subpersonal (that is, not viewable to the conscious self) neurological processes, and his project is to detail these processes, removing any notion of a substantial self somehow providing, like a hand moving a puppet's mouth, the representations we have.[35] In our natural attitude, we tend to reify the *representation* of *ourselves* as the representer of these representations, a confusion that he allows may have certain beneficial effects evolutionarily speaking, but is nevertheless a fiction that has deleterious effects, such as locking up millions of prisoners each year using dubious notions of free will and the suffering that comes with self-consciousness, such as the knowledge of one's death. There is no *who* that represents, only a *what* that is representing.[36]

In a manner akin to what Lacan called the infantile mirror stage, the self, for Metzinger, is a fiction that allows for the self-organization of complex bodily processes. As Metzinger argues, we are naïve realists about having unmediated access to this consciousness, when in fact, there is no thinker behind the thinking. This discussion of the mediation of the self to itself, through the unconscious or language, has been at the center of philosophy for more than one hundred years. To borrow Cartesian language, the self has no formal reality, but it has objective reality as the correlate of the organism's self-representation. This is best seen in Metzinger's rewriting of Plato's allegory of the cave.[37] In the original allegory, the education of the philosopher first necessitates "turning about" from the false images of sense experience, then taking the arduous path upward toward the world above the cave, that is, the world of the forms lit by the sun or Good beyond being. In Metzinger's telling, the task is not to climb out the cave, but to realize that the phenomenal self is but another shadow on the wall, with no one in the cave; this is what he'll later call the "ego tunnel." "What exists," then, "are information processing systems engaged in the transparent process of phenomenal self-modeling."[38] These processing systems don't just represent the self to itself, but also represent the outside world. But, as in the lesson from Sellars' critique of "myth of the given," these appearances are always mediated through signification and there is no direct encounter with the world except through concepts. As is well known, Sellars' attack on the "myth of the given" targets modern empiricism, which, simply put, argued that sense data are foundational for knowledge. No doubt, there is affection and sentience caused by material causation, but this is not sapience, which is conceptual. Sellars writes,

> One couldn't have observational knowledge of any fact unless one knew many other things as well. And let me emphasize that the point is not taken care of by distinguishing between knowing *how* and knowing *that*, and admitting that observational knowledge requires a lot of "know how." For the point is specifically that observational knowledge of any particular fact, e.g. that this is green, presupposes that one knows general facts of the form X is a reliable symptom of Y. And to admit this requires an abandonment of the traditional empiricist idea that observational knowledge "stands on its own feet."[39]

For Metzinger, our concepts of the world, while not one-to-one with that world, are just accurate enough to keep the human organism from any number of dangers.

Of course, Metzinger is not the first to attack Descartes' reified mental substance, and his prose, however right Brassier finds him in many ways, has the annoying tone of treating his opponents as not having advanced since the days of seventeenth-century substance philosophy. Nonetheless, like Sellars, Metzinger argues there is a temporality to this mental self-image: "As soon as the system does not need a globally available self-model, it simply turns it off," as in sleep, but also in an evolutionary future, when there would be this final death of the most stubborn of mental images.[40] In other words, Metzinger provides a naturalist answer to why the manifest image arose, which for Sellars was a conjecture. He thus, for Brassier, provides an "inapparent," scientific image (from unapparent neurology) for the manifest image of the "man-in-the-world," completing the Sellarsian project. Metzinger writes in *The Ego Tunnel: The Science of the Mind and the Myth of the Self* (2009), "There will likely be a conflict between the scientific view of the acting self and the phenomenal narrative, the subjective story our brains tell us about what happens when we decide to act."[41] As Brassier puts it, we can now "envisage systems capable of generating sophisticated conceptual representations of themselves and their world without benefit of a PSM," that is, the self as we understand it.[42]

Anyone who has read Metzinger also knows that this is not just a descriptive project, but part of a wider sociological and political project to replace the manifest image with the scientific one. For Metzinger, sounding vaguely Buddhist, the continuance of the self only augments suffering, since through self-reflection of one's place in the world one has knowledge of one's death and other affects relating to the deaths and pains of others. In this way, he offers a vaguely utilitarianism doctrine, for the reduction of this unhappiness, that follows from his ontological depiction of the mental. For example, he imagines a "post-biotic" artificial intelligence who (a) pities the human for living in a constant fiction about his or her role in the world (including having free will and strong agency) and (b) offers up the concept of fully naturalized thinking that would not be self-reflexive and hence does not suffer as humanity does.

The upshot of this whole analysis, as Brassier argues, is that we can now answer "whether it is possible to envisage systems capable of generating sophisticated conceptual representations of themselves and their world without" phenomenal selfhood.[43] We can have a fully naturalized account of subjectivity's rise. But just because there isn't phenomenal self-reflexivity—"the view from nowhere"—the brain still can provide concepts "without exemplifying phenomenal selfhood," in similar manner to a computer that is able to do complex computations without self-awareness.[44] This is not just a decentering as in the work of various deconstructionists of the last 40 years, but a non-centering, a view that makes many of the anti-humanists of the 1960s' generation appear positively nostalgic for humanism.

Here we should pause: all manner of facile arguments have been made against supposed "reductionism" (even if Metzinger is not, strictly speaking, a reductionist for Brassier)[45] and often a number of philosophers think just using the term replaces substantive arguments. For example, in a recent work critically and excellently examining the rise of neuromarketing and the laughably naïve ways in which MRI scanning and its uses have been reported in the national media, Sally Satel and Scott Lilienfeld suggest, in their eminently readable *Brainwashed: The Seductive Appeal of Mindless Neuroscience* (2013), that when it comes to reductionism, it must be rejected on, among other grounds, its threat to civic, legal, and moral notions of freedom. But this is not an argument and, in any case, perhaps these notions of freedom need updating given the ruptures from numerous philosophical points of view over the last 150 years. The legal system should be rethought if it still engages with Augustinian notions of free will—for a host of reasons after Freud. Again, standing up for old-fashioned values requires more than just waving the flags of freedom and civic virtue.

Clearly, Metzinger's account would upend these notions, while also performing an Ockham's razor to subjectivity: the quickest way to account for all manner of mental abilities is through neurobiology. Despite critics, this view from nowhere need not be "amoral"—it's not literally killing human organisms—since the "view from nowhere" happens also to be the place from which proper knowledge as traditionally thought to be is dispensed and thus with it the place from which ethical decisions are thought to be made. For many in the history of philosophy, decisions about what we can know and how to act should be done without regard to our subjective emotional states and partial needs. Having this "view from nowhere" would make the organism, as Brassier says, egocentric only in the limited need to protect itself according to evolutionary adaptation—which has always been allowable in most moral systems. Is Brassier not delivering on the old Kantian dream of purely objective rational agents who would lack hypothetical imperatives, that is, self-serving whims? Since there would be no "self" that could make itself an exception, this organism could think only in terms of universalizable duties. "[It] is possible," Brassier maintains, "to imagine systems endowed with the same cognitive capacities as humans, but whom the transparency constraint, specifically as pertaining to the PSM, would not obtain."[46] Thus, this would be an end to "humanity," providing not an anti-humanism, but a non-humanism that recognizes there was never a humanity to begin with, properly speaking, since the manifest image relied on an anthropocentric fiction. Brassier writes:

> The hypothesis of nemocentric consciousness [that is, a consciousness with no sense of self] provides a possible *model* for the *new type of experience* that could be *engendered* [here, in sum, is the pedagogical enterprise Metzinger and Brassier share] were scientists to succeed in

> objectifying their own neurobiological processes of objectification. The nemocentric subject of a *hypothetically completed* neuroscience [this hypothetical is important, since many don't share the view that it can be completed] in which all the possible neural correlates of representational states have been identified *would* provide an empirically situated and biologically embodied locus for the *exhaustively objective* "view from nowhere.[47]

Finally in this section, we should emphasize the changes in Brassier's positions since *Nihil Unbound*, most notably that, by way of Sellars, he sees Badiou and Meillassoux's account of thinking as too theoretical and removed from the natural sciences. That is, Sellars provides a Kantian-inspired explanation of practical reason while also accounting for how this arises from materiality; there is no such account in Badiou or Meillassoux, the latter of whom relies on an "intellectual intuition" that reaks of the correlationism his work was to critique. This leads Brassier to rely less on a "metaphysics of extinction," which follow on just the type of approach Meillassoux uses with the arche-fossil, than on his transcendental account of nihilism broached below.[48]

The subject of reason

In this way, he has abandoned all aspects of the "manifest image," and Brassier, unlike the other speculative realists, picks up the Kantian heritage concerning concepts. Rightly understood, Kant's writings on both practical and theoretical reason do not deny that the human being is fully embodied and thus given over to physical biology. The transcendental in Kant is an "as if" relation of reason to the empirical—one should make maxims as if one could perform one's will in the world and so on. Following on this, what is indispensable about the manifest image for Sellars, Brassier notes, is "its normative valences as the framework which allows us to make sense of ourselves as rational agents engaged in pursuing various purposes in the world."[49] But does not the proposed dissolution of the self disallow any normative claims—both understood in terms of an ethics and in that concepts are rule bound and "inferential" in the philosophical meaning of the term? Brassier's answer: "it does not, so long as we distinguish the *phenomenon* of selfhood from the *function* of the subject."[50] Brassier writes, "the manifest image is indispensible insofar as it provides the structure within which we exercise our capacity for rational thought," and that without this "science's investigation of reality would become pointless."[51] He continues, with the second question here the most pertinent: "Is this to say that the manifest image subordinates the ends of enquiry to human interests? That the manifest image predetermines our understanding of what a person [a 'subject,' not a 'self'] is? I think the answer to both questions is no."[52] What then is this agent or subject, but again, not a self?

> An agent is a physical entity gripped by concepts: a bridge between two functions implemented by causal [physical] processes but distinct from them. And the proper metaphysical framework for explaining the neurobiological bases of subjective experience is that of a scientific realism rooted in an account of conceptual normativity that supervenes [i.e., simplistically put, depends], but cannot be identified with, socially instantiated and historically mediated linguistic practices.[53]

Here, in short order, is Brassier's critique of all manner of post-1960s' Continental philosophy, since he believes they identify all norms, even conceptual norms, with historically mediated linguistic practices. But as with the above, he would also warn against conflating norms with the activity of neurological systems. In this, Brassier shares with Sellars a view that conceptuality is not merely in the "self," but follows rules that bind all those that utilize concepts; the "subject" is "gripped by concepts," and thus the subject is a "bridge between two reasons, a function implemented by causal processes [the materiality of the brain] but distinct from them." Hence, as in Sellars, the subject is bound by rules for how intersubjective conceptuality works. To cite the most used of examples, concepts are not lonely atoms, but as with words, they rely on a given grammar and relation to other words in given sentences, and there is no such thing as a private language. In a natural language, such as French or German, words can only be used in certain sentences correctly and not in others—thus the arduous work of non-native speakers to be understood in a new language. After structuralism in Continental philosophy, natural languages are not taken to represent objects outside of language, that is, the sign "tree" equals a real tree somewhere, but rather each signifier or word only exists in a negative relation with infinite other words: a tree is not a chair, which is not a table, and so on *ad infinitum*. Similarly, concepts for Brassier and Sellars are not representations of real objects but, as Kant held, rules for combining and separating representations. In this way, sentience (sense) does not, as Brassier holds, equal sapience (thought), that is, there is an irreducible gap between conceptual rationality and sense data. He writes:

> Conception is answerable to normative standards of truth and falsity, correctness and incorrectness, which develop from but cannot be collapsed into the responsive dispositions through which one part of the world—whether parrot or thermostat—transduces information from another part of the world—soundwaves or molecular kinetic energy. Knowledge is not information: to know is to endorse a claim answerable to the norm of truth *simpliciter*, irrespective of ends.[54]

This would appear to trap Brassier and Sellars in idealism: true knowledge comes from rationality and not from the senses—with the upshot that we are trapped in conceptual schemes. (This is precisely John McDowell's critique of Sellars, namely that he returns to a form of Cartesian dualism where the space of reasons can be disconnected from causes. For McDowell, the world provides both causes *and* reasons.) But this is where Brassier and Sellars argue that modern philosophy (understood as the period up to Kant) provides a false choice: it is not rationalism or empiricism that is the answer, since as Kant held, "thoughts without content (*Inhalt*) are empty (*leer*), intuitions without concepts are blind (*blind*)." As Brassier puts it, "There is no cognitive ingress to the real save through the concept. Yet the real itself is not to be confused with the concepts through which we know it. The fundamental problem of philosophy is to understand how to reconcile these two claims."[55] Taking this as his dictum, Brassier practices a transcendental realism that recognizes that the real transcends a conceptual scheme concerning it and hence does not fall to the myth of the given. This would include, for Brassier, the intellectual intuition of Meillassoux, the sense data of empiricists, and even the intentionality that founds phenomenology. Hence there is no easy leap from the epistemology concepts provide to the ontology of the real. Brassier writes:

> We gain access to the structure of reality via a machinery of conception which extracts intelligible indices from a world that is not designed to be intelligible and is not originarily infused with meaning. Meaning is a function of conception and conception involves representation—though this is not to say that conceptual representation can be

> construed in terms of word-world mappings. It falls to conceptual rationality to forge the explanatory bridge from thought to being.[56]

For Brassier, using the Kantian language, it's within the phenomenal that the concept of the noumenal appears, even in its nonappearance. Among our concepts is a concept of what transcends conceptuality, and the task is not to confuse, as Metzinger points out with the self, the representations, say, of objects, with that which transcends representations, namely the *an sich*. Brassier writes that we must follow Kant's critical project in the

> acknowledgement that reality is neither innately meaningful nor inherently intelligible, [which] entails that the capacities for linguistic signification and conceptual understanding be accounted for as processes within the world—processes through which sapient creatures gain access to the structure of a reality whose order does not depend upon the conceptual resources through which they come to know it.[57]

Thus reasons given in thought—through inferential moves among concepts—are not the same as physical causes, though ontologically speaking we can also say that thoughts are causally produced by neurological processes. Transcendental realism, as Peter Wolfendale puts it, is the "position that shows that the structure of thought itself implies that there is a real structure of the world"—including that structure that gives rise to thoughts in the first place—"in excess of the structure of thought."[58] But this also implies that the task Brassier has given himself is a new Critique: to provide an account for the "structure" of thought, namely an epistemology, that could be wedded to an ontology of the real "in excess" of these concepts. This is the task for philosophy, over and above any scientific endeavor. As he puts it,

> This is not to say that we cannot draw ontological consequences from science: on the contrary, we can and we should. But the relationship between science and metaphysics is complicated: science says nothing about how to tell the difference between what is and what is not ultimately "real." It becomes difficult to let science dictate metaphysics once we acknowledge that what science says is real continues to undergo fundamental revisions. That's why I endorse a "transcendental realism" according to which science knows the real but the nature of this "real" is not strictly speaking objectifiable. The basic idea is that we know the real through objects, but that the real itself is not an object.[59]

Thus this is a realism where there can be no correlation of words and things, no empirico-transcendental doublet, and thus we have a realism that transcends "objects" as understood as part of our manifest image of the world in terms of substantiality. Again from Brassier:

> Acknowledging the autonomy of the in-itself, transcendental realism faces the problem of determining what is real. This cannot be addressed independently of scientific representation. For those of us who take scientific representation to be the most reliable form of cognitive access to reality, the problem is one of granting maximal (but not, please note, incorrigible) authority to the scientific representation of the world while acknowledging that science changes its mind about what it says there is. Accordingly, the key question becomes: How can we acknowledge that scientific conception tracks the in-itself without resorting to the problematic metaphysical assumption that to do so is to conceptually circumscribe the "essence" (or formal reality) of the latter? For we want to be able to claim that science knows reality without resorting to the Aristotelian equation of reality with substantial form.[60]

The regulative ideal of all science, for Brassier and Sellars, is a coming together of the phenomenal and noumenal, which though ideal, would see the end of self-recursivity and when "man"—at the very moment this word would no longer make sense—can see "himself" for what he is not, along with all the objects that fill "his" manifest experience. As Daniel Sacilotto nicely puts it, "the immanence of the Real awaits . . . purged of positive content."[61] Such would be the living death to which we accede at the limits of all horizons, for Brassier, in the death of the sun and all thought that ends with it, at which point nothing, or the *nihil*, would be unbound from our correlationist conceptions.

CHAPTER 7
THE TRANSCENDENTAL MATERIALISM OF ADRIAN JOHNSTON

We saw in the last chapter that Ray Brassier weds scientific thinking to a transcendental realism that looks to evacuate old notions of the self, while not abandoning the subject of reason. In this chapter, we continue through Continental responses to recent neuroscientific research, in particular with Adrian Johnston and his "transcendental materialism," while setting up the discussion in the next chapter of Catherine Malabou and her considerations of plasticity as the new "motor scheme" of history. Like Brassier, though from different directions, both Malabou and Johnston argue for an end to Continental philosophy's antipathy to philosophical naturalism. As we will see, despite their numerous philosophical differences, Malabou is closer to Brassier and his attention to Metzinger's nemocentric universe. Where I will begin in this chapter, though, is Johnston's transcendental materialism. This will enable me to return to the question of the nemocentric real in the next chapter as part of thinking the stakes of speculative realisms as reinscribing what Foucault called the end of man.

Toward an existential materialism

In the past several years, Johnston has become a transformative thinker in Continental philosophy, deserving of wide reading by those interested in new forms of subjectivity and materialisms that follow after the structuralist and constructivist paradigms of the past 50 years. As with all the writers discussed in this book, Johnston's work is formed out of a complicated intellectual background that necessitates him delivering his positions after many pages of ink spilled concerning German idealism, Žižek's neo-Lacanianism, recent work in neuroscience, Freudian metapsychology, and Hume's empiricism. The reader might thus get worried—no, not another dozen pages going over the history of philosophy before you tell me what he thinks! Let me try an end run around such a summary by citing Jean-Paul Sartre, who is not often found in Johnston's work, but warranted by an important (though *only*) self-description by Johnston of his transcendental materialism as an "existential materialism."[1] Against the backdrop of 1950s Marxism, Sartre, best known for his work on human freedom in *Being and Nothingness* (1943), attempted a difficult synthesis of Communist theory and existential freedom in his *Critique of Dialectical Reason* (1959), along with its preface, published separately in English as *Search for a Method*—a highly readable work compared to the door stop that is the rest of the book. Sartre was confronting Marxists, directed by tedious apparatchiks in Moscow, who argued for an historical and economic determinism.[2] In the first section of *Search for a Method*, "Marxism and Existentialism," Sartre argues for the continued use of existentialist terms, despite his clear aim to recognize Marxism as the "philosophy of our time":

> We cannot go beyond [Marxism] because we have gone beyond the circumstances that engendered it. Our thoughts, whatever they may be, can be formed only upon this humus; they must be contained within the framework which it furnishes for them or be lost in the void or retrogress.[3]

Given his own references to Lenin, Mao, Žižek, and Badiou, for Johnston, communism is still very much still the "philosophy of our time," though he also agrees with Sartre that it must not lose sight of the singular. For Sartre, existentialism is a "parasitic system which lives on the margins" of Marxism, which is "the real science."[4] That said,

> *without living men, there is no history*. The object of existentialism—due to the default of the Marxists—is the particular man in the social field, in his class, in an environment of collective objects and of other particular men. It is the individual, alienated, reified, mystified, as he has been made by the division of labor and by exploitation, but struggling against alienation with the help of distorting instruments and, despite everything, patiently gaining ground. The dialectic totalization must include acts, passions, work, and need as well as economic categories.[5]

We will have to break off from Sartre here. But it's important to note that subjectivity is literally *nothing* for Sartre; it is the freedom or intentionality that is neither a mystification nor is a Cartesian substance, even as attempts to explain it through causal physical relations end up explaining it away. It is a "void" at the heart of being, which Sartre likens to the differences between actors playing roles that, however unchanging the script, will always perform the ineliminable difference among their styles even if every word is predetermined. The self comes through its very stylization of what it is given in a script or a personal history. Our existence is a "formal transcendence" of the ego for Sartre, and the term "transcendental" in Johnston's transcendental materialism is analogous. As Johnston puts it, "by contrast with certain versions of dialectical materialism, the strongly emergent subject of transcendental materialism can and does achieve, at least from time to time, full-fledged independence from its ontological-material grounds."[6] Formally transcendent, the ego in Sartre and in Johnston's materialism is a no-thing, and the task is to think forms of subjectivity that account for freedom or autonomy without, as Metzinger and Brassier would point out, reifying such a process as a substantial entity beyond or behind the physical brain—a veritable ghost in the machine.

Johnston argues for "points of forced freedom,"[7] over and against not just Marxist determinisms, but also neurological and materialist varieties, such as Thomas Metzinger's, that would deny any notion of human freedom. As Johnston puts it in a 2011 interview:

> I think that even if there's something there that's ineliminable, nevertheless, especially at the level of our experience of ourselves, in our practices, there can be the threat of, at least experientially, irreducibility being occluded, lost from view—a sense of dissolution or of being levelled down, reduced away, taken up without remainder into these non- or anti-individual matrices [such as history or neurobiology]. I think that's certainly a danger and *a lot of how we position ourselves could be seen as a reaction to that threat.*[8]

Hence, while it's true that much of Johnston's recent work has aimed to allow naturalism within the frame of Continental philosophy, he should also be read as pushing back against neurobiological reductionism that, in some ways, Brassier valorizes and Malabou, for her part, sees as a window onto fundamental ontology. In short, Johnston "refuses to dismiss all things subjective as epiphenomenal, namely, as purely illusory qua causally inefficacious."[9] The irony is that Johnston finds the self to be an illusion, but a causally effective one.

Johnston's first book, *Time Driven: Metapsychology and the Splitting of the Drive* (2005), is an excellent reading against the view that for Freud the unconscious is atemporal. For Freud, the human relation to temporality is through what Heidegger called phenomenological clock-time, which in consciousness just sees time in terms of a metaphysics of presence: now, then now, then now again, *ad infinitum*. But since in the unconscious the past is never past (thus one suffers symptoms rising from immemorial conflicts) and is anchored into the repetition of various traumas, it is said to be "timeless." Johnston shows, by way of Lacanian theory and influenced by Slavoj Žižek's own readings, that in fact Freudian drives are fully temporal. The trauma of the living is always in relation to multiple *real* times: repetition, progressive time, and so on. However, Johnston's first work offers that there is no simple "drive," but all are co-implicated and "split." But I think it's also the case that he begins there mapping and contesting considerations of time that are important for his later work. Indeed, the "transcendental" aspect of his materialism is precisely bound up in what Sartre thought it was, namely the temporality of existence itself. This temporality is what Derrida called the "quasi-transcendental" timing that disallows the locking-in of any subjectivity to the absolute presence of the now, and thus dislocates the immanence that Johnston supposes of naturalistic systems: time is precisely what Johnston calls the "transcendence in immanence" of the very gap of subjectivity. As we near the end of this book, this will help me build my own argument for the *arché* of time, one that I have argued must be thought, even if temporarily, as all things are, for any realism worthy of the name. Does this not inform Johnston's attacks on the non-temporal, Platonic "formalisms" of one side of Lacan, Badiou, and Meillassoux in his recent works? Against a tradition that describes what is transcendent as atemporal, beyond being, and thus the unity of all that is real, I think Johnston, read through what he says in his first book regarding temporality, joins those who would counter with a pure immanence, if there were such a thing, which is the night in which all cows are black. As such he sets to thinking an "immanent-monistic emergence of a disharmonious ontological-material multitude or plurality."[10] This is what enables his "conflict ontology" of recent works and it's this part of his work with which I mostly make peace, whatever its conflict.

In *Žižek's Ontology: A Transcendental Materialist Theory of Subjectivity* (2008), Johnston pledges allegiance to Žižek's post-Lacanian project. For those who reduce Žižek to a series of jokes and the worn-out magic trick of the reversal ("Most people think bacon comes from pigs, but is not the reverse truly the case? That the pig only exists to become bacon, that it, in a sense, comes from it?), Johnston aims to show the joke is on them, demonstrating how Žižek's work derives from crucial elements of German Idealism, especially Schelling. As with all of Johnston's work, a quick summary is difficult, but at its heart, the book aims at thinking of the unconscious not as having ever-descending depths of content, as in Romantic and some of Freud's own depictions, but as "a radical indeterminacy and groundlessness covered over by various psychical layers seeking to avoid this void."[11] Johnston continues,

> Confronting the unconscious, instead of involving a realization that one is a puppet dancing on the end of personal-historical strings held firmly in the grasp of a libidinal puppet-master, might very well amount to coming face-to-face with an abyssal autonomy, an anonymous groundlessness situated as the extimate kernel of one's subjective existence.[12]

The extimate here, following Lacan, is *both* at the very heart of oneself and intimate, and is not one's own or under one's will or sovereignty. Therefore, where Sartre posited the void as consciousness itself, Johnston thinks of the void as the unconscious. In his recent monumental book on Hegel, Žižek makes the point that the "Lacanian" split subject is driven, not just by the famous triad of how it imagines itself over and against the big Other of the social symbolic order and its Real material/animal existence, but also by its non-appearance of the self to itself. Here, as is typical, Žižek uses a joke: two men are at a theatre, knocking back a few drinks while in the audience. At some point, one of the men gets up to use the toilet, embarrassingly lurching around for the WC. Finally, desperate to relieve himself, he pops through a door and spots a potted plant. Frantic, he relieves himself right there. After some copious urination, he zips up and eventually finds his way back to his seat. "What a pity," his friend tells him as he sits down. "You missed the best part! Some man just came on stage and pissed in the potted plant!" Žižek provides the moral from here: "The subject necessarily misses its own act, it is never there to see its own appearance on the stage, its own intervention is the blind spot of its gaze."[13] In the movie theatre, is this not the split between what Žižek calls the void of the subject, the pure *cogito* that has exited the room, and the subject as he appears to the Other in the social symbolic pissing on the plant?

This language of voids, blind spots, gaps, and fissures litters Lacan-inspired prose like misbegotten dropped crumbs that lead the lost nowhere. But conceptually, this is not difficult: in the analyst-analysand relationship, the analysand often provides the details of her life in a narrative that leaves in gaps, ambiguities, and holes. You are sitting on the couch of stereotype, perhaps even visiting the analyst because a boss, friend, or family member "suggested" counseling. They think it evident that you can be "fixed" by this expert psychoanalyst, a "subject supposed to know," as Lacan called it, and having put down your check for the assistant in the waiting room, you are literally invested in it, too. You enter the analyst's office and after some awkward patter—yes, you say, it's nice to meet her, though it's not, since being there means something has gone horribly wrong in your life. Then you are met with the most damning question, some variant of the simple "Why are you here?" You begin to detail your story of woe. How would *you* detail such a thing? You need not purposely leave anything out, but you think it important to discuss your husband's weird bedroom tics as the reason for your infidelity, or think you're throwing a bone to the analyst by saying your anxiety attacks spring from some childhood trauma. You provide a necessarily Imaginary self—you obviously don't narrate everything, but detail what you imagine is meaningful—all while using the conventions of everyday language and in the face of a societal Other, the analyst, representing the social Symbolic, whose judgment worries you. Looking at the situation, an outsider might think you are just telling the analyst what you think she wants to hear: you are not such a bad guy, it's your parents fault for your kleptomania, and so on. If only we could have a recording of your every interaction and thought since birth, then we would have the "real" you. We would know all your relationships with your parents, friends, and so on, and even your weak moments of apathy and self-disgust—nothing will be hidden from your repressing inner gaze, not your earliest erotic thoughts of a parent or the fact that you are currently parked in a handicapped spot. But for Lacan, there is no big Other, no omniscient God or recording device, not least since "we" would filter this Real through our own Imaginary and own expectations formed by the Symbolic when we hear the recording device. Psychoanalysis is thus a hermeneutic enterprise that worries over its ability to comprehend and thus invariably reduce subjects to a pre-given narrative through its acts of interpretation. You are not a substantial *cogito* or even the repository of an eternal memory in an unconscious that is hidden, but still there, just below the conscious level. "You" are just there fumbling on the couch, caught between what you imagine of yourself, how that is affected by the Symbolic, and the Real circumstances of your material being, which in turn, is not something "out there" but is caught up in the effects of what you imagine yourself to be and the social symbolic given your very specific history. Thus the self skims the surface of the very language you speak, which also means it's in the gaps and fissures of what is not said and what is left out, that is, what shakes loose from the clichés and grammar of everyday language. This is what Lacan means by saying that the human being is the *parlêtre*, the speaking being.

Now, let's look again at Thomas Metzinger's *Being No One*, discussed in the last chapter. Despite Metzinger's dissolution of the self, Johnston gives a reading of his book that sees it not as reductive, as he views the eliminative materialism of Paul Churchland, which describes all but biochemical accounts of the self as mere "folk psychology." Recall that Metzinger's task is to provide for a naturalist account of how the "self" came to be. For Johnston, Metzinger demonstrates why each person cannot accept the Churchlandian view, that is, there is a first-person aspect that is reducible to such neurobiology. "The nice thing Metzinger does is to say that we now have neuroscience to explain why it is that we can't accept eliminativism as true, although it is true."[14] Thus while Metzinger takes his role to be pointing out the illusion that is the self and hope for its dissolution, Johnston reads this positively as demonstrating a "transcendental or necessary illusion of much of what we take for granted at the folk psychological level being 'real.'" Where the cognitivist Metzinger unmasks the self as an unnecessary illusion, Johnston stands up to say, I agree, except that it is a *necessary* illusion. Here he agrees with Žižek in *The Parallax View*:

> [M]aterialist reductionists who claim that "there really is no self" are right, but they nonetheless miss the point. At the level of material reality (inclusive of the psychological reality of "inner experience"), there is in effect no Self: the Self is not the "inner kernel" of an organism, but a surface-effect. A "true" human Self functions, in a sense, like a computer screen: what is "behind" it is nothing but a network of "selfless" neuronal machinery. Hegel's thesis that "subject is not a substance" has thus to be taken quite literally: in the opposition between the corporeal-material process and the pure "sterile" appearance, subject is appearance itself, brought to its self reflection; it is something that exists only insofar as it appears to itself. This is why it is wrong to search behind the appearance for the "true core" of subjectivity: behind it there is, precisely, nothing, just a meaningless natural mechanism with no "depth" to it.[15]

There is a temporal point here that Johnston discusses in *Žižek's Ontology* in line with his notion of freedom, which is not an index of any consciousness or self-willing act:

> [A]n autonomous act involves the momentary, sudden return of the abyss of freedom, namely, the resurfacing of the archaic void within the realm of the here and now. . . . The unprecedented novelty of a genuine act of freedom interrupts the chronological-linear flow of historical temporality, introducing something there that cannot be accounted for in historical terms as an outgrowth of what came before.[16]

The Real for Lacan, which is "the impasse of formalization," is given assorted names in Johnston, including corporeality, animality, and matter, which is different than "reality," the imaginary-symbolic form of existence that is disrupted by this Real. But interestingly, the "real real," the "true real" in Lacan, Johnston maintains, is "precisely what the ways of the sciences enable to be accessed lucidly and rigorously in its truth."[17] This, in a sense, will be the opening through which Johnston will drive his naturalism, seeming to repeat Brassier's delineation between transcendence and the scientific image of man in the world. But questions are bound to arise: what notion of freedom comes out of this Lacanian structure? Can Lacan be naturalized as Johnston wishes, without shifting Lacan's categories? Or is he linking materiality, historicity, neuroscience, and subjective freedom in ways that sound good—who would want to say down with freedom? Pay no attention to material history! Don't read anything from science!—but are just ultimately irreconcilable?

The politics of the event

Before smacking into these problems head-on, let's first look to *Badiou, Žižek, and Political Transformations: The Cadence of Change* (2009), where Johnston investigates the political import of his claim that immanent genesis can produce transcendent affects at both the subjective and political levels. How do systems rupture as a result of mutations from *within* those systems? How do they produce "events" that mark a new system on the scene, thus transcending any epistemology of what is taking place *now*? These "events" are the mark of a certain transcendence irreducible to previous systematic causes, which we'll see puts him at odds with Malabou's immanentism.

In *Žižek's Ontology*, Johnston asks, "In light of what is presently known regarding the deterministic influences operating at historical, psychical, and biological levels, is there space left for a subject that could be said to be free in any meaningful sense?"[18] His answer is affirmative, which is important for the naturalism discussed in the next section:

> Being free is a transitory event arising at exceptional moments when the historical, psychical, and biological run of things breaks down, when the determining capacities of natural and cultural systems . . . are temporally suspended as a result of deadlocks and short circuits being generated within and between these multifaceted, not-whole systems.[19]

In *Political Transformations* Johnson extends this thinking to offer a discussion of the "exceptional moments" of political and historical events. But *Political Transformations* also touches upon classical philosophical problems that arise from both transcendental and immanent accounts of change: if all change is immanent, then how is something *new* to come into existence? On the other hand, if what is new is wholly transcendent, then how is this "Other" to disrupt an immanent system such that this change can be even noticed? The ghost that Johnston wishes to exorcize is the specter of political quietism. At each turn, Johnston tests theories of the event against its potential abuse as an excuse for political quietism and determinism. There is good reason for this, since any theory of praxis that can breathe life in what some suppose as contemporary political inertia will upend two depictions prevalent in Continental philosophy: the need for a turn to a micropolitics in light of the dominant order, for example, as found in Julia Kristeva and her depiction in her trilogy on revolution of patrimonial, docile subjects, or a simple awaiting for the transcendent moment to come, as for example in Heidegger. As Heidegger famously put it in his 1966 *Der Spiegel* interview, published posthumously a decade later, "only a God can save us," which, in turn, can only mean politically that no one can. Hence, while engaging the works of Badiou and Žižek, Johnston will worry over those who "tend to favour models of change that risk discouraging in advance precisely the sorts of efforts at transforming the world today that they so ardently desire."[20]

Johnston begins *Political Transformations* by summarizing the most influential part of Alain Badiou's writings, which gestures toward a thinking of the event and the subject's formation as "faithful" to this occurrence. Many commentators have argued, convincingly in his view, that Badiou's thinking of the event is too transcendent and leaves behind too many considerations of what happens politically prior to the purified events of revolutionary action. Working through the competing literature on this point, Johnston calls for a Lacan-inspired thinking of "pre-evental" desire that would make any event inspirational in the first place.[21] In light of his writings on affect in *Self and Emotional Life: Philosophy, Psychoanalysis, and Neuroscience* (2013), another way to put this is that politics must answer to the traumas of misfelt feelings, those affects that are not immediately available to us yet are potentially productive of this "pre-evental" desire.

Before continuing further, it's worth recalling Badiou argues in *Being and Event* (1987) and *The Logic of Worlds* (2006) that truths are meta-historical and radically discontinuous from any previous regime. According to Badiou, there has been a cult of historicism (he seems to place doctrinal Marxism as well as Heidegger-inspired notions of historicity here) that cannot make its way out of the continuity of history to the radically *new*. For Badiou, an event has "no common measure, no common chronology, between power on one side and truths on the other—truths as creation."[22] In this way, Badiou conforms to one side of the age-old philosophical *aporia* of accounting for historical change. Is there an elsewhere from beyond the immanence of what is available now such that the *new* can appear within history as a *creatio ex nihilo*? Or, is it the case, as Spinozists and Malabou would claim, that transcendentalism is too otherworldly to think how such events would occur from within a given historical or natural structure? For Badiou, the "event" is not simply a reform, revision, or change within a dominant "state ideology," which only describes what is the state of things within a given political regime. He argues, as Johnston notes, that capitalist ideologies are perpetual motion machines that present mere change as events (for example, elections of new presidents and prime ministers) while also depicting actual revolutions as but "temporary, correctable glitches in the functioning of the established system."[23] Statist ideology thus acts as the cop on the beat that moves the revolutionary masses along claiming there is nothing to see. But we act, if at all, in a temporality he calls the "future anterior," which is the "real political time" for Badiou.[24] The political subject, on his account, acts according to a working fiction "as if" the event had *already* occurred, and thus the subject of the event may never in the end *know* if the event indeed has taken place. This epistemic ambiguity for the subject is an important element of Badiou's theory. Indiscernible, the subject must "force" through "courageous discipline" *after the event* the circumstances such that the event *will have* taken place. As a depiction of radical change, there is much that

Badiou offers here: political movements never can know if ontologically the breaking point of a given system has already occurred when they have to act. Yet, without this "forcing," which Badiou links up with revolutionary and often violent *praxis*, the truth of this event cannot be brought into a system of knowledge: the fact that this event happened only rises to the level of "the encyclopedia of established, recognized knowledge" if the subject is faithful to the event at issue. For this reason, the paradigmatic moment of revolutionary action, for Badiou, is the act of "nomination" in which a revolutionary group names and brings about performatively the event this naming entails. This nomination is a "subtraction" of the new from the current "set" of circumstances.

Responding to all of this, Johnston contends that, strictly speaking, there are in Badiou two events: $Event_1$ and $Event_2$. The former, Johnston argues, is the ontological rupture in which, in terms of one set or "world," nothing precisely happens, since the occurrence cannot be marked in terms of the prevailing order. The second event occurs through the declaration by an "anonymous hero" of the previously unacknowledged event. Johnson argues not that Badiou refuses to think the "pre-evental," that he doesn't detail at all actions that would bring about revolutionary events. Instead, he argues that Badiou fails to deal with what happens *between* $Event_1$ and $Event_2$. Badiou maintains that there is a given set for historical systems and that only through a subtraction process of what is unavailable in that set can transformational change come about. Political actors, then, do not produce events but are produced by them, since only subjects through their fidelity and militant discipline to the event gives rise to them in the first place.

If Badiou provides an account of a disciplined "fidelity" to the event *after* its occurrence, there is still no neat cordoning off of the temporal "before" and "after." As we've noted, Badiou argues that one must always act "as if" the time of the event had indeed arrived.[25] The task is to step out of statist time such that one is faithful to the event that one could then, by discipline, redeem in the past. This is the upshot of Badiou's discussions of Christian grace, which he pointedly argues, in *Logic of Worlds*, is different from the "Franciscan theology" found in Agamben's work, since the latter merely calls for a monastic awaiting for the event still to come.

Johnston emphasizes the intra-evental, since Badiou leaves largely undiscussed what would motivate political subjects. Johnston's line of approach is "to suggest the viability of a third materialist position" between history as it is lived, which Badiou calls in *Logic of Worlds* "democratic materialism," and the heroic life of the engaged subject, the life as lived in the "materialist dialectic."[26] This third position, transcendental materialism, describes an interstitial, *intra-*, and *inter*-evental space "within which a human being struggles to exceed his or her status as an all-too-human individual (along with the entire surrounding environment connected with this identity) while not (at least not yet) being clearly identifiable a proper subject vis-à-vis a distinct event-level happening."[27] Not just a "materialistic dialectic," this is "a materialism striving to account for how *more-than-corporeal* structures of subjectivity immanently surface out of the *odd materiality of human corporeality*,"[28] a repeating chorus from Johnston's earliest writings to his most recent. Thus, in line with his long attempt to sketch out a "metapsychological" account of how transcendental and irreducible events, such as freedom, are generated themselves from corporeal materiality, his discussion of political transformations shows there is a similar movement in the material development of history.

Neuroscience and the disenchantment of nature

With these political stakes in mind, which are never far from view in his work, we can now turn to Johnston's two most recent works, his contribution to the Catherine Malabou co-authored book, *Self and Emotional Life: Philosophy, Psychoanalysis, and Neuroscience* (2013) and *Prolegomena to Any Future Materialism: The Outcome of Contemporary French Philosophy* (2013). The latter is the first book in a planned trilogy, but provides enough of a sketch that the reader sees more than just the outlines of his transcendental materialism. The second volume, *A Weak Nature Alone* (projected 2015), proposes to extend what he has already argued in previous works, namely that "nature" is not an all-power one-All, whole and complete as one finds, he believes, in various forms of Spinozism. The Real or Nature is divested of any overarching meaning; he here agrees with Brassier's disenchantment of existence. But he also agrees with Heidegger's critique of depictions of the world as a single being or whole, since "antagonisms and oppositions" are at "the very heart of material being,"[29] that is, the "material *an sich* is itself inconsistent."[30]

> The natural does not amount to Nature-with-a-capital-N as the One-All of another big Other [God-like or systematic through and through], whether as a flawlessly coordinated clock-work mega machine (as in Laplace's Demon and mechanistic materialism) or a (w)holistic

> cosmic super-organism . . . . Instead of a seamlessly self-integrated and consistent with itself (i.e., "strong"), the *Grund als Ur/Un-Grund* of the Otherless expanse of the natural is "weak" *qua* fragmentary and inconsistent, shot through with irreducible negativities thwarting any totalizing synthesis of the field of innumerable material beings.[31]

This is hence both an atheistic project, but also, with the third volume, *Subject also as Substance* (projected 2016), a critique of Spinozistic philosophy. For Johnston, as well as Žižek,[32] Spinozism provides no moment of negativity in which being reflects back upon itself, since it is always caught in perpetual cause-and-effect relations; it also is a system that lacks personality, as Hegel argued.[33] Moreover, given its single plane of being—here we see the route Johnston is charting: a middle course between Plotinion teleology and transcendence and Spinozistic naturalism and absolute immanence—there can be no distinctions made between being and appearance, the virtual and the actual, since all that exists is appearance; nothing is more or less, according to Johnston. And thus one can't hold to a distinction between objects and the subject that enacts itself through nature and by which nature reflects back upon itself.

This critique of Spinozism also matches his take on object-oriented ontology, since he argues it is without an "acknowledgement or concession that there is some sort of fundamental difference-in-kind . . . that makes a subject something which can't be considered an object."[34] Updated Spinozisms, such as Jane Bennett's work and presumably Grosz's naturalism covered in Chapter 5, don't fare any better in his view. These works, for Johnston, are driven to an "anti-humanism," fomented by what one could call the moral blackmail of an ecological politics, where ecological commitments lead to flatter ontological ones. But this, Johnston suggests, reverses it: a politics should follow from ontological commitments, not the other way around.

Perhaps a recent example of what Johnston has in mind is Michael Marder's *Plant-Thinking: A Philosophy of Vegetal Life* (2013), where Marder argues against the denegation of vegetation as found in the philosophical tradition, from Aristotle to Heidegger and beyond. No doubt, this kind of work, from its very title, is too easy to ridicule: why would one want to think like a plant? What next, thinking like a rock? But one wonders if the language Marder uses makes it easily digestible for those raised in the posthumanist movements. By depicting the treatment of vegetation as a form of "oppressed" in the tradition, Marder calls for "respect[ing]" the "alterity of plant-life," even if, to be honest, Marder's description of plant life appears ontologically no different than the tradition he describes. After all, it was always ascribed with life over simple things, and he calls plants the "non-thing" within the thing, an "elusive vitality." In any case, it is not enough now to be attuned to the otherness of the animal, and the animal that we are, but also plant life.[35] After all, unlike the human, the plant is always already open to the other: "What if consistent with this conclusion, the advantage of a plant-soul and plant-thinking is that they let the other pass through them without detracting the other's alterity? What if they grow so as to play this role more effectively, to welcome the other better?"[36] In short, plants have an "inherent respect for alterity," unlike, of course, those humans who have consorted in a long "violence of metaphysics."[37] Does not the talk of "plant liberation" or the "violence Aristotle unleashed against plants" and all manner of language borrowed from revolutionary anti-colonial, anti-racist, and anti-patriarchal politics, risk borrowing on the real-world suffering of countless individuals for a program that amounts, at the end of the book, to a call for localvorism and "respecting" nature, a nature open and welcoming of the Other?[38] This only repeats a fully modern tradition, found in so much ecological thinking, which denotes the natural as peaceful and holistic. Hence Marder duplicates a tradition of the binary opposition between nature and culture that he wishes to displace, not least since it requires of all "plants" to have a common "thinking," despite the heterogeneity of such beings. When Marder tells us that plant thinking is to be valorized because it does not install any distance to and from the others of nature, is this not precisely repeating Kant and many others who depicted the human as transcending and cut away from nature? This is what Johnston is critiquing under the thinking of Nature as the one-All. Or to put it in a slightly different Lacanian language, is this not the ultimate fantasy of the subject, that something *else* is obtaining full satisfaction, without any lack in its relationship to the Other, while my own being is imperfect precisely inasmuch as I can never have this satisfaction? That plants have no distance from and violence with the other, unlike the human in me? As Derrida noted long ago—we have kept with Marder for reasons that hopefully are apparent, given the discussions of nature and flat ontologies we have been discussing—simply overturning a traditional binary opposition, say, between humans and plants, does not displace that opposition.

Johnston argues forcefully against such naturalistic pieties. More to the point, he begins from the human to work his way outward: "what is meant ... by the weakness of nature can be best appreciated starting with reference to human beings."[39] As such, the starting point for his "materialist ontology must be reverse-engineered starting from a theory of subjectivity."[40] Thus his transcendental materialism moves from the reality of the subject to the subject of reality, since the one is an "index or symptom" of the other. The notion of the Real and its access is a difficult topic in Lacan, and wedding Lacanianism to the natural sciences as a path to that Real is anything but obvious. Lacan is highly formalist—thus his avowed "structuralism" and late use of topological theory—and however complicated this notion, the "Real" in Lacan seems to cut off discussions of ontology, as Lacan himself noted, that would derive from his metapsychology. Indeed, Johnston seems to move in *Prolegomena* between two different Lacans when needed: in the first chapter, when he wants to offer a rapport between Lacanianism and naturalism, he rebukes those who would conflate the Real as "akin to Kant's sphere of the *noumena*."[41] He then will report Lacan's own words on not being Kantian and being a materialist, but these disavowals do not lessen the force of Lacan's own writings—and Johnston piles up the evidence of antinaturalism himself. He writes:

> The Real underlying and making possible both the emergence of speaking beings out of living beings [note for the following: the historical instantiation of language, of the speaking being, in Lacan's French, the *parlêtre*] as well as the symptoms . . . of these thus afflicted animals [having entered the "reality" of the Symbolic-Imaginary world] is not some ineffable *je ne sais quoi*, some mysterious noumenal "x."[42]

Important feminist and queer theories rely on Lacan's denaturalization of sex and the phallus, and thus one can feel an attempt to naturalize Lacan as anything but a step forward for many influenced by him, since this risks renaturalizing the bases for relations of power. While discussing Malabou's own work, we will come back to this point, since the onus, after much great work on the alliance of various naturalisms to vicious biopolitical apparatuses, is on those, like Johnston, Malabou, Grosz and others covered in this book, to show how at this juncture, such an implication is avoided. In any case, having set up this non-Kantian Lacan in Chapter 1, in Chapter 3, when arguing against Lacan's view that there is no thinking before or outside of language—as Lacan himself puts it, "the symbolic universe exists first, and the real universe comes to settle down in its interior"[43]—Johnston then describes how, by "*following closely* [my emphasis] in Kant's footsteps," Lacan marks out the Real as the pre-/non symbolic reality of an archaic prehistory. But this would also be case then, *mutatis mutandis*, for the non-symbolic as such in Lacanianism. What seems like a view only a simplistic reader of Lacan would make in Chapter 1 becomes an insightful way to think of the limits of Lacanianism in relation to science in the Chapter 3. This discussion, for speculative realists, is central, since the accessibility of the *an sich* is at issue. But there is also a methodological matter: Lacan claims not to be an ontologist, as Johnston notes,[44] not because of a false modesty (as if Lacan were ever given to such), or because he was leaving it to others to extend his thought, as he suggested in a 1972 seminar, when he declared "one surely will be found one day to make an ontology with what I am telling you." Rather this is because he was operating within a precise area of metapsychology regarding the production of the subject through signification. Embedded in that metapsychology, not least through Lacan's engagement with Heidegger, is an implicit ontology of the subject—one that Johnston admirably and clearly lays out over his last several books—but one must wonder about a materialism that works from *within* a given account of subjectivity to an account of the real *an sich*. This, formally at least, is the move of every idealism. In other words, the subject *an sich* may be an archipelago of incompletions and gaps, but what merits the broad claim that from the finitude of the subject, that the following is the case:

> [T]here is just a weak nature, and nothing more. *All that exists* are heterogeneous ensembles of less-than-fully synthesized material beings, *internally conflicted*, hodgepodge jumbles of elements-in-tension—and that is it. What appears to be more-than-material (*especially subjectivity and everything associated with it*) is, ultimately, an *index or symptom* of the weakness of nature, Other-less, un-unified ground of being.[45]

This formulation is constant in Johnston's work: the subject is not alone in its strife, but rather is an "index or symptom" of a "weak nature" speculatively discovered in subjectivity itself. What, then, we could ask, provides the ontological warrant for these claims? This is what, I think, necessitates Johnston's move to the natural sciences, since by an intellectual division of labor, he can use the biological sciences for an account of a "weak nature." "Freudian psychoanalytic metapsychology here contains the nascent potentials for the formulation, in conjunction with *select resources* from today's natural sciences, of a conflict ontology, a theory of the immanent-monistic emergence of a disharmonious ontological-material multitude of plurality."[46] This, as he recognizes, means choosing those scientific results and areas that bolster his ontology; such choices, are ineradicable to philosophical naturalisms, which often provide narratives that bracket the very controversies and debates in which scientific claims about, say, brain plasticity or evolutionary development are made. We are always presented with the meat of the issue, never the grisly factories in which it is being produced.

In *Self and Emotional Life*, Johnston chastises those who would "pla[y] off an irreducible nonnatural subject, portrayed as a mystery *utterly inexplicable* in scientific terms." He argues that the days of scientific mechanism are largely over in the recent literature.[47] This account of naturalistic mechanism, on loan from early modernity, is very much theological, according to Johnston, since this nature is a big Other "to the extent that it is made into the repository of every possible answer to any query capable of 'scientific' formulation."[48] More on this will be covered in the second book of his trilogy, which will have to account for his seeming move from what Sellars and Brassier describe as the "space of causes" to a view of nature that differs from this. In any case, despite adhering to a certain account of the biological sciences, in *Prolegomena*, he notes that he doesn't wish to posit a "scientific" psychoanalysis, which would have the effect of dissolving the clinical patient and her individual psychopathologies. He writes about this well: "I am not in the least bit interested in trying to reduce away without remainder the singularity of *more-than-biomaterial* subjects [my emphasis] . . . indifferently subjected to treatment as the fungible patients of a replicable clinical framework, system, or method, a poor (and impoverishing) imitation of the natural sciences."[49] He calls for, then, a "double move of, one, *supplementing* Freudian-Lacanian psychoanalysis with a naturalist/biological account of the material *underpinnings* of *denaturalized/more-than-biological subjectivity*, and two, supplementing the neurosciences with a sophisticated, systematic metapsychology theory of subjects whose geneses, although tied to brains, involve much more than bare organic anatomy."[50] In other words, the "irreducible nonnatural subject" of psychoanalysis is "utterly inexplicable" in scientific terms: "a scientifically backed account of the genesis and structure of subjects that comes to evade the grasp of the sciences themselves."[51] If psychoanalysis needs to take up neuroscience, while not making one the palace slave of the other, then it's notable that this neuroscience upends his Lacanianism only around the edges (Lacan's notion of prehistory, for example, is jettisoned). No word is yet given on how this would change psychoanalytic practices—not just the framing of the metapsychology that one presumes has the upshot for Johnston of making it more palatable to those outside psychoanalysis. Otherwise put, if one looks through his recent works, one sees only how neuroscientific accounts of affect, for example, mirror claims already made by Freud or Lacan, not the other way around, which can lead the reader to wonder if he is only picking those scientific accounts that mirror his transcendental materialism, rather than testing the insights of Freud and Lacan.

Many working on the philosophy of mind, including Johnston and Malabou, write at times as if full Cartesian dualists are still around, though they are as rare in philosophy departments as alchemists and flat earthers. The downside to this is that it causes both not to sharpen just what they mean by the mental/physical relation, other than it not being dualist. Malabou at points will simply say the mental *is* the brain, while at others saying there is an ineradicable dialectic between them. In contemporary Anglo-American philosophy, there are whole ranges of accounts of the relation of the mental to the physical, some of which we noted in the last chapter, none of which posit some substance behind the mental besides naturally describable physical properties. For his part, Johnston opts for a dual-aspect monism:

> I am tempted to characterize my transcendental materialism as an emergent dual-aspect monism [why only a *temptation* at this point?], albeit with the significant qualification that these "aspects" and their ineradicable divisions (such as mind and matter, the asubjective and subjectivity, and the natural and the more-than-natural) enjoy the heft of actual existence (rather than being, as they are in Spinoza's dual-aspect monism, epiphenomena deprived of true ontological substantiality).[52]

Let's leave aside the reading of Spinoza, since substance in his case is the infinite power of existence as is expressed in the causal relations of physical and mental attributes, and thus the modes are anything but epiphenomenal. Johnston ends his analysis positing "emergent subjects [that] also come to have *significant repercussions* for the biomaterial bases that are the necessary-but-not-sufficient aleatory conditions of possibility of their very existences."[53] This in turn means we must think "dialectically" a "bi-directional flow of causal influences between matter and mind."[54] Hence we have property, not substance dualism: there is a single plane of existence out of which a transcendental subjectivity emerges as a "recursive, self-relating structural dynamic of cognitive, affective, and motivational subjectivity—a subjectivity fully within but nonetheless free at certain levels from material nature."[55]

At this point, despite what some of his rhetoric might suggest, Johnston is not on the vanguard pushing forward a neuroscientific endeavor. In fact, his target is often the materialist reductionists who take an Ockham's razor (and who might not be tempted to, if the alternative was reading Lacan's dense prose?) to subjectivity and just say it's physical processes that provide the quickest and cleanest explanations of mind and, let's throw it in, too, culture. But Johnston counters that many of these critics have views of physical processes that are too neat and clear. For example, human beings have a biological complexity such that any self-depiction of wholeness, as found in the Lacanian mirror stage, is an illusion. Johnston cites the "kludge" model of evolutionary neuroscience to argue that each human being is a happenstance of intricate physiologies. These intricacies, he says, produce "discordances, glitches, etc.," that are "generated in and by" the organism's "intricacy-induced auto-disruptions."[56] The weak nature found in our evolutionary and genetic make-up provides for the "denaturalization" at the heart of the natural, supplying the "internal yet irreducible transcendence-in-immanence with respect to natural history itself."[57] That is to say, precisely because nature is not a one-All or fully deterministic structure—the human is nothing other than product of multi-level processes often at odds with one another—there are "grey areas" where "things can happen otherwise that would be dictated by the rules and regulations of default systemic business as usual."[58] For example, the symbolic arises precisely through the finitude and dependency of the infant inasmuch as its needs are not fully cared for; in short, imperfect parenting is the source of culture. But for Johnston the Symbolic, too, is not a one-All, given slippages in language, incoherencies, and so on, and we are not fully signified in and through language or history. The human being is thus capable of "achieving autonomy from both nature and culture" because of "events of simultaneous encounters with two overlapping voids: the negativity of a barred Real plus that of a barred Symbolic," that is, the overlapping of underdetermining processes of nature and denaturalization. The question that arises is whether or not we can know at the micro-level the causal relations that give rise to this supposed "autonomy." Is it not possible, if given the time, to work backward and reverse-engineer all the determinations or causes that gave rise to spontaneous acts? For Johnston, this very model presupposes a one-All of nature, which he believes is both epistemologically and ontologically impossible. We are not just cut off in some Kantian way from such God-like knowledge, since nature itself is not a meticulous mechanism operating with the effortlessness of a high-end automobile.

Obviously it's also not possible to provide a one-All of Johnston's work and his particular readings of the philosophers that have influenced him. As we've seen, though, his transcendental materialism stands on a tripod of dialectical materialism and its critique of the commodification of the individual, naturalist accounts of evolutionary neuropsychology, and Lacanian metapsychology. At this point, one helpful way to clarify further this project is to proceed through his rejection of other forms of speculative realism. For example, we have already seen that Johnston faults object-oriented ontology for its flattening out of a specific human distinction in its depiction of everything as objects, a problem he believes is shared by Jane Bennett's discussion of actants.

Johnston's engagement with Meillassoux has been more extensive, taking up, for example, the last fifty pages of his *Prolegomena*. His central claim is that Meillassoux, like Badiou, favors a formalist approach to ontology. (Johnston is also critical of those places in Lacan that reject out of hand the biological sciences.) This formalism is quite apparent, as we pointed out in Chapter 3, in the depiction of the four worlds by Meillassoux. If the world of matter arrives *ex nihilo*, then there is an *a priori* conception of a purely formal existence understood through set theory, which is a strange claim for a materialism to make, since the material would be the effect of this formal ontology. But the crux of Johnston's claims against Badiou and Meillassoux is their choice of "sciences." While Meillassoux argues that the qualitative difference of life arrived from matter without any explanation, Johnston claims that a materialist philosophy should note the many naturalistic accounts of how such did occur, without the need for creation *ex nihilo*. But hyper chaos also leads Meillassoux to think a God-to-come, and in this way, Meillassoux distributes, as Johnston notes, all the previous predicates of the God of onto-theology onto hyper chaos (creation *ex nihilo*) and the God-to-come (justice and redemption). Once hyper chaos is introduced, one deals with "uncaused effects," and one has no epistemic warrant—recall Chapter 2's discussion of Russell's claim that one cannot prove the world was not created 5 minutes ago—to limit these creations to those he mentions. In place of explanation, Meillassoux provides only mystification, Johnston argues.[59] Here Johnston provides his take:

> Transcendental materialism, allied with [biological] sciences and implacably opposed to both posturing scientisms [that would reject human autonomy] and mystical obscurantisms, arguably accounts in a much more satisfactory and plausible manner than the speculative

> creed of the twin lords of hyper-Chaos and the God-to-come for what preoccupies both Meillassoux (at least occasionally) and me: the immanent natural emergence of what is transcendent(al).[60]

We can break off here from his criticisms of Meillassoux, though for those interested in his writings, Johnston's close reading of him is important. The speculative realist that I wish to juxtapose with his work, however, is Ray Brassier, since their approaches to neuroscience mean, as Johnston puts it, that they are "fellow travelers."[61] But, he also explains that against Brassier, "there are good scientific supports for the idea that a subject that is not capturable by the sciences emerges out of what the sciences look at."[62] Recall from the last chapter that Brassier distinguishes the "self," which can be jettisoned with advances in neuroscience, and the normative function of the "subject" as gripped by concepts, which cannot be. Any agency would have to come not from a self, which is an after-image of subpersonal neurological processes, but from the being that is subject to the rule formation of concepts. But this picture of the human being is, of course, not uncontroversial, given its definition of the human being, as in Kant, as subject to rationality, with the implicit upshot that the affects of humans are simply in causal relations with the physical world. In fact, only insofar as it is gripped by concepts can there be a manifest image of man-in-world and thus a proper notion of the human in the first place. But it's notable that Brassier's account is not just one-sided in terms of a certain Kantianism, but also in its treatment of neuroscience, which borrows, loosely speaking, from those cognitivist approaches of such thinkers as Paul Churchland and Thomas Metzinger. That is, these approaches tend to picture the brain in terms of a cognitive-computer that is itself at variance with many neuroscientific accounts in recent years, at least as depicted by Johnston. The neuroscience of affect, for example, sees the co-implication of the cognitive and the emotional, with the consequence that affects are communal and formed through and beyond the social Symbolic.

As in his other recent work, Johnston's contribution to *Self and Emotional Life* takes up the relation between psychoanalytic and neuroscientific accounts. In shortest order, Johnston argues for what he calls "misfelt feelings"—where one's manifest emotions are different from the affective life of the organism, including the unconscious—particularly by arguing that Lacan, far from being the formalist champion of the signifier per stereotype, long considered the nature of affect in relation to the unconscious. But as one would expect from above, he is also out to demonstrate that the field of affective neuroscience backs up the claims of his psychoanalytic account. He writes:

> A properly formulated neuro-psychoanalysis . . . engages in the double move of (1) complementing Freudian-Lacanian psychoanalysis with a naturalist or biological account of the material underpinnings of denaturalized or more-than-biological subjectivity and (2) complementing the neurosciences with a sophisticated, systematic metapsychological theory of subjects whose geneses . . . involve much more than bare organic anatomy. . . . . One can and should strive to develop a scientifically shaped (although not purely and strictly scientific) account of how humans defying and escaping explanatory encapsulation by the sciences become what they are.[63]

If Brassier was concerned to demonstrate the possibility of forms of cognition that did not require self-reflection, Johnston takes off from unreflected, in fact, unfelt or unknown feelings. This undercuts common sense and long-held Western views of autonomy: if I don't even know what I am feeling, how I can begin to act on those feelings with any sense of volition? How can I be said to will some event if I don't know why or even perhaps for what "deep" purpose? Isn't this also the fear of the rising neurosciences described by Johnston and Brassier? That our supposed freedom is an illusion, a trick of rather sophisticated processes developed over millennia, for no other reason than this trick helps in survival? Moreover, from Plato to Kant and beyond, has not freedom been reserved for those who can knowingly rule over themselves through the use of reason? Our emotional life, then, would be a mark of our animality. For Johnston, following from Lacan, our affective existence is lived in the shadow—but not as mere shadows—of the often slipshod and underdetermined manner in which we are formed by the Symbolic and the material processes of the Real.

We can now return to where we began with Johnston, to see what his response to Brassier might be. Recall that for Brassier, existentialism was a false reaction to nihilism, which tried to give meaning to a concrete existence unflattered by our human comings and goings. But without addressing this directly, Johnston holds that the whole question of meaninglessness is premised on a world pregiven as meaningful, by way of the Lacanian Symbolic-Imaginary reality and as an effect of the Real. Otherwise put, to paraphrase his argument concerning the first-person illusion, Brassier has to work to persuade us of a nihilism that we stubbornly refuse. Implicit in

Brassier's account is a certain heritage borrowed from pre-Death of God theologies: without God there can be no meaning, since God is the only possible guarantor of immortality, or put in terms of *Nihil Unbound*, thought finds its obliteration in the fact of its future end. For Johnston the death of God provides that there is, as we've seen, no big Other, including the big Other of the Symbolic of social constructivism and the big Other of a Nature said to be at peace with itself. While he would challenge any supposed voluntarism of Sartre, Johnston nevertheless provides the language of an existential materialism that he believes to be the prolegomena to any future materialism. Here, we end with his own phrasing of this near the end of his first book:

> Despite the apparent bleakness . . . of an assessment of human nature as being perturbed by an irreducible inner antagonism, there is, surprisingly . . . a liberating aspect to this splitting of the drives. Since drives are essentially dysfunctional, subjects are able to act otherwise than would be dictating by instinctually compelled pursuits of gratification, satisfaction, and pleasure. Severed from a strictly biological master-program and saddled with a conflict-ridden, heterogeneous jumble of contradictory impulses . . . the *parlêtre* has no choice but to bump up against the unnatural void of its autonomy. [As in Sartrean bad faith] this void is frequently avoided. . . . Humanity is free precisely insofar as its pleasures are far from perfection, insofar as it enjoyment is not absolute.[64]

CHAPTER 8
MALABOU'S PLASTICITY OF THE REAL

The continued analyses of Freudian psychoanalysis in Continental philosophy, as in Johnston, are at best puzzling to thinkers not from this tradition. No one, the view goes, would seek out the advice of a doctor whose only textbooks were from a century ago and thus why would any patient, in the throws of agonizing depression, anxiety, and so on, turn to psychoanalysts still influenced by Freud? There has been a decades-long ritual of mocking Freud's work as unscientific and tied to biological, not to say cultural, views, that are said to be nothing short of antiquated. The number of practicing Freudian-influenced analysts has fallen precipitously in the English-speaking world in the last half century, even as his concepts such as repression and the Oedipal complex remain stubbornly in our everyday language, to the consternation of many analytic philosophers of mind and psychology. The famed talking cure is now reduced to a soft whisper in much of the Western world while Lacan's work has been, perhaps, judged even more suspect by those outside Continental philosophy, since at least Freud wasn't said to be pathologically obscure. Yet, Continental philosophy's major thinkers were to a man and woman long readers of Freud, even as there have long been critics of Freudianism in Continental philosophy, from feminist depictions of his misogyny and heteronormativity, to Deleuze and Foucault's critiques of the political model it imports into the psychological sphere, to neo-Marxist accounts of the "bourgeois science." One wonders what this area of philosophy would look like if it were no longer tied, at least in terms of a long reaction complex, to Freudian metapsychology instead of the numerous other fields in psychology, especially those based on recent neuroscientific research. This marks a crucial difference between Catherine Malabou and Johnston. Malabou argues that the founding concepts of Freudian theory in terms of sexuality need to be rethought in terms of "cerebrality," especially as it relates to neuroplasticity. Thus while Johnston aimed to show how fundamental psychoanalytic ideas are anything but dislodged by twenty-first-century neuroscience, for Malabou they are to be reconsidered through the new figure of "neuronal man."[1] As she puts it in *The New Wounded* (2012), "nothing less would be required today than the complete theoretical reinvention of psychopathology."[2] This is not to say that Malabou avoids Freud, or that she agrees with outright dismissals of his writings, but her long engagement with him gives rise to sketches of his systematic limitations.[3]

We turn to Malabou because she has identified neuroplasticity as a synecdoche for her plastic ontology, which is gaining wide influence. Just as Johnston looked to the subject to think a transcendental materialism that could then be read alongside the ontologies of such thinkers as Badiou, Malabou uses the neurological conception of plasticity as an example of a mutability that remains an important, if underdeveloped, trope in such thinkers as Kant, Hegel, Heidegger, and Derrida. More than that, she also thinks "plasticity" is the "new motor scheme" that replaces previous Western modes of discourse, and thus is a passkey to thinking what is at stake in the world today. In this way, she joins the speculative realists in bypassing previous constructivisms and even deconstruction to access what she calls the "malleable real." In a 2011 interview, she noted that her work "does relate to speculative realism in many ways":

> First of all because it is a realism, what I am trying to do is a philosophy which insists on materiality, because in fact what they call a realism is in fact a materialism. . . . Speculative Realism means that what is challenged is "finitude" and the way in which subject and object relate on the basis of the unknowability of the "thing" per se; and so it is a whole refutation of Kant, and of the limits which he presented as absolutely un-transgressable. In a way Speculative Realism tries to go beyond these limits, but not in the sense of "yes metaphysics is possible," of dogmatism, which can [be] prohibitive. . . . Can we speak of a reality then? Is it possible to speak of something real without the presence of the human subject. Is it possible to have a speculative approach to the real when no finite being is on earth? . . . . The self-arrangement of reality into a meaning, the self-hermeneutical arrangement of the Real, without what Kant calls the Transcendental Subject, the thing per se.[4]

For a thinker focusing on plasticity and change, Malabou is herself remarkably consistent in her writing. A philosopher of immanent becoming, she aims through her notion of plasticity to identify a necessary ground of mutability at work in order for Hegel's system, Heidegger's ontico-ontological difference, and Derrida's *différance* to get underway. More than just a mutable ontological "foundation," she also argues it is an organizing principle—a "motor scheme" or something like a Foucaultian *epistemé* or Kuhnian paradigm—for the modern day, replacing an earlier era dominated by writing. Neuroplasticity is central for her since it calls into question old metaphors of the brain as a computer running genetic hardware, with little chance of alterability over time. Immanent mutability is irreducible for her in the brain and, for that matter, texts and being itself. She will thus critique those moments of non-immanence in recent philosophies, for example, Heidegger and his quasi-transcendental account of temporality, in which *Dasein* is always out ahead of itself in its futurity, and Derrida's thinking of the Other that is never wholly given in the here and now. But she also critiques recent feminism in a formally similar way by arguing that it depicts feminine identity as coming wholly from the outside, by way of social construction, instead of identifying an element of the feminine that is immanently mutable and irreducible to construction. Without recognizing this, she argues, the anti-essentialism of (some) recent feminism is implicated in the very violence against women it denounces.[5] Thus whether it concerns ontological, biological, or political structures, Malabou attempts to account for immanentist change: "The most recent and current research in neurobiology reveals a new kind of brain organization that may work as a model to understand *all kinds of organization* [my emphasis] today: society, for example." In this way, she goes on, she is developing "a new materialism, which implies this concept of society as a whole, as a *closed totality* [my emphasis] without any kind of transcendence. . . . I don't believe in transcendence at all."[6]

Instead of taking her work chronologically, which others have done well,[7] I will elaborate her critical distance from Johnston's work, while also introducing her conception of cerebrality. Having done that, we can turn to her ontological conceptions of the real as plastic. Here, it seems to me, are the six main hypotheses of her work: (1) "From sex to the brain": she argues that material brain trauma will "replace . . . within the psychopathology to come."[8] (2) An analysis of these traumas will reveal "the traits that all of the new wounded," whose pathologies can only be explained materially, "have in common."[9] (3) There exists "destructive plasticity," which is not thematized properly either by recent work in neuroscience or psychoanalysis.[10] (4) Plasticity is not just neuronal, but a "motor scheme" or epistemological frame to understand contemporary existence. This motor scheme has replaced the previous motor scheme of writing, which informed Derrida's *Of Grammatology* as well as mid-twentieth-century computer programming, the linguistic turn, discussions of DNA, and so forth. (5) Ontologically, plasticity is the very stuff of existence; it's a ground that destabilizes any stable meaning or foundation for existence.[11] (6) This includes the notion of identity, which, following Heidegger's notion of *Wesen* (essence), is a non-substantial "way" or mutability and flux, which can also be an "explosive" change producing new identities unmoored from previous ones, as in the brain traumas she discusses. We can also add (7), namely her thus-far-underdeveloped but intriguing conception of "plastic reading," which argues that texts are themselves mutable over time and thus open to new meanings to be imagined. This is precisely what she attempts to do with Hegel, Heidegger, and even such figures as Oliver Sacks.[12]

Malabou's work is best known for its reflections on the question, to cite a title of her 2004 book, "What should we do with our brain?" In mirroring Lenin's "What is to be done?" Malabou's question reflects on three trajectories: (1) how should Continental philosophy deal with the findings of contemporary neuroscience? (2) What is the nature of the brain and what does it do? (3) What political and ethical questions arise out of the ontological status of the brain? Malabou raises these most recently in terms of what she calls the "new wounded," those victims of brain damage, among many others, who lose any continuity from the person they once were. In *What Should We Do with Our Brain?*, she begins by noting the three modes of plasticity discussed in the writings of the neuroscientists Marc Jeannerod, Antonio Damasio, Joseph LeDoux, and Jean-Pierre Changeux: developmental plasticity, the growth of neuronal connections through the genetic-developmental process; modulational plasticity, the changes in these neuronal connections due to one's relations to one's environment; the reparative plasticity marked by the compensation and healing of neuronal lesions.[13] Plasticity for Malabou, as she first discussed in 1996 in her reading of Hegel, is "a capacity to receive form and a capacity to produce form."[14] From 2004 onward, Malabou has also emphasized a third quality of *plasticité* given its relation in the French to *plastiquage*, the word for plastic explosive. Just as Johnston looks to find ways to describe how transcendent events arrive out of immanent change, Malabou, avoiding any talk of transcendence, looks to find a means for discussing the explosive change available through immanent processes of neurobiological plasticity. In *What Should We Do with Our Brain?* Malabou argues that it is plasticity that enables us to think differently than the binary oppositions of freedom and determinism and nature and culture. Far from eliminating freedom, the new brain sciences on her account offer a morphology of the synaptic system that is reactive to and in turn formative of its environment.[15] As Ian James puts it, "this means that the cerebral subject is without preformed essence or fixity. . . . It is exposed . . . to a future which is without identity."[16]

In her early works, plasticity took on a positive valence, as it does in many popular books on the subject, which equate plasticity with self-renewal and, let's face it, a hope for an eternally youthful brain that ceaselessly recreates itself (if one puts down a money order for this or that software, with the dubious premise that puzzles and the like set off such processes). Her work, though, has focused more and more on the darker aspects of this explosive power of plasticity, namely the changes to the brain that tear apart notions of a continuous self-identity—and thus there can be no awaiting, as we'll see she argues, for a Derridean messianism.[17]

> Experience plays a major part in forming neural connections. These connections are highly modifiable—their shapes change—which shows that the brain is not a rigid structure, closed in on itself. On the contrary, it is open to external influences and affects. Plasticity means a new kind of exposure of the nervous system to danger and, consequently, a new definition of what "event," "suffering," and "wound" mean. When the brain is damaged, it is our whole "self," our subjectivity itself, which is damaged or altered.[18]

If anxiety over being-towards-death was the affect of a war-weary and post-death-of-God West in the early twentieth century, it is now a common fear of aging and the neuronal diseases that often go with it, such as Alzheimer's, that lead both to a cultural obsession with youth and the shutting away from sight of our elderly, now infantilized parents in nursing homes and long-term care centers in an aging West. But the new wounded are not just these patients, but also sufferers of accidents and even those taking part in and suffering from the widespread assaults of war and its tragic posttraumatic stress disorder. Her paradigm of the new wounded, taken from the early pages of Antonio Damasio's *Descartes' Error* (1997), is the mid-nineteenth-century railroad worker Phineas Gage, who managed to survive an iron rail striking his head, though with great damage to his prefrontal cortex. In Malabou's words, the Gage who "survived" the accident became a "new, *unrecognizable person*."[19] He was left without affect and maintained no continuity of identity from his past self to his current one.

Clearly, the "new wounded" raise questions about classic notions of the self and identity, which are themselves questions of the one and the many: what unites a given self over time, despite its various changes? What if this self doesn't even recognize its previous incarnations, through memory or other means? Is the self, then, one or many? For Malabou, this question has become all-important, since she argues that victims of rape, torture, and other social, though no doubt physical, violence face similar symptoms as those with neuronal lesions.

A deconstructed real

For Derrida, whose philosophical relation to Malabou is crucial, the self is always already constituted through its relation to the outside, whether it is language it uses to define itself in *Of Grammatology* (1967) or the relation to the Other that is "older than I" in his later writings. But for Malabou, who was a doctoral student of Derrida, contemporary neurobiology enacts not only a deconstruction of the self, but one that is fully materialist. While Derrida had argued that this "heteroaffection" is prior to any "autoaffection" in the self, Malabou argues,

> Autoaffection, which is the root of all other affects, is subjectively invisible. It thus seems that the neurobiological approach provides us with a radical concept of heteroaffection. This concept does not follow from the deconstruction of subjectivity; it describes the very essence of subjectivity. The subject is fundamentally, immediately, biologically, a stranger to itself, which never encounters itself. . . . This situation is determined by the structure of the brain, and not by that of consciousness, which is derived from the brain.[20]

In other words, the full deconstruction of subjectivity has come about not through Derrida, but through the work of neuroscientists. She argues that deconstruction, with its links to Derrida's early work on writing, needs to be supplanted by a new philosophical scheme. "There are new configurations—new changes," she writes in *Plasticity at the Dusk of Writing*, and we must have a "tool" that "is adequate to them, and this is no longer the case with writing."[21] Malabou seeks to escape the metaphors of writing (margins, trace, marks, inscription, and so on) around which Derrida's early work took shape, forcing her to detail a different metaphoric, or better, metamorphic system.

For Malabou, "grammatology" will have to be replaced by "neurology," since the latter science is helpful in critiquing non-plastic conceptions of being. It remains unclear, however, just what Malabou has in mind by "motor scheme" and its ontological implications: was being always mutable, or is this a non-question since the schema was not yet available to think being this way? Despite her declaration of realism in places, at other points she seems correlationally trapped in the very schema she produces. Malabou argues that her notion of "plasticity . . . is only a scheme," and "it will itself be replaced by another scheme," and yet "to think," she writes, "is *always* to schematize, to go from the concept *to existence* by bringing a transformed concept into existence."[22]

In any case, the plasticity of neuronal circuits is paradigmatic of what is underway logically before and historically after writing, since they self-organize and "modify their connections during the activity required by perception or learning."[23] In this way, neurology is apt since the metaphors used for the brain are "assemblies, forms, or neuronal populations"—and not graphic.

> The word *plasticity* thus unfolds its meaning between sculptural molding and deflagration, which is to say explosion. From this perspective, to talk about the plasticity of the brain means to see in it not only the creator and receiver of form but also an agency of disobedience to every constituted form, a refusal to submit to a model.[24]

Where Derrida had discussed the programming of DNA, plasticity escapes this paradigm, on her account, since it reshapes itself and thus is irreducible to writing: "plasticity forms where DNA no longer writes."[25] Malabou sees "neuro-plasticity" as a metonymy for the plasticity of personal identity, political communities, and reality itself. "Plasticity," she writes, "is slowly but surely establishing itself as the paradigmatic figure of organization in general."[26]

> Existence reveals itself as plasticity, as the very material of presence, as marble is the material of sculpture. It is capable of receiving any kind of form, but it also has the power to give form to itself. Being the stuff of things, it has the power both to shape and to dissolve a particular facet of individuality. A lifetime always proceeds within the boundaries of a double excess: an excess of reification and an

> excess of fluidification. When identity tends toward reification, the congealing of form, one can become the victim of highly rigid frameworks whose temporal solidification produces the appearance of unmalleable substance. Plasticity situates itself in the middle of these two excesses.[27]

Malabou thus reasons that the ontological difference between Being and beings should be re-formed in terms of this plasticity. It's also the case, for her, that the "biological and social mirror each other," and in terms of social critique, the task is to evaluate contemporary capitalism for not being plastic enough, rather than too destructive of the traces of the past.[28] "I am insisting," she notes, "upon the community between different kinds of systemic plastic organizations,"[29] a thinking of politics as without essence mirroring the plastic patterns she finds in neurology. Thus, while Derrida was content to end his preface to *Of Grammatology* arguing that "perhaps patient meditation . . . on and around what is still provisionally called writing . . . are the wanderings of a way of thinking that is faithful and attentive to the ineluctable world of the future,"[30] Malabou offers instead that the brain provides "the image of another world to come."[31] For Malabou, then, the point is to move past what is contingent and accidental to this epoch—and then to name what is essential. For her, plasticity must replace *différance* since the latter misses the very form of what allows change. "The entire question is to know," she writes, "what renders possible the modification and extension of a word ["writing"], the transformation of a concept at a given moment in the history of thought."[32] In this way, while *archi-écriture* or writing in Derrida's sense is the condition of possibility of any writing, it is plasticity on Malabou's account that designates the mutability of one "form" of writing into another, and this "modifiability" is "not reducible to the single operation of writing."[33] This would be the "nonwritten part of writing, which interrupts the trace of the trace to substitute for it for an instant the formation of the form"[34] The dangerous supplement to deconstruction on her account is the ever-malleable and explosive force of plasticity: "there are no graphics and no tracing without metamorphosis. I have called this new condition of supplementarity 'change.'"[35]

Derrida argues in his earliest work that the metaphysics of presence must ignore the trace structure of time in order to isolate a given form as the *eidos* or outer appearance of a given concept or thing, that is, it makes things available to thought in the presence, in all meanings of the term, of its appearance. While discussions of his critique of the metaphysics of presence can be notoriously unclear, Derrida is basically assailing a reductionism of time to one mode. For example, the concept of time has been traditionally reduced to the present of "now time," and post-Heideggerian deconstructions of the history of the ontology of time attempt to work out how untenable this conception is. Derrida's task, as with Heidegger before him, was to isolate how this reductionism is replicated in the privileged categories of metaphysics, such as the presence of the subject to his or her speaking. The latter is said to be more originary than writing, a conclusion that would not just give mastery to the speaker over what he or she says, but also is belied by all matter of new forms of writing irreducible to phonetic writing, such as the notations of set theory.

Important to Malabou's concerns, Derrida argues that such metaphysical concepts reduce time to a given "form," an "outer appearance" of it. Any given "form," he argues in numerous early works, is but a "self-evident" *eidos* presupposed by a given metaphysics, and this form must be left unquestioned lest the whole system tremble.[36] In this way, the "form" of "writing" is said to be speech, and the "form" of speech is the conscious subject. As such, forms tend to become a repeatable formula, and the trace structure on Derrida's account renders possible *possibility* or *change* in the first place. Derrida argues as much in "*Différance*":

> An interval must separate the present from what it is not in order for the present to be itself, but this interval that constitutes it as present must, by the same token, divide the present, that is, in our metaphysical language, every being, and singularly substance of the subject. In constituting itself, in dividing itself dynamically, this interval [of any given present] is what might be called spacing, the becoming-space of time or the becoming-time of space (*temporization*). And it is this constitution of the present, as an "originary" and irreducibly nonsimple (and therefore, *stricto sensu* nonoriginary) synthesis of marks . . . that I propose to call arche-writing, arche-trace, or *différance*.[37]

Does not Malabou's repeatable formula of plasticity, as form and reductive *eidos*, name itself outside of time, since it only ever names itself no matter the site she is investigating? Why must the "becoming-space of time or the becoming-time of space" announce itself for her only in one language, the language of plasticity, for all time, as it were? This is why this non-origin origin in Derrida—excuse me for the terrible phrasing—comes under different names in different sites, not all reducible to "writing," as Malabou says.

The immanence of the new wounded

From her earliest work, in any case, Malabou has been attempting to think a mutability without this trace structure, which I think she finds in the "new wounded." Disparate scientific endeavors demonstrate, for Malabou, that cognitive abilities are grounded in the affective brain, and thus any attempt to reduce the definition of the human organism to rationality is bound to fail. Here she agrees with Johnston, though it's worth pointing out that she thinks psychoanalysis is indebted to a view of the mind that cannot pass muster after the recent neuroscientific revolution, and she is keen to point to those places in Freud's texts where he refused any status to neurological injuries. Her main claim is that Freud is beholden to a hermeneutics of the self, which would provide interpretations that would give meaning to these traumas within the history of a subject that has, because of these traumas, disappeared. Clearly, with millions of sufferers, the "new wounded" confound previous ethical and ontological categories; the expanding list of experts in biomedical ethics testifies less to our knowledge than a disavowal of deep cultural conflicts over the meaning of living and dying and its borderlines.

At the beginning of *The New Wounded*, to my mind her most impressive work and a good entry into her thinking, Malabou says she was led to write the book in part because of her grandmother's suffering with Alzheimer's disease. Her grandmother had become someone else and in the last stages lost any attachment or affect for her world—all while indifferent to her own suffering. Malabou writes movingly about this:

> Why wasn't I comforted by this turn of events? After all, to desert life in this way, to die before being dead, isn't this the most beautiful way to die? To die to death itself? No longer to know oneself mortal? No long to have to die *in person*? [This lack of personhood will become important.] Such thoughts, however, brought me no solace. I was perfectly aware—along with everyone who must endure the same spectacle in their own lives—that this presence, this disaffection, this strangeness to oneself, were, without any doubt, the paradoxical signs of profound pain.[38]

This "depersonalization" is an empirical counterpoint to the Hegelian notion of the person, and though she doesn't mention it, it is also an analogous to the third-person view of the self that recognizes the enunciating "I" as a fiction and which Malabou calls neuroscience's ultimate deconstruction of the subject. Bear with me as I move between two quotations, one from Malabou and her citation from Metzinger:

> There could no power of acting, no feeling of existence, no temporality without this originary delusion of the first person.... As the cognitivist Thomas Metzinger writes: "Nobody ever was or had a self.... No such things as selves exist in the world.... All that ever existed were conscious self-models that could not be recognized *as* models. The phenomenological self is not a being, but a process—and the subjective experience of being *someone* emerges if a consciousness information processing system operates under a transparent self-model . . ." The transparency of the self-model and the anonymity of the emotional brain are the disenchanted wonders of the new psychosomatic and libidinal space.[39]

Let's leave aside whether or not there would be no "temporality" without the "delusion of the first person." In both the "new wounded" and the case of "the anonymity of the emotional brain," there is a similar structure of a loss of self. The new wounds are suffered not through psychobiographical trauma, but from sheer contingent accidents, as in the case of Gage, that have nothing to do with Freud's theory of the drives. "Cerebrality is," she writes, "the causality of a neutral and destructive accident—without reason."[40] Their etiology, thus, is nothing other than brute material causes, which from one's mental point of view are a creation *ex nihilo*, since for Malabou consciousness never sees itself for what it is, blocked from the actual physical processes that produce it. However, she suggests, for most of us caught in folk discussions of the mental, as the Churchlands would call them, these horrific events are what provide the evidence of who we are as material beings and what we do with our brains—at the very moment we no longer know who we are.

Malabou also claims that the new wounded evince "emotional indifference and 'flatness,'" a veritable lack of the kinds of affect one would find in Freudian neuroses. In this way, she writes, "the new wounded . . . have replaced the possessed or the madmen of ancient medicine and the neurotics of psychoanalysis." Just as we have moved to a new motor scheme of plasticity, she also argues that there is a new form of trauma to match, and she gives it the widest applicability: "The specter of such phenomena hints at the scope of a *posttraumatic condition* that *reigns everywhere today* [my emphasis] and demands to be thought."[41] This comes on top of her claiming that victims in war are "comparable *in every respect* to those of patients with brain lesions."[42] Stacey Smith, among other commentators, takes this claim to be highly problematic, since Malabou's examples are on the extreme end of the spectrum and even within those examples, each takes place within progressive stages of trauma, such as Alzheimer's disease.[43] In other words, she makes the rather exceptional the rule for her analysis.

Moreover, while she piles on multiple descriptions by patients that they are a "new person" and so on, personhood and identity are, speaking loosely, inherently intersubjective: "Gage" has a meaning beyond brute materiality in the brain and one's class, racial, and sexual identities are not so plastic. At several places in her work, Malabou claims, "current neurobiological analyses of the relationship between the brain and subjectivity do not involve a reductionist approach."[44] But in rounding down what Derrida called the heteroaffection from the Other, which she rejects in the name of immanence, she also implies that the Symbolic is nothing but the effect of neural processes:

> I continue to defend the thesis that the *only valid philosophical path* [my emphasis] today lies in the elaboration of a new materialism that would precisely refuse to envisage the least separation, not only between the brain and thought but also between the brain and the unconscious. It is thus such a materialism, as the basis for a *new philosophy of spirit*, that determined my definition of cerebrality as an axiological principle *entirely articulated in terms of the formation and deformation of neuronal connections* [my emphasis]. The "symbolic" is obviously not far away, since the elementary form of the brain is the emotional and logical core where the processes of auto-affection constitute *all identity* and *all history* [again, my emphasis].[45]

We can clarify this through her critique of Foucault in *The New Wounded*, where she argues that genealogy follows from the neurological, and any attempt to think the history of the brain relies on the very powers it would wish to historicize. To be simplistic, the task of a Foucaultian genealogy is to look to histories of practices and their formation within social milieus: prisons, for example, have a relatively short history in the West and must be understood alongside a crystallization of disciplinary practices arising after the eighteenth century; to think the contingencies that led to these institutions is also to appreciate that the prison industrial complex is not an implacable social institution. Thus a Foucaultian might start with a discourse on neurobiology not by discerning what is new, but seeing how it follows from practices and institutions discernable through a genealogy. Foucault also placed practices of subjectification within a "will to know"—to interrogate and discipline the subject through processes of normalization. But doing all of this would place these milieus at a level of explanation outside of neurobiological accounts: "I think that situating the subject beyond the pleasure principle [that is, the non-affect of the "new wounded"] also obviously places the subject beyond the will to know," Malabou counters.[46] She lists two reasons. I will cover the second first, namely that this neurological rule of no one meets up with Foucault's notion of the death of man and so the "neuronal is not the opposite of the genealogical, as Foucault thinks it is, but is its mirror."[47] Let's leave aside Foucault's own comments on the practices of the natural sciences, which have produced critiques of him as anti-realist. It's true, as I mentioned in Chapter 6, that these neuronal depictions go beyond the empirico-transcendental doublet Foucault describes at the end of *The Order of Things* and thus a certain *episteme* of man, though any discussion of the political application of biology and the "will to know" needs to address Foucault's 1970s work on biopower.

Malabou's work is impressive and at its most important when it lays claim to the shifting ground beneath our feet and the new concepts needed to keep up with it. This appears less the case though, when she provides her other reason for rejecting Foucaultian genealogy, where she practices the very reductionism she claims to avoid:

> [A] genealogical critique of cerebrality is undoubtedly possible, but it avoids the question of what genealogy itself, in its structure, *owes* to the neuronal model [my emphasis]. Readers of Foucault might not have sufficiently taken into account the fact that neuronal functioning, organized in centerless networks that depend on ever-changing punctual interactions, is precisely the biological counterpart to the schema of micropower. The very form of the genealogical critique would thus be *derived* [my emphasis] from one of the powers it examines: that of cerebral organization. . . . It is time to recognize that, for at least half a century, the form of political critique *largely follows* [again, my emphasis] the very neuronal model that it sometimes attempts to deconstitute.[48]

This, I admit, is an imprecise if revealing passage. First, it's not clear why a mere "biological counterpart" should trump a genealogy of the biopower of neuroscience. After all, this is at best a metaphor on loan ("owed") from the biological sciences, and it's not clear how much this was prevalent at the time Foucault was writing. (Malabou's writings on the brain are premised on the fact that plasticity is different than the model available in the 1960s and 1970s.) More pertinently, state and micropolitics of power are on a completely different level of description, which do not simply repeat neurological concepts. Not to put too fine a point on it, but disciplinary power and prisons and police officers don't act like synapses—never has a synapse racialized minority synapses—never mind that Foucault has various models of power, not just those operating in networked fashion.[49] But following from the quotation above, Malabou seems to be arguing that power is an effect of neuronal processes, with a double upshot, as Hannah Procter notes: (1) to understand politics, one must first have a grasp on the science of neurobiology; (2) this science has access to structures disinfected of the networks of power Foucault describes.[50] Put me down as dubious on both counts.

Foucault's relationship to the natural sciences is not straightforward. On the one hand, his genealogies were almost wholly focused on what the French call the human sciences. Indeed, his work investigates the pretentions of the use of "science" for pedagogy, psychology, sociology, and so on, especially as those disciplines developed in the twentieth century in France. But Foucault was also lead by the question he announced in "What is Enlightenment?": "In what is given to us as universal, necessary, obligatory, what place is occupied by whatever is singular, contingent, and the product of arbitrary constraints?"[51] The epistemic sovereignty of the sciences and its political uses cannot be denied, and there have been various biopolitical moves to take what is contingent and cultural and exporting it onto nature as an ontological given. Given Malabou's move from contingent sciences—the result of a motor scheme she finds only a couple of decades old and derived from findings far newer—to an ontology of the real, she would seem to repeat this move, especially given her avowed shift from these epistemically fallible findings to neuropolitics. A politics of the brain has long been with us—the histories of racialization as well as claims about sexual differences rooted in neurology are well known. But it's more worrisome given that she differentiates between the "I" of her texts, who has a brain and "knows it," and those "docile" and have a brain and don't know it.[52] As she puts it, "In this sense, we are still foreign to ourselves, at the threshold of this 'new world,' which we fail to realize makes up our very intimacy itself. 'We' have no idea who we are, no idea what is inside 'us'"—though presumably "we" performatively would not be the person writing these very words.[53] One can also ask, at the late date of 2004, when she wrote *What Should We Do with Our Brain?*, years after the U.S.'s declared "decade of the brain" in the 1990s and long after brain plasticity was the stuff of popular books and college courses, just who precisely was this "we" that had "no idea what is inside us"? Those who disagree with her accounts do not just do so because they don't know who they are, and don't know about the advances in neurosciences the past few decades.

More troublesome is her depiction of those suffering under the "*la grande exclusion*." One should always worry about a politics painting the non-elite as the "docile," "disaffected" marginalized, which she describes in her *La grande exclusion: L'urgence sociale, symptôme et thérapeutique* (2009) on the model of Alzheimer's and other "new wounded."[54] Such a view from on high always renders invisible implacable differences. Otherwise put: it's true that neoliberalism has had its pernicious effects, that inequalities are disavowed, that the great traumas involved are anaesthetized through drugs, alcohol, new media and so on, but one must not confuse the aims of an affectless technocracy with the lives of those marginalized because of it. Thinking of the "*grande exclusion*" on the model of a neurologically defined "new wounded"—to say, in short, that the marginalized are brain damaged, since for her lack of affect is always material—borders on offensive, especially as Malabou follows affective neuroscience in making affect a necessary condition for rationality. Those most damaged by degrading poverty and processes of racialization and patriarchy—that is, those facing the sharp end of the states of sovereignty—heroically take care of their children, find love, cheer each other on in moments of joy and reinforce community bonds in moments of despair, and perform micropolitics of "conviviality" discussed well in the work of Paul Gilroy[55]; they, whoever this "they" is, live anything but the affectless lives of the new wounded.[56]

That said, in *What Should We Do with Our Brain?*, Malabou is attentive to the ways in which the neurosciences have given rise to "ideologies" of self-production and "flexibility." "The error," she writes, "is in thinking that neuronal man is simply a neuronal given and not also a political and ideological construction (including of the "neuronal" itself)."[57] Borrowing from the analyses in Luc Boltasnki and Eve Chiapello's *The New Spirit of Capitalism*, first published in France in 1999, Malabou differentiates plasticity from flexibility, which is the anticipation of constant neural self-renewal in the face of ever-changing working conditions. Instead, one is expected to be a constant "entrepreneur," employed in networked, less hierarchical work environments, but without the salaries and employment security of a generation ago.

> If I insist on how close certain managerial discourses are to neuroscientific discourses, this is because it seems to me that the phenomenon called "brain plasticity" is in reality more often described in terms of an economy of flexibility. Indeed, the process of potentiation, which is the very basis of plasticity, is often presented simply as the possibility of increasing or decreasing performance. . . . *Suppleness, the ability to bend, and docility* [my emphasis] thus appear to join together in constituting a new structural norm that functions immediately to exclude.[58]

Everyone is expected to be a freelancer, to be "flexible" to the infinite needs of employers who require you to know the ins and outs of a job you don't even have. As per Tom Friedman, *New York Times* columnist and somnambulant repeater of whatever cliché fills the chatter of the managerial class's cocktail bars: job seekers must be "relentlessly 'entrepreneurial' because they understand that many employers today don't care about your résumé, degree or how you got your knowledge"—that's so *yesterday*—"but only what you can do and what you can *continuously reinvent* yourself to do."[59] "Finally," he adds for job seekers caught in the worst employment environment since the 1930s, "if you can't find a job, try to invent one."[60] As Malabou puts it, "in effect, anyone who is not flexible deserves to disappear."[61] Against this general atmosphere of flexibility, Malabou writes,

> neuronal functioning and social functioning interdetermine each other and mutually give each other form (here again the power of plasticity), to the point where it is no longer possible to distinguish them. As though neuronal functions were confounded with the natural operation of the world, as though neuronal plasticity anchored biologically—and thereby justified—a certain type of political and social organization.[62]

Boltasnki and Chiapello are scathing in their book for those who look to naturalize and, if one can excuse the word, neuronalize neoliberal instantiations of power, and Malabou avowedly seeks this naturalization, indeed ontologicization, of plasticity to demonstrate the ability for something new beyond "flexibility."[63] Yet it's hard to differentiate just where Malabou would delineate her own approach from that critiqued by Botasnki and Chiapello, except by providing a positive valence to plasticity and a negative one to flexibility.

> Plasticity is the systemic law of the deconstructed real, a mode of organization of the real that comes after metaphysics and that is appearing today in *all* [my emphasis] the different domains of human activity. . . . Today, new metamorphic occurrences are appearing at the level of social and economic organization and at the level of "gender" or individual sexual identity. From the start I have said that the privileged regime of change today is the continuous implosion of form, through which it recasts and reforms itself continually.[64]

But this destructive/constructive plasticity would seem to mirror the creative destruction of neoliberalism, where the trauma of disruption means there is no memory of yesterday, where, as she puts it about her own immanentist ontology without ontological difference in *The Heidegger Change*, "all is equally exchangeable." Another straightforward quotation, this from *Plasticity at the Dusk of Writing* (original French 2005):

> When plasticity is taken into account, it becomes possible to deconstruct the substantive appearance of existence and to think of identity as something mobile, *whose many frontiers, psychic as well as political, are constantly being drawn, erased, redrawn, and negotiated* [my emphasis]. Fleeing frontiers [for another world] is simply not an option. In this way, existence would be the plastic drive within the closed form of the world, within the closure of globalization.[65]

As such, she notes in a 2008 interview, "Well, we have to admit that *there is no alternative* to capitalism; this is something that is, I think, inescapable today."[66] Everything is subservient to this "motor scheme," though, as in China, "capitalism is multiple" and it teaches us, she says, "how a single form is able to differentiate itself almost infinitely."[67] Mark Fisher manages, in his recent *Capitalist Realism*, to bring together the notions of plasticity and contemporary capitalism: "Capitalist realism . . . entails *subordinating oneself* to a reality that is infinitely *plastic*, capable of reconfiguring itself at any moment. We are confronted with what [Frederic] Jameson . . . calls 'a purely *fungible* present in which space and psyches alike can be processed and remade at will.'" The problem with Malabou's account of immanence is that it appears totalizing—depicting "a closed totality," to repeat an earlier citation—while using capitalism as its avatar, giving us a plasticity that is able "to differentiate itself almost infinitely." This is not to tag her ontological accounts as mere Ideology, a tedious reading easy to produce with just about any thinker. The problem is that her account suggests a one-All with absolute monadic interiority, where there is no Other to the system, whether it's the brain or even subjects described in the third person. How does this not fall to what Johnston describes, following Hegel, as a middle-of-the-night Spinozism in which all cows are black, especially when the "subjects of accident" are said to be without affect, docile, and without community, without the personality of "subjectivity"? How does her discussion of the world as a "totality" not fall to the Heideggerian critique of treating the world as just simply one large being? Finally, how is this neuronal account not reductive, not just in the Churchlandian sense, but also reductively casting judgment on the victims of war and all the new wounded as non-aware, non-affective?

> We have to stop thinking that politics is an expression of consciousness: it is something else. I think we are at a similar moment but with new forces, which are, yes, biological. For me, the political gesture is to try to figure out what this new non-awareness is. So political awareness is dependent on a new political unawareness and we have to understand what it is.[68]

In online lectures on Foucault and Agamben, who could never be read as arguing for thinking politics as an "expression of consciousness," she calls for a positive biopower and is largely dismissive of their work since they have not done the requisite scientific accounting for discussions of life and so on. This provides access to the reality of life as such, outside cultural invocations of it. But married to the immanentist interiority is a methodological sameness: there is only one key to this "motor scheme," and only one way to understand personhood as the neuronal relation of self to self—a strange depiction given her Hegelian roots. In giving description to these forms of power, one need not utilize Foucaultian genealogy, but perhaps there is more than one "*valid philosophical path today*" for investigating what is going on beyond the processes of the brain.

TIME FOR A CONCLUSION

> Since Aristotle, every philosopher who has studied time has agreed at least on one point: the extreme difficulty, if not impossibility, of thinking its "reality."
>
> Dominique Janicaud, *Chronos: Pour l'intelligence du partage temporel*[1]

What will be the future of speculative realism? In philosophy of science one often speaks of a Peircian ideal, an image of a future in which science has filled in all the gaps it can't currently explain and has a community of people that adhere to its deepest insights. There can be no such ideal for speculative realism, since each thinker we have covered has very different views for what that future would be—greater attunement to objects, or thinking of oneself as a vectorial subject haunted by essential specters as well as by the coming of God in a future world, or a nihilist watching as it has taken many long years for humans to accept the death of the self, or one of the many other paths thrown out here like the scrawls of an infant on a blank page. What speculative realism will have accomplished is a shift from the era of interpretation and minute textual analyses to a "post-metaphysical" plundering of the real while also shifting Continental philosophy back to traditional metaphysical questions about the nature of being, philosophy's relation to scientific understanding, and so on. But the challenges are not easy. Its turn to realism often means stomping at times inelegantly across subfields long covered in analytic philosophy, such as philosophy of science, philosophy of mind, epistemology, and so on, while also reinvigorating different ways of thinking these fields. Those offering a materialist naturalism will need to turn in full to answering critics about whether or not they are naturalizing status quo categories, while constructivists have already begun borrowing the language of materialism to such an extent it will be hard to see the difference between them and their avowed enemies. Further prognostications would only be a symptom of hubris: we know the treatment of philosophy in the contemporary era and one wonders if there will be anyone to look back philosophically on much of anything, let alone this movement known as speculative realism. Philosophy's history teaches humility: who could have predicted the changes wrought under the proper names of Descartes or Marx? But let me surmise something of this Speculative Realism future: it will have had to take up the reality of the future and the reality of time in an atmosphere hostile to it. Sure, such a movement as I call for here will have been temporary, as all things are, a mere bubble in a longer history—we declare no new brands or movements here. Where I wish to bring us here is a consideration of a realism of time. If there is a future for philosophy, it is not one that breaks inexorably with the past—the more the protests on this, the less you should believe it—not least since the "new" as a philosophical term is anything but and has its own history in the Western tradition. To speak philosophically is to speak a language developing over millennia and thus when we speak about the "real" or about "time," we speak in a language that comes with an inheritance, just as speaking French requires knowing a grammar in order to make any sense. This is, of course, a central premise of Heidegger's *Destruktion* of the history of ontology and later forms of deconstruction in such figures as Derrida and Irigaray. The speculative realists hold—to a man and woman in these chapters—that there is something outdated about these figures, trapped constantly spinning yarns about a tradition now being surpassed. In other words, they were merely rereading texts meant to correspond to a real but never discussing the latter, a correlationism that would deny the real it's due in favor of all-too-human sign systems and pietistic poetizing. But while I think Heidegger's grasp on philosophical history is a grip that almost strangles it, the insistence that movements are wholly new and that the word "tradition" is a synonym for "naïve" leads me to speak up to point out the repetitions of a past we can't easily escape. I hope to show that speculating on the reality of time is anything but foreign to their work and, as I've tried to point out at intermittent points in this book, is one that those in speculative realism should take on, lest they give themselves over to the idealism of objects, mathematics, and so on.

Of course, you may take arguing for a realism of time as banal and as congratulating myself for defending a truism of everyday life, like defending a well-balanced diet and the cuteness of puppies. But the temptation to find a standpoint outside of time—for an atemporal truth untouched by time has been with us since Parmenides—is an abiding one, which we have seen already within these pages. The dismissal of Heidegger et al. risks thinking, as Harman puts it, that they have "nothing to teach us" about time, which is anything but the case. What's interesting is that for over a century, Continental philosophy has been critiquing the "metaphysics of presence," the view that time should be thought reductively as "now, now . . . then now . . ." In physics and Anglo-American philosophies of time, it's precisely this depiction that is said to follow from any view of the passage of time, which is said to be upended by twentieth-century physics in the form of relativity theory and quantum mechanics. Almost every article on time begins by saying something like, "we tend to think there is something like the present," but in fact after relativity theory they say there is no such thing and therefore no concept of time. The false choice, then, has been between a metaphysics of presence, critiqued by Heidegger and Derrida, but also in certain places, by Hegel, and a block theory of the universe that depicts any change in time as illusory. As Einstein once put it to calm a sobbing widow in a funeral oration, "the past, present, and future are only illusions, even if stubborn ones."

This is also why I would argue that one cannot make philosophy a mere handmaiden of the sciences, since physicists often insist time doesn't flow at all. Or at least one needs to treat science as if it's stopped—as if for all time—in order to turn its physics into a metaphysics. It's true that relativity theory rid the physical universe of simultaneity—Newton's idea that there was an absolute time that clocked the whole of the universe—and philosophers have long argued in line with John McTaggart that the very tenses of past and future lead to contradiction.[2] These arguments direct neurobiologists to argue, like Metzinger, that temporal flow is but another illusion of the transparent self model, a model that may be evolutionarily advantageous but does not represent a reality in which there is a past, present, and future. To put it another way, this block universe is modeled from a timeless point outside the universe in ways that vary from physicist to physicist but, as the cosmologist Lee Smolin argues, reproduces the Platonic view of the world.[3] Like the Platonists before them, this end of the flow of time is a salve to our mortal worries:

> And what if science were able to explain away the flow of time? Perhaps we would no longer fret about the future or grieve for the past. Worries about death might become as irrelevant as worries about birth. Expectation and nostalgia might cease to be part of human vocabulary. Above all, the sense of urgency that attaches to so much of human activity might evaporate.[4]

We should leave aside these strange messianisms that await human beings finally catching up to their illusions, lessening our suffering as we have seen Metzinger points out, where death becomes a thing of the past and "urgency" goes away. Recall that Catherine Malabou argues that the final deconstruction of the human takes place in the neurosciences and its depiction of the nemocentric—the view from nowhere and no one. Is this not also the dream of a view from "no when," as Huw Price called it? Would this not be the last hope—the hope for the end of all hope and expectation? This is where I would say there is a world of difference between *deconstruction* and *destruction*, between accepting the tenuous line of being and appearance and announcing the end of the latter in the name of the former. Even Wilfrid Sellars, whose scientific realism forms the basis for Brassier's thought and much recent work in the Pittsburgh Hegelian school of philosophy, could not bring himself to give up time to the scientific image, arguing that present moments are an inexorable part of reality.[5] Sellars' notion of the essence of time being in the present has a long history and so do all the theories of time from Aristotle to Boltzmann and beyond. We are still formulating questions about the distinction between the measure and what is measured, concerning the existence of the future and the past, and so on. My hypothesis is quite simple and hopefully timely: the moment someone steps forward with a supposed new viewpoint of physics is when you can hear the not-so-faint echo of lines from Aristotle or Plato or Bergson—though we should not deny these advances. The destruction of time has passed us by before, and perhaps we can define the human as simply this: the stupid bastards always holding onto illusory notions after being told time and again to drop them.[6]

The difficulty of taking time as real is no doubt also made difficult because much work on Heidegger, Derrida, Deleuze, et al.,[7] tended to think time in terms of the time of life and less about the reality of time—in short as correlationist. Let me take up the most radically correlationist of these figures, if one believes the critiques of various speculative realists, namely Derrida, with the upshot that showing what is still available in his thought highlights questions of realism and anti-realism that have been the subject of this book.

It's said Derrida would trap us in a textual idealism that could never speak to the real, but I would argue his theory of texts is founded on the anarchic *archē* of the reality of time. But it does more than this, since it thinks time both as something absolute, without falling into the Newtonian view of absolute time as a container of the world, and as relational, which is considered in every book on the matter as making time epiphenomenal. Moreover, since the temporality is thought in and through texts, Derrida's work would rethink any conceptual schemes posited as being outside the time being denied; the very writing of philosophy requires always thinking through and in time. Thus, Derrida's emphasis on writing, which is seen as the ultimate correlationist anti-realism,[8] in fact serves as a "speculative" move to the real. In other words, how can the question of anti-realism be broached except in time? How can there even be an illusion of change without changes in the very illusion under discussion?

The *locus classicus* for the charge of Derrida's textual idealism comes just near the midpoint of his early work, *Of Grammatology* (1967), where he declares "there is no out-side text [*il n'y a pas de hors texte*]." For speculative realists, this would be the original scene of the crime of deconstruction. Reading Rousseau's texts to demonstrate an implacable logic of "supplementarity" intrinsic to them, Derrida pauses to consider whether someone disputing his reading of Rousseau could not simply point to the "reality" of Rousseau's life beyond any given text. If everything is a "text" for Derrida, then does he not deny the reality of the world as such? Moreover, doesn't his text risk just producing a hermeneutic "commentary" that would look to stand in for the text itself, to state a truth it does not itself announce? He writes:

> Yet if reading must not be content with doubling the text, it cannot legitimately transgress the text toward *something other than it* [my emphasis], toward a referent (*a reality that is metaphysical* [my emphasis], historical, psycho-biographical, etc.) or toward a signified outside the text whose content could take place, could have taken place *outside of language* [my emphasis], that is to say, in the sense that we give here to that word, *outside of writing in general. . . . There is nothing outside of the text* [there is no outside-text; *il n'y a pas de hors-texte*]. And that is neither because Jean-Jacques' life, or the existence of Mamma or Therese *themselves*, is not of prime interest to us, nor because we have access to their so-called "real" existence only in the text and we have neither any means of altering this, nor any right to neglect this limitation. . . . [I]n what one calls the real life of these existences "of flesh and bone," beyond and behind what one believes can be circumscribed as Rousseau's text, there has never been anything but writing; there have never been anything but supplements, substitutive significations which could only come forth in a chain of *differential* references, the "real" supervening, and being added only while taking on meaning from *a trace* and from an invocation of the supplement, etc. And thus *to infinity*, for we have read, in the text, that the *absolute present* [my emphasis], Nature, that

> which words like "real mother" name, have always already escaped, have never existed; that what opens meaning and language is writing as the disappearance of natural presence.[9]

No doubt, this long citation risks your patience; time is marching on after all. But Derrida's take is incisive, even if it risks an anti-realism, discussing all "reality" as derisively "metaphysical." Derrida, like Heidegger before him, set out to critique the "metaphysics of presence," though the terminology Derrida tends to use in *Of Grammatology* is "transcendental signified." In any set of texts, there are, of course, a whole slew of signifiers (words, but also structures that *themselves* are signifiers of reality). To keep things as simple as possible, what Derrida argued in *Of Grammatology* is that his structuralist forbearers, such as Saussure, recognized the play of language in writing—that its meaning shifts in different contexts—but sought some pivot point that transcended this "play." For Rousseau, this was Nature, something that he could indeed write about, but had a fixed "reality" in the world beyond the texts he was writing. Saussure argued the same for consciousness. But, Derrida notes, all such argumentation is taking place within language itself; it cannot transcend all signifiers and language, since all such terms are *within* language and thus are given over to the very structures Saussure and Rousseau discuss, and these structures are "founded," if one can use the word, on the time-spacing of *différance* (difference/deferral). In other words, Saussure says that no term has a "positive" meaning: a tree is only knowable in terms of what it is not: not a chair, not a blade of grass, etc. But when it comes to "consciousness," Saussure argues that somehow this term is outside the contexts of language, despite the fact that, of course, it is a word, and thus its meaning will shift in a given context on his account. And, in the citation above, in Rousseau this is "Nature," something incorruptible and "real" beyond culture and language and the changing ways in which "Nature" differs in given contexts. Derrida's take is that "Man," or "Nature," or "God," or the self-present subject both *grounds* and are *put out of play* in these "metaphysical" discourses. This is not merely the facile claim that these words are pulled into language and one can't think except in language, but rather that both Rousseau and Saussure bypass the very linguistic structures they delineate in their works on the matter, putting these terms outside the vagaries of time.

Thus, where Heidegger critiqued the metaphysics of presence for reducing Being to one kind of being (be it God or matter), Derrida in his earlier work seeks to find the "transcendental signified" that centers a given philosophical discourse. In this way, Derrida is said to trap us forever in "readings" of texts, forming a new (anti-?) scholasticism creating different interpretations of philosophical works without ever speculating on the real. There is, it would seem, "no outside-text." As Lee Braver puts it:

> There is nothing outside the text because our experience is always linguistically mediated; this makes both subject and object *effects* of language, rather than entities that precede it from the outside to master or anchor it. Language impersonally structures our selves and our world, and our actions depend on passively taking on these structures.[10]

There is much that is disagreeable in this passage, for example, that linguistic mediation is equated with efficient causality ("subject and object" are "*effects* of language"), and as if anyone but a naïve realist believes in the immediacy of objects (let alone subjects). In any case, those who tell this story of Derrida face two problems, *at least*:

(1) Inasmuch as Derrida is given to putting the very word "reality" in quotation marks, he can be said to note its shifting meaning in different contexts. But *who would deny this*? Are not the many arguments over realism really just about its different uses in multiple contexts? *For real.* Moreover, those who do speculative metaphysics claim to bypass naïve realism, about which they are equally scathing. Is not Derrida's emphasis on textuality and *différance* simply a reference to the implausibility of any naïve realism—the naïve realisms of unmediated presence, to consciousness, to "man," to nature, and indeed to "objects" forever hidden from view? The whole problem is contained in Braver's formulation: Derrida is not suggesting objects are the "effect" of some "cause" known as linguistic structures. That, certainly, would be a linguistic idealism, if such a thing even exists. Words do not create Being. Such would make the speaker of language an infinite being—"In the beginning was the Word."

(2) But—and this will be the most difficult part of our discussion ahead—neither is Derrida formulating a linguistic update of Kant's concepts of the understanding, where linguistic structures merely filter an *an sich* forever inaccessible to us on this side of the language barrier. This, at least, is Braver's contention, and meets up with Christopher Norris's early claim that Derrida's work amounted to a new "transcendental deduction" of the conditions of possibility for knowledge.[11] This would make Derrida's entire project an *epistemological* adventure, an irony given his proximity to Heidegger's *Destruktion* of the history of *ontology*.

No doubt, many of Derrida's earliest exponents presented his work in terms of his textualism, but he is less an heir to the linguistic turn than continuing a line of thought from Husserl and Heidegger regarding temporality. Derrida's *speculative* move is to look to the specific temporality of texts as a pivot to a *real time*; it is *différance* as difference/deferral[12] that is the condition of possibility for all of Derrida's claims about deconstruction and indeed his claims about texts. He writes:

> The concept of text or of context which guides me does not exclude the world, reality, history. Once again (and this probably makes a thousand times I have had to repeat this, but when will it finally be heard, and why this resistance?): as I understand it (and I have explained why), the text is not the book, it is not confined in a volume itself confined to the library. It does not suspend reference—to history, to the world, to reality, to being, and especially not *to the other*, since to say of history, of the world, of reality, that they always appear in an experience, hence in a movement of interpretation which contextualizes them according to a network of differences and hence of referral to the *other*, is surely to recall that *alterity* (difference) is irreducible.[13]

There is his "metaphysics," and we can use this word since Derrida often said that we couldn't but speak metaphysically, and though this is taken to be "anti-metaphysical," he can no more be anti-metaphysical than I can be "anti-" the floor on which one stands; he was always "taking on the tradition," as Michael Naas discusses it, in both senses of the term. But one could point out we should not simply accept Derrida's own defense on the matter, though his later work, which privileges the "to come" of a future worthy of the name rather than his early emphasis on writing, brings home this point. He writes:

> The deconstruction of logocentrism, of linguisticism, of economism (of the proper, of the at-home [*chez-soi*], *oikos*, of the same), etc., as well as the affirmation of the impossible are always put forward *in the name of the real*, of the irreducible reality of the real—not of the real as the attribute of the objective, present, perceptible or intelligible thing (*res*), but of the real as the coming or event of the other, where the other resists all appropriation. . . . The real is this non-negative impossible, this impossible coming or invention of the event the thinking of which is not an onto-phenomenology. It is a thinking of

> the event (singularity of the other, in its unanticipatable coming, *hic et nunc*) that resists reappropriation by an ontology or phenomenology of presence as such. . . . Nothing is more "realist," in this sense, than a deconstruction.[14]

As he's suggesting, this would not be a realism in the epistemological sense, where truth is the relation between the representation and represented, between a perception of the sign and its signified in an intelligible concept, in a correspondence theory of truth. At the least, he can respond that we are on a path towards a thinking of time that is not *merely* theoretical, if such a thing can be thought, since as Heidegger noted well, our relation to time is pre-theoretical, and is prior to or the condition of possibility for Dasein's "practical," circumspective care structure. Heidegger's project, one to which Derrida responds and follows, is to think time not from the point of view of eternity. From the *Timaeus* to the *Confessions*, this is the shared axiom of Platonism, and, skipping quite a lot here, the well-named "presentism" and "eternalism" of contemporary philosophies of time, however opposed, share a theoretical view that can only theorize time in terms of conceptual schemes of tenses that freeze time.[15] There is much to unpack here, but I want to argue that Derrida's early work specifically targets the relation between writing and time, and thus between any supposed conceptual scheme and the time of discursivity, that is, between differentiation (time-spacing) and its marking of existence, or marking *as* existence. Derrida thus refuses the gesture of the "view from nowhen,"[16] as Huw Price calls it, and we should all tense up when the time of writing, as Augustine noted well in his own thinking of the temporality of poetry, is reduced to the atemporal problems of tenses.

And yet, one could rightly say that Continental philosophy in the twentieth century is no nearer to giving us a "realism" of time. Husserl's early work could only think a time in the circuit of the constituting subject. Heidegger's 1920s lectures foundered in trying to get out of the circuit of *Dasein*, that is, to move from the time of *Dasein* (*Zeitlichkeit*) to the time of Being (*Temporalität*), or what he later dubbed "true" or "authentic" time" (*die eigentliche Zeit*) in *Time and Being*, which nevertheless must be given in a given experience:

> In order to move beyond the idiom [of *es gibt*] and back to the matter [*Sache*], we must show how this "there is" ["*es gibt*"] can be experienced [*erfahren*] and seen [*erblicken*]. The appropriate way [*der geignete Weg*] to get there is to explain what is given [*gegeben*] in

> the "It gives" ["*Es gibt*"], what "Being" means, which—It gives [*das—Es gibt*]; what "time" means, which—It gives [*das—Es gibt*].[17]

Is this thinking, too, still within the circuit of a giving (*geben*) that is received through an experience and a certain seeing, however many caveats Heidegger will provide? Levinas, too, responding to Heidegger, would critique a thinking of time as related to the eternal, but would find time in the duration or *durée* of the relation between the Same and Other, and thus not outside the circuit of certain humanism, one could argue.

> There is the time that one can understand in terms of presence and the present, and in which the past is only a retained present and the future a present to come. Re-presentation would be the fundamental modality of mental life. But, in terms of the ethical relationship with the other, I glimpse a temporality in which the dimensions of the past and the future have their own signification. In my responsibility for the other, the past of the other, which has never been my present, "concerns me": it is not a re-presentation for me. The past of the other and, in a sense, the history of humanity in which I have never participated, in which I have never been present, is my past. As for the future—it is not my anticipation of a present which is already waiting for me, all ready, and like the imperturbable order of being, "as if it had already arrived," as if temporality were a synchrony. The future is the time of pro-phecy, which is also an imperative, a moral order, herald of an inspiration . . . a future that is not a simple to-come [*à-venir*]. The infinity of time doesn't frighten me; I think it is the very movement of the to-God [*a-dieu*] and that time is better than eternity which is an exasperation of the "present," an idealization of the present.[18]

There is a fundamental insight here, namely a link between infinite displacement and time, and beyond the eternal, it is this Levinas to which I respond. Following this, there is, in Derrida, a linking of time to infinity that is infinitely different, if we can speak that way, from the thinking of time in relation to the eternal. Platonism begins where we move from time directly to the *concept* of time, and treat the latter as the former.[19] It is this conceptualization that provides a supposed "temporal idealism." The marks of signification (and here we are thinking of textuality in the widest sense, taking up precisely the *écriture* of Derrida's early writings) are nothing but the *traces* and *tracing out* of the difference/deferral of temporalization. The real is temporalization, in Derrida, even if all discussions of time risk bringing us back to a metaphysics of time, even if *naming* time risks removing time from itself in the name of its concept and conceptualization, which would make it anything but timely. This was precisely the move of Platonism. But you might say: how to address and respond to time as other to conceptuality? Why not just turn to the matter (*die Sache*) of time itself? Directly and head-on, if you will, without all this "reading"—all this deconstruction? In *Being and Time*, Heidegger sought to do so, to open up the question of time as such (*Temporalität*) through the time (*Zeitlichkeit*) of *Dasein*, through a phenomenology of the appearance of time to *Dasein*. This move led him to think the transcendental care structure of a being asking after its own being, and thus hopefully (and speculatively) giving us the transcendental structure of time (*as Temporalität*) as the condition of possibility for *Dasein*'s being in the world and its own timeliness. That this failed is well known, and led Heidegger to forestall a third division of *Being and Time* that was never to appear officially. Phenomenology reached its terminus in an inability to pivot from the *Dasein-Zeitlichkeit* dyad to an "independent" *Temporalität*, since as a science of appearances, despite whatever withering (*Destruktion*) of clichéd language covering over the *phenomenon*, could not help but circle around a creeping anthropology of *Dasein* in its acts of boredom and being-towards-death. Thus while Heidegger's perspicuous phenomenologies of factical existence rendered as an abstraction clock time and philosophical conceptions of the now of *Dasein*'s being-in-the-world, the *aporia* of the phenomenological method only meant circling back to *Dasein*. Thus Heidegger would attempt other "methods"—most notably, forms of poetizing—in order to speak to the givenness of time as such. Heidegger's early failure (though, given its import, that is too strong a word) is but another sign of a certain truth, though not a truth that can be adequated to a given real. Recall Augustine's oft-repeated quotation on time:

> For what is time? [*quid est enim tempus*] Who is able easily and briefly [*facile breviterque*] to explain that? Who is able so much as *in thought* to *comprehend* it, so as to express himself concerning it? And yet, what in our *usual discourse* do we more familiarly and famously [*familiarus et notius*] make mention of than time? . . . We understand it also, when in speaking with another we hear it named [*cum alioloquente id audimus*]. What is time then? If no one asks me [*sinemo ex me quaerat*], I know [*scio*]; but if I were desirous to explain it [*explicare*] to one that should ask me, I know not [*nescio*].[20]

Like the ghost in Hamlet, we are asked to speak to time, to speak of it, and finally respond to it. Is this not the thought of anyone writing on time: "The time is out of joint: O cursed spite / That ever I was born to set it right"?[21] It gives, and yet when I must speak, I bite my tongue, like many would say Derrida does concerning all metaphysical questions. On the one hand, we can read this as repeating a classical distinction between discursive thinking—that which can be spoken—and the soul or *animus* that merely "sees" through the intellect the matter at hand. Yet we attempt to speak of time, and nevertheless it lies beyond signification or the *representatem* of knowledge. This would seem merely to repeat Platonism's distinction between the sensible (sign) and the intelligible (signified). Yet even Augustine indirectly contests this aspect of Plato, since time is *sensible* via the soul as it is literally marked out on notes of poetry, and this time is itself not speakable as the quotation above stipulates. Augustine's resolution to the difficulties of time arrives in his *Confessions* Book XI when he ponders the timing of a given psalm:

> Who therefore can deny [*negat*—if only I had the space to work through this whole discourse of "denial" and "negation" that forms around all these discussions of time—from Augustine to Hegel to Heidegger to Levinas, but beginning in Plato's turnabout from becoming to the eternal] that things to come are not as yet? Yet already there is in the mind [*in animo*] an expectation [*expectatio*] of things to come [*futurorum*]. And who can deny [*negat*] past things to be now no longer [*non esse*]? But yet is there still in the mind a memory of things past. And who can deny [*negat*—again!] that the present time hath no space [*praesens tempus career spatio*], because it passeth away in a moment [*in puncto*]. But yet our attentive *marking of it* [here the crucial point: time and its marking] continues so that that which shall be present proceedeth to become absent [*set tamen perdurat attention, per quam pergatabesse quod aderit*]. The future therefore is not a long time, for it is not [*quod non est*]: but the long future time is merely a long expectation of the future. Nor is the time past a long time, for it is not [*quod non est*]. I am about to repeat a psalm that I know . . . [etc. etc.]

There has thus always been linked a relation between time and *aesthesis*, time and experience (*erfahren*). Time, thus written out (of metaphysics), would be but a signifier, a mimesis or *representatem*, of the eternal, the ever self-same, the *one* ever standing in the present, a truly transcendental signified, which is the mark of the intelligible as such. One thus sees the radicality of Heidegger's project in the 1920s. As he noted, it was past time to think temporality not as anchored in the eternal. But he also attempted to disentangle what was also axiomatic to Platonism: that time was a specific mark of the sensible, whether that sensible is the world of becoming, the sensibility of the *animus*, or the transcendental aesthetic of Kant. As Derrida puts it, "Here we are touching upon the point of greatest obscurity, on the very enigma of *différance*."[22] This ecstatic structure stands out ahead of itself, toward the future worthy of the name. This brings us to the ethics and politics of Derrida's later work. I realize I'm moving fast here. But for Derrida, the structure of the future is that which we must welcome without delay, since of course, this is temporalization itself. This would be a future that would be wholly other, not the future as thought from the present—or a block time that has already mapped it all out—and thus there's precisely, as in Levinas, a symmetry between the relation to temporalization and the coming of the Other; it cannot be made the object of a correspondence theory of truth, nor be the *significatium* of Augustinian knowledge. It is not to be represented—"comprehended" [*compris*] in Levinas's sense—since it's slipped away before you've done so, and thus cannot be given in an experience or correlation, though it is no less real.

Is this not the message of Aristotle's often non-Platonist *Physics*? Heidegger thinks time in *Time and Being* as the *es gibt* (it gives or there is) of Being, which has withdrawn "in favor of the gift that It gives. That gift is thought and conceptualized from then on exclusively as Being with regard to beings."[23] This exchange and response of the gift (*die Gabe*) to the giving (*geben*), this *signifier* of a timely *signified* that is beyond signification, that is, what Heidegger calls "true time extending," is generally lost in the discussion of the ontico-ontological difference, the metaphysics of presence, the dismantling of a tradition, and the iron grip we find in Heidegger's readings of various authors. No doubt, Heidegger occasionally read less with a lens than with a hammer. In particular, when he reads Aristotle's still contemporary meditations on time in the *Physics* as "metaphysical" in the sense of anchoring time in the now. But this is not *entirely* the case, or perhaps we should say, "it is not . . . or scarcely is." That is, Aristotle begins his account in the *Physics* with the *aporia* that time is made up of nows, which in turn are made up of the past and the future, and thus is made up of what is *not* (the future just about to be and the past that is no longer, and thus time would be what is *not*, since it is made up of non existents [that which is *mē on*]). Hence, while Aristotle gives us an account of time as anchored in the now, it is only to reveal the *aporia* of common or exoteric views of time. First, Aristotle does not think time on the basis of the eternal ("time is the moving image of eternity" as in the *Timaeus*), which is the starting move of more than a millennium of thinking on the matter, from the *Timaeus* to Augustine's *Confessions*. That is, Aristotle shows that one cannot find a *paradigma* or *idea* of time, since all fail: it is not a line (*grammē*), it is not a point (*stigmē*), it is not a number (*arithmēma*), it is not a sphere (*sphaira*), it is not change (*kinēsis*), it is not movement (*metabolē*), etc. Indeed the best Aristotle can broach is that time is "what is counted," but it is not a number, and thus we can disturb the facile summation that Aristotle thinks time is the measure of movement: it is that which is *numbered* and thus is "prior" to *mathēsis* and any given signification. It gives itself to number: "time is a numbered number." As Derrida rightly interprets this, "This means paradoxically that even if time comes under the rubric of mathematics or arithmetic, it is not *in itself* [my emphasis], in its nature, a mathematical being,"[24] a point that Aristotle makes clear when he argues that 100 men and 100 horses have the same number but are different. And by declaring a non-reductivity to time through the marking out of the *aporiai* of time to the now, Aristotle thus escapes the full grasp of Heidegger: he can't make time present to thought; time as such (if there is such a thing) is not given over to conceptuality.

Thus as "realists" of temporalization, we must acknowledge that attempts to give time mean a slippage or movement of *différance*, that is the movement from any *form* of time. Derrida writes:

> Let us take [this] as a marker in the history of aporetics that will become a law and tradition: From the moment time is apprehended on the basis of the present now as a general *form* [my emphasis] and only modifiable or modalizable in such a way that the past and future are still presents-past and presents-to-come,[25] this predetermination entails the aporetics of time that is not, of a time that is what it is *without being* (it) [*sans l'être*], that is not what it is and that is what it is not, which is to be *without being (it)* [*qui est de l'être sans l'être*].[26]

Time, too, comes to us as if by surprise, like the Other. It comes in events and the non-anticipatable, which Derrida thinks in terms of the death, not just of the Other, but of all Others of the Other. I would like to mark this out: the use of the "trace" in Derrida both to mark the relation of *time* to *writing* (in the general sense), one that is the non-presence of time (we have only available its trace), and to mark the deferral of each signifier to another as this deferring, othering, alter-able structure of writing, which is the self-negating of time, that is not a *thing* or being (*ousia*), that negates itself in the passing of any now (*nun*), and thus could never be made present (*parousia*) as such. And this trace would link us to a thinking of the trace of the Other that always interested Derrida, an Other that would come to us not "as if" from the future, but as the future of what can never be present, here and now. Derrida writes, this trace . . .

> is thus that the difference between Being and beings, the very thing that would have been "forgotten" [according to Heidegger] in the determination of Being as presence, and of presence as present—this difference [read always for Derrida: *deferral* and *differentiation*, or the becoming time of space and the becoming space of time—of which writing is the eminent example] is so buried that there is no longer any trace of it. The trace of difference is erased [in metaphysics as read for Derrida]. If one recalls that difference (is) itself other than presence and absence, (is) (itself) trace, it is indeed the trace of the trace that has disappeared in the forgetting of the difference between Being and being. . . . Beyond Being and beings, this difference, ceaselessly differing from and deferring (itself), would trace (itself) (by itself)—this *différance* would be the first or last trace if one still could speak here of origin and end [which would] give us to think . . . a writing exceeding everything that the history of metaphysics comprehended in the form of Aristotelian *grammē*, in its point, in its circle, in its time, and in its space.[27]

Yes, this can be infuriating prose. Nevertheless, Derrida will note that "if one allows that the linearity of language entails this [linear,] vulgar, and mundane concept of temporality (homogeneous, dominated by the form of the now and the ideal of continuous movement, straight or circular), which Heidegger shows to be the intrinsic determining concept of all ontology from Aristotle to Hegel, the meditation on writing and the deconstruction of the philosophy become inseparable."[28] And thus, *mutatis mutandis*, so too any rethinking of writing, as in Derrida, makes a *speculative* move to a "real time" and thinking of the event that traces itself out in/as writing (in the widest sense), and thus beyond any tenses of conceptual schemes that require the writing of time. As he puts it: "Now if *différance* is (and I also cross out the "is") what makes possible the presentation of the being-present, it is never presented as such."[29] And as derived from the Latin *differre*, it means "in this sense to temporize, to take recourse . . . in the temporal or temporal mediation of a detour that suspends the accomplishment or fulfilment of 'desire' or 'will.' . . . This temporization is also temporalization and spacing, the becoming-space of time, the 'originary constitution' of time and space."[30]

This unconditional, infinite *tracing* (which is neither present nor absent, given the contradictory logic or *logos* of time, as Aristotle himself teaches: "time [*chronos*]" is that which "is not" or which "is barely and scarcely") means also that there is no present in which the Other *is*, and thus the Other comes to me from a future that transcends our epistemologies of the present but is nevertheless real. This is Derrida's metaphysics, if you will, there at the border between a thinking of metaphysical temporalization and a metaphysics of Levinas, announced early in *Of Grammatology*: "The future can only be anticipated in the form of an absolute danger. It is that which breaks absolutely with constituted normality and can only be proclaimed, presented, as a sort of monstrosity. For that future world and for that within it which will have put into question the values of sign, word, and writing, for that which guides our future anterior, there is as yet no exergue"—no writing that can masterly present time and this future anterior as such.[31]

Such would be our humility before declaring the future of speculative realism. The task of philosophy has for long been to turn us upward from time to the non-temporal, from the sensible to untimely laws beyond them, and thus we have an argument that to speak to the real is to speak to what is timely and work backwards from there—in the face of a future that may be monstrous. Such is a difficult thought—like building a house on a mudslide. Such a thought is not reflective of eternal becoming since such would be an idea of an eternal time that would not allow time to be other than its concept, to be finite and thus turn itself over into stasis and death. This time would not be correlationist, since like the future of extinction in Brassier, it cannot be made present to thought except through the indirection of the very writing of the discourses about it. This is my speculative gambit and unlike speculative realists returning to a certain Platonism, time is on my side.

NOTES

Introduction

1. Ray Brassier, "I am a nihilist because I still believe in truth: Ray Brassier interviewed by Marcin Rychter." *Chronos* 4 March 2011. Available at http://www.kronos.org.pl/index.php?23151,896 (Last accessed 1 September 2013).
2. Lee Braver, "On Not Settling the Issue of Realism." *Speculations IV* (2013): 9–14, 13.

Chapter 1

1. Quentin Meillassoux, "Continency & Absolutization of the One," lecture delivered at the Sorbonne, trans. Benjamin James Lozano, accessed at http://www.speculativeheresy.files.wordpress.com/2011/03/contingency-and-absolutization-of-the-one.pdf, 1 May 2012, p. 6.
2. Maurice Merleau-Ponty, *Phenomenology of Perception*, trans. Don Landes (London: Routledge, 2013), p. 432.
3. Meillassoux, "Time without Becoming," lecture at Middlesex University, London, 8 May 2008. Accessed at http://www.speculativeheresy.wordpress.com/resources/, 1 May 2012, p. 1. We'd be remiss if we didn't mention other excellent accounts of Meillassoux's depiction of correlationism, namely in Paul J. Ennis, *Continental Realism* (Winchester, UK: Zero Books, 2011), and Graham Harman's *Quentin Meillassoux: Philosophy in the Making* (Edinburgh: Edinburgh University Press, 2011).
4. Meillassoux, "Time Without Becoming," p. 1.
5. Meillassoux, *After Finitude*, p. 15.
6. Ibid., p. 5.
7. We should emphasize that this does not deny that in Anglo-American philosophy, there is not a school of thought that defends "naïve realism," in particular those who work in philosophy of perception and who defend disjunctivism. See William Fish, *A Philosophy of Perception: A Contemporary Introduction* (London: Routledge, 2010), especially chapter six, for an excellent and eminently readable overview of these positions. My thanks to Richard Sebold for this reference.

8. Graham Harman, in his *Philosophy in the Making*, distinguishes between "strong" correlationism, which describes the thinkers we discuss here, and "very strong correlationism," which describes postmodern relativists who are said to believe everything is socially constructed (18–23). This is not a distinction found in Meillassoux, and in any case, a social constructionist would be something like a "naïve" idealist—unable to think reality outside the play of concepts.
9. Another helpful point I owe to Richard Sebold.
10. Ian Hacking, *The Social Construction of What?* (Cambridge, MA: Harvard University Press, 2000).
11. For an excellent summation of these positions as staked out by Meillassoux, see Harman's *Philosophy in the Making*, p. 23. However, a minor quibble: Harman argues that for the absolute idealist, "the things-in-themselves are unknowable and also completely unthinkable" (23). If he has in mind here Hegel or any of the German idealists, such as Fichte, this misses the import of their "speculative" approach, which mirrors, in some sense, Meillassoux's own method: they take seriously the *reality* of thought as *absolute*, or that the correlate between thinking and being is real. The in-itself is not some *outside*, but is thought in its very activity, which is thus eminently knowable and thinkable. Thus rather than get caught up in the *content* or *reference* of what we think, it is the *form* of thought itself that centers their work, and this is their true legacy for all future philosophers, including Meillassoux, who borrows much from them in attempting to think the *absolute* through the speculative method.
12. The terminology in the philosophical literature can be confusing on this count, since in the contemporary period, Platonic "realists" abound. But this merely means that these philosophers take either ideas or mathematics to be unchanging reality beneath the changing semblances of our world.
13. George Berkeley, *Principles of Human Knowledge: Three Dialogues* (London: Oxford University Press, 1999), p. 33. We will cover more on this in terms of "Stove's Gem" in Chapter 4.
14. Ibid.
15. Immanuel Kant, *Critique of Pure Reason*, trans. Werner S. Pluhar (New York: Hackett, 1996), Bxvi.
16. Ibid., A30, my emphasis.
17. The sharp reader will of course note that it's really a Copernican Revolution in reverse. For Copernicus, the solar system no longer revolves around the sun, nor humanity, while for Kant knowledge does indeed revolve metaphorically around the subject.
18. Ibid., A42.
19. Ibid., A101.
20. Ibid., B275.
21. Ibid., B69.

22. This is what led him to rewrite his fourth paralogism of the so-called A edition of the *Critique of Pure Reason* as a "Refutation of Idealism" for the B edition.
23. Ibid., p. 275.
24. Meillassoux, "Continency & Absolutization of the One," lecture delivered at the Sorbonne, trans. Benjamin James Lozano, accessed at http://speculativeheresy.files.wordpress.com/2011/03/contingency-and-absolutization-of-the-one.pdf, 1 May 2012.
25. Reductive materialists argue that all psychological states can be reduced to what is physically occurring in the brain or the body. Eliminative materialists go further, since they argue there are only physical states, while reductive materialists still hold out some value to discussing mental states.
26. We'll look in Chapter 4 at how Bruno Latour and Graham Harman argue for an "irreductionism," which calls for an end to this philosophical one-upmanship: we can have the mind and brain, economics and morality, and so on.
27. Michael Dummett, "Realism." *Synthese* 52 (1982): 55–112, 55.
28. Dummett, *The Interpretation of Frege's Philosophy* (Cambridge, MA: Harvard University Press, 1981), p. 434.
29. John McDowell, *Mind and World* (Cambridge, MA: Harvard University Press, 1996, 2nd edn), p. 11. He comes back to this image throughout his work, arguing, "we can reinstate friction between thought and world," p. 66.
30. Dummett, "Realism," p. 111. We will come upon Wilfrid Sellars' critique of naïve realism when discussing Ray Brassier's work in Chapter 6.
31. Ibid., p. 109.
32. Hilary Putnam, *Reality and Representation* (Cambridge, MA: MIT Press, 1988), p. 114.
33. Lacanian theory in Continental thought takes this notion of a fundamental illusion seriously. For Lacan, the Real is but a third member of a tri-partite structure of being-in-the-world. The Real is fundamentally an empty kernel at the heart of human existence onto which the Imaginary and Symbolic project some "reality." The point of Lacanian theory is not to point out that we must get the "real" right because of some illusions that others are dogged by, but rather that the illusion that a given "reality" is *real* is fundamental. The Real is thus, in Lacan's words, "impossible," an in-itself that will ever escape symbolization, because that would mean a processing of the Real through the work of the imaginary into the coding of the Symbolic. We will return to these points at some length in our discussion of Adrian Johnston's work in Chapter 7.
34. Meillassoux, *After Finitude*, p. 5.
35. Maurice Merleau-Ponty, *The Visible and the Invisible*, p. 4. On Merleau-Ponty's notion of expression, see the excellent study by Donald A. Landes, *Merleau-Ponty and the Paradoxes of Expression* (London: Bloomsbury, 2013).
36. Merleau-Ponty, *Phenomenology of Perception*, p. 432.
37. Ibid., p. 15.

38. Merleau-Ponty, *The Visible and the Invisible*, p. 162.
39. Marie-Eve Morin, "Martin Heidegger," in Paul Ennis and Peter Gratton (eds), *The Meillassoux Dictionary* (Edinburgh: Edinburgh University Press, 2014).
40. Michael Cerbone, "World, World-Entry, and Realism in Early Heidegger." *Inquiry* 38(1995): 401–21, 401.
41. William Blattner, *Heidegger's Temporal Idealism* (Cambridge: Cambridge University Press, 1999), p. 3.
42. Hilary Putnam, "A Problem about Reference," in Michael J. Loux (ed.), *Metaphysics: Contemporary Readings* (London: Taylor & Francis, 2002), pp. 496–524, 517.
43. Hilary Putnam, *Meaning and the Moral Sciences* (London: Routledge, 1978), pp. 125–6.
44. Martin Heidegger, *Being and Time*, trans. John Macquarrie and Edward Robinson (San Franciso, CA: Harper & Row, 1962), pp. 248–9. Published in German as *Sein und Zeit*, 7th edn (Tübingen: Neomarius Verlag, 2001), pp. 204–5.
45. Heidegger, citing Kant at *Being and Time*, pp. 249/205.
46. Here it's worth citing Meillassoux: "the end of metaphysics, understood as the 'de-absolutization of thought,' is thereby seen to consist in the rational legitimation of any and every variety of religious (or 'poetico-religious') belief in the absolute. . . . *by forbidding reason any claim to the absolute, the end of metaphysics has taken the form of an exacerbated return of the religious*" (Meillassoux, *After Finitude*, p. 45, emphasis in the original).
47. Heidegger, *Being and Time*, pp. 246/202, my emphasis.
48. See his first chapter in *Glance of the Eye* (Albany, NY: SUNY Press, 1997).
49. Putnam, "A Problem," p. 521.
50. Heidegger, *Being and Time*, pp. 96/67–8. This move also grounds Merleau-Ponty's phenomenology. See *The Visible and the Invisible*, chapter one, where Merleau-Ponty grounds the "time of science" and the "cleavage between the 'subjective' and the 'objective'" in a fundamental openness to the world (*The Visible and the Invisible*, trans. Al Lingis [Northwestern University Press, 1968], pp. 19–20).
51. Heidegger, *Being and Time*, pp. 255/211.
52. Ibid., pp. 114/83.
53. Lee Braver, *A Thing of This World* (Evanston, IL: Northwestern University Press, 2007), p. 165.
54. Heidegger, *Being and Time*, pp. 98/69.
55. Ibid., pp. 97/68.
56. Despite what Heidegger writes about such entities not being merely "usable for something" (*Being and Time*, pp. 99/70).

57. We will return to this point, but it's notable that all functionalist accounts must elide the second division of *Being and Time*, if not much of the other work of Heidegger's early period.
58. Cited in Meillassoux, "Time Without Becoming," p. 5.
59. Heidegger, *Being and Time*, pp. 255/212.
60. Ibid., pp. 95/66–7.
61. Ibid., pp. 101/71.
62. Ibid., pp. 187/147, 61/36.
63. Ibid., pp. 60/35.
64. Heidegger, *Basic Problems*, pp. 170/241.
65. Heidegger, *The Fundamental Concepts of Metaphysics: World, Finitude, Solitude*, trans. William McNeill and Nicholas Walker (Bloomington: Indiana University Press, 1995), p. 205. Originally published as *Die Grundbegriffe der Metaphysik. Welt—Endlichkeit—Einsamkeit* (Frankfurt am Main: Vittorio Klostermann, 1992), p. 300.
66. Heidegger, *Basic Problems*, pp. 170/242.
67. Heidegger, *Fundamental Concepts*, pp. 201/295.
68. Heidegger, "*Einblick in das was ist. Bremer Vorträge*," in *Gesamtausgabe* 79 (Frankfurt am Main: Vittorio Klosterman, 2nd edn, 2005), p. 5.
69. Ibid., p. 13.
70. Ibid., p. 5.
71. In Chapter 4, we will show how Levinas, after Heidegger, reads the latter as still too reductive of the world of things.
72. Heidegger, "Introduction to 'What is Metaphysics?'," in *Pathmarks*, p. 284.
73. Heidegger, "*Einblick*," pp. 20–1, my translation. This section is also in Heidegger's essay, "The Thing," *Poetry, Language, Thought*, trans. A. Hostadter (New York: Harper & Row, 1971), pp. 181–2.

Chapter 2

1. Harman, *Philosophy in the Making*, pp. vii–viii.
2. Meillassoux, *After Finitude*, p. 10.
3. Here is his definition: "An arche-fossil . . . designates the material support on the basis of which the experiments that yield estimates of ancestral phenomena proceed—for example, an isotope whose rate of radioactive decay we know, or the luminous emission of a star that informs us as to the date of its formation" (Ibid.).
4. Ibid., p. 17.

5. Ibid., p. 18.
6. Ibid., p. 17.
7. John Nolt, "An Argument for Metaphysical Realism." *Journal for General Philosophy of Science* 35 (2004): 71–90, 71.
8. A point made also, rightly, by Graham Harman: "In [Meillassoux's] view, the correlational circle of human and world is not a trivial error or word game, but rather the starting point for all rigorous philosophy" (Meillassoux, *Philosophy in the Making*, p. 3). This also forms the basis for my discussion in "The Speculative Challenge and Post-Deconstructive Realism," in Peter Gratton and Marie-Eve Morin (eds), *Jean-Luc Nancy and Plural Thinking* (Albany, NY: SUNY Press, 2012), pp. 109–25.
9. Ray Brassier, Iain Hamilton Grant, Graham Harman, and Quentin Meillassoux, "Speculative Realism." *Collapse* 3 (2007): 429.
10. Meillassoux, "Time Without Becoming," p. 2.
11. Ibid., p. 5.
12. As Harman puts it, "In [Meillassoux's] view the correlational circle of human and world is not a trivial error or word game, but rather the starting point for all rigorous philosophy" (*Philosophy in the Making*, p. 3).
13. Ibid., p. 13.
14. To be precise, Meillassoux seems to have a use of the word "realism" that he doesn't specify. In several places, including the discussion in "Speculative Realism," he is willing to take on the word "realism." But for the most part, he argues that neither he nor the correlationists are "anti-realists." Thus the argument, for him, seems to be less about realism and anti-realism than the "anti-absolutism" of the correlationists ("Time without Becoming," p. 7). Ultimately, as we will see, Meillassoux identifies the "absolute" as the principle of contingency, yet he also rejects realism in favor of a "materialism," though he cannot, for all that, be clear on how a *relation* (however absolute) is itself *material*. He also, in several places in *After Finitude*, uses the word "real" synonymously with the "absolute." For our purposes above, we use the term "speculative realism" since what is "real" has not been just "external," but *independent* of "our representations—conscious, linguistic, historical ones" (ibid.).
15. Ibid., p. 27.
16. Ibid., p. 28.
17. *L'Inexistence divine*, p. 162. This is precisely what is called elsewhere Platonic realism.
18. Meillassoux, *After Finitude*, p. 5.
19. Ibid., p. 15.
20. Ibid., p. 10.
21. Ibid., p. 8.

22. Ibid., p. 17.
23. Ibid., p. 18.
24. "Time Without Becoming," p. 5.
25. Nolt, "An Argument for Metaphysical Realism," p. 73.
26. Hallward, "Anything is Possible: A Reading of Quentin Meillassoux's *After Finitude*," in *The Speculative Turn: Continental Materialism and Realism* (Melbourne: Re.Press, 2010), p. 135.
27. As Harman notes, "Eventually we need to ask why a temporal discrepancy is more important for Meillassoux than the spatial discrepancy between human observers and unwitnessed events in distant galaxies and abandoned houses" (*Philosophy in the Making*, pp. 13–14). It's not clear that Meillassoux ever properly answers this question, though for Nolt it's the structure of physical temporality that is at least the one undeniable fact.
28. Ibid., p. 21.
29. Ibid.
30. Meillassoux, *After Finitude*, pp. 44–5.
31. For a diversity of these philosophies, see this special issue of the open access *Analecta Hermeneutica*, "Refiguring Divinity: Continental Philosophy of Religion," 4(2012):http://www.journals.library.mun.ca/ojs/index.php/analecta/issue/current/showToc (Last accessed 1 September 2013).
32. Markus Gabriel, *Transcendental Ontology: Essays in German Idealism* (London: Continuum, 2011), p. ix.
33. Gratton, "After the Subject," p. 67.
34. In reviewing Berkeley's naïve idealism, Brassier notes he "reveals the hidden logic of every correlationist argument," namely "that things *depend* [his emphasis] for their existence on being thought or perceived and are *nothing apart from* our thinking or perceiving them" (Brassier, "Concepts and Objects," *The Speculative Turn*, pp. 47–65, 57).
35. Nolt, "Metaphysical Realism," p. 75. Nolt uses the term "depends" throughout his essay.
36. Meillassoux, *After Finitude*, p. vii.
37. Hallward, "Anything is Possible," pp. 137–8.
38. Merleau-Ponty, *Phenomenology of Perception*, p. 432, my emphasis.
39. Nathan Brown, "The Speculative and the Specific: On Hallward and Meillassoux," in *Speculative Turn*, pp. 142–62, 144.
40. I owe this point about Spinoza and much else to the late Jim Bradley, my former Memorial University colleague.
41. Paul Ennis, *Continental Realism*, p. 27.
42. There is a short lesson here. Even if one agrees with Meillassoux, we should probably end the pretence, so often found in recent works, that everything

offered is something new under the sun. No doubt, the Earth spins and a new day is born, but there is also a history of philosophy upon which we often just go round and round. This is the greatness and pathos of our given traditions—even as we take them on in the double sense.

43. See Brown's reply to this point, "The Speculative and the Specific," pp. 144–7.
44. Meillassoux, "Time Without Becoming," p. 4.
45. Nolt, "An Argument for Metaphysical Realism," p. 85.
46. Ibid.
47. Ibid., pp. 85–6, my emphases.
48. Ray Brassier, Iain Hamilton Grant, Graham Harman, and Quentin Meillassoux, "Speculative Realism." *Collapse* 3 (2007): 414. See also, *After Finitude*, p. 82.
49. See Brassier, et al., "Speculative Realism."
50. Nolt, "An Argument for Metaphysical Realism," p. 86.
51. *After Finitude*, pp. 22–4.
52. Ibid., p. 25.
53. He writes, taking up the embodied conditions of possibility for the transcendental subject, "we thereby discover that the time of science temporalizes and spatializes the emergence of living bodies, that is, the emergence of the conditions for the taking place of the transcendental" (*After Finitude*, p. 25).
54. "Time Without Becoming," p. 3.
55. Martin Heidegger, *The Basic Problems of Phenomenology*, trans. Albert Hofstadter (Bloomington: Indiana University Press, 1982), p. 325.
56. Ibid.
57. *After Finitude*, p. 136n. 1.
58. Harman, *Quadruple Object*, p. 63.
59. "Speculative Realism," pp. 427–31.
60. Adrian Johnston, "Materialism, Subjectivity, and the Outcome of French Philosophy." *Cosmos and History: The Journal of Natural and Social Philosophy* 7.1 (2011): 167–81, 173.
61. Slavoj Žižek, "Censorship Today: Violence, or Ecology as a New Opium for the Masses," available at http://www.lacan.com/zizecology2.htm (Last accessed 1 September 2013).
62. "Time Without Becoming," p. 5.
63. *After Finitude*, p. 23.
64. Ibid., p. 27.
65. Ibid., p. 44.
66. Ibid., p. 39.
67. Ibid.

68. "Interview with Meillassoux," in *Philosophy in the Making*, p. 164.
69. *After Finitude*, p. 59.
70. Ibid., p. 64.
71. Ibid., p. 55.
72. Ibid.
73. Ibid.
74. Ibid., p. 56.
75. Ibid., p. 59.
76. Ibid., p. 60.
77. Brassier, *Nihil Unbound*, p. 67.
78. *After Finitude*, p. 64.
79. Ibid.
80. Ibid., p. 59.
81. Ibid., p. 60.
82. Ibid.
83. Ray Brassier et al., "Speculative Realism," pp. 430–1.
84. See Ray Brassier's translator's note in *After Finitude* (132n. 6).
85. "Time without Becoming," p. 9.
86. *After Finitude*, p. 66.
87. Ibid., pp. 67–8.
88. Meillassoux, "Excerpts from *Divine Inexistence*," in Graham Harman, *Philosophy in the Making*, p. 155.
89. *After Finitude*, p. 53.
90. Lee Smolin, *Time Reborn: From the Crisis in Physics to the Future of the Universe* (New York: Houghton Mifflin Harcourt, 2013), p. xxv; see also 119. It should be noted that Smolin's contentions are deeply controversial among physicists.
91. "Speculative Realism," p. 435.
92. Ibid., p. 77.
93. *After Finitude*, p. 64.
94. Ibid., p. 97.
95. Ibid., p. 101.
96. For our purposes, we need not explain Meillassoux's particular use of set theory, other than to move to the conclusions on these points that he believes it provides. For his own quick and clear explanation, see *After Finitude*, pp. 134–5. But we should also note that Badiou, whose use of set theory in *Being and Event* (1987) forms the background for Meillassoux, has come under heavy criticism by mathematicians working in the area. His use reflects "*a priori* commitments rather than necessary truths of the set theory," as

Ricardo L. Nirenberg and David Nirenberg summarize their line of attack ("Badiou's Number: A Critique of Mathematics as Ontology." *Critical Inquiry* 37.4 [2011]: 583–614, 583). And while we're mentioning Alain Badiou, Adrian Johnston's "The World before Worlds: Quentin Meillassoux and Alain Badiou's Anti-Kantian Transcendentalism." *Contemporary French Civilization* 33.1 (2009): 73–99, discusses the crucial differences between Meillassoux and Badiou, despite overall similar trajectories. For Meillassoux's own elucidation of his relation to Badiou, see his interview in *Philosophy in the Making*, p. 169. But whatever their differences, it's my view that the impasses Meillassoux has between the world as it appears and the set theory he uses to describe it—namely, his treatment of the world as a "set"—are more clear in Meillassoux's work than Badiou's more byzantine structure, which makes Meillassoux a hermeneutic shortcut to the heart of problems facing the Badiouian project.

97. *After Finitude*, p. 98.
98. Ibid., p. 99.
99. Despite the very different language, there is a logic here similar to Heidegger's discussion of the worldhood of the world in *Being and Time*: the world is not some *whole* or *all*, since that would confuse the world as being just like the objects of the world.
100. Paul Livingston, "Georg Cantor," in Paul Ennis and Peter Gratton (eds), *The Meillassoux Dictionary* (Edinburgh: Edinburgh University Press, 2014).
101. *After Finitude*, p. 104.
102. Ibid., p. 105.
103. Ibid., p. 107.

Chapter 3

1. Meillassoux, "Time without Becoming," p. 11.
2. This is why Harman notes that, despite his clarity of prose, Meillassoux has produced "few if any literal disciples" and is a "thinker of rare solitude" (*Philosophy in the Making*, p. 7). But Harman also states that though Meillassoux's claims about contingency of the laws of nature are the "least convincing" in *After Finitude*, it is the seed of an idea that "deserves to grow for a season before exposed to the frost of critique" (Ibid., p. 150). But here I disagree: many seasons have passed since Meillassoux first broached these ideas in his doctoral dissertation, then in *After Finitude*, and in numerous essays since. Meillassoux has, to continue the metaphor, long been letting this seed grow and it's bloomed in all of his work. It's time to see if it can survive the cold light of day.
3. See his post at http://itself.wordpress.com/2012/01/21/my-experience-of-reading-meillassoux/ (Last accessed 15 May 2013).
4. *The Works of Philo Judaica: Vol. 1*, trans. C. D. Younge (London: Hadden Brothers, 1855), p. 110.

5. Ibid., p. 349.
6. "Time without Becoming," p. 11.
7. Ibid.
8. See, for example, "Time without Becoming," p. 6; *After Finitude*, p. 121.
9. Peirce writes: "To suppose universal laws of nature capable of being apprehended by the mind and yet having no reason for their special forms, but standing inexplicable and irrational, is hardly a justifiable position. Uniformities are precisely the sort of facts that need to be accounted for. Law is par excellence the thing that wants a reason. Now the only possible way of accounting for the laws of nature, and for uniformity in general, is to suppose them results of evolution." "The Architecture of Theories." *The Monist* 1.2 (1891): 161–76.
10. "Appendix: Excerpts from *L'Inexistence divine*," in *Philosophy in the Making*, p. 176. As Graham Harman notes, *L'Inexistence divine* was originally the title of his doctoral thesis published in 1997. The "Appendix" includes approximately twenty per cent of the total volume, selected and translated by Harman, of a 2003 version of the text. As we'll see, many of these ideas are also found in a 2010 text, so there's no reason to think Meillassoux has abandoned these ideas given the publication of *After Finitude* in the meantime. See "The Immanence of the World Beyond," in Conor Cunningham and Peter M. Candler (eds), *The Grandeur of Reason* (New York: SCM Press, 2011).
11. We will suggest below that Meillassoux's rationalism cannot apprise itself of the full "immanence" he seeks. This is also a point picked up, indirectly, by Adrian Johnston in "The World Before Worlds: Quentin Meillassoux and Alain Badiou's Anti-Kantian Transcendentalism."
12. Giorgio Agamben, "Absolute Immanence," in *Potentialities: Collected Essays in Philosophy* (Stanford, CA: Stanford University Press, 2000), p. 226.
13. Hasana Sharp, *Spinoza and the Politics of Renaturalization* (Chicago, IL: University of Chicago Press, 2011), p. 216. For more on that work, see my review in *Society and Space* (2012): http://www. societyandspace.com/reviews/reviews-archive/hasana-sharp-spinoza-and-the-politics-of-renaturalization-reviewed-by-peter-gratton/ (Last accessed 1 June 2013).
14. "Excerpts from *L'Inexistence divine*," p. 177.
15. Ibid.
16. Ibid., p. 179.
17. Ibid.
18. "The Immanence of the World Beyond," p. 444.
19. "Excerpts from *L'Inexistence divine*," p. 189.
20. Ibid.
21. See also *L'Inexistence divine*, p. 292. We will see this non-Whole return in Chapter 7, when Johnston discusses Lacan. He argues that Meillassoux's notion comes from Lacan, with Badiou as the intermediary.

22. Ibid., pp. 290–5.
23. Ibid., p. 294; "Excerpts from *L'Inexistence divine*," p. 187.
24. Ibid., p. 189.
25. Ibid., p. 180.
26. Ibid., p. 184.
27. Ibid., p. 185.
28. For a concise counter-argument against Russell, see Joseph Wayne Smith and Sharyn Ward, "Are We Only Five Minutes Old? Acock on the Age of the Universe." *Philosophy of Science* 51 (1984): 511–13.
29. "This essential excess of life and thought beyond matter implies a scission that ruptures all continuity, leaving the divine and the soul to fill the resulting chasm" ("Excerpts from *L'Inexistence divine*," p. 180).
30. Ibid.
31. Ibid., p. 181.
32. Ibid., p. 191.
33. Kearney, *The God Who May Be: A Hermeneutics of Religion* (Indianapolis, IN: Indiana University Press, 2001), p. 24.
34. Ibid., p. 37.
35. Ibid., p. 28.
36. Ibid., p. 29, my emphasis. Kearney's arguments are much more substantive than I can provide here, and not just limited to the text of Exodus. The point, though, is to show a different mode of argumentation about a possible God in Meillassoux. Much can and should be written about the relation between these two thinkers.
37. Ibid., p. 30, my emphases unless otherwise marked.
38. Ibid., p. 38.
39. "Immanence of the World Beyond," p. 450.
40. Ibid., p. 459.
41. Ibid., p. 460.
42. Ibid.
43. In this essay, Meillassoux does not stick to his previous capitalization of World to differentiate it from the "world" of the virtual or factial. For continuity and less confusion for the reader, I will adjust the quotations from this essay to keep it in line with these important distinctions.
44. Ibid., p. 462.
45. Ibid., p. 463.
46. Ibid.
47. Ibid., p. 454.
48. Ibid., p. 451.

49. Ibid.
50. Ibid., p. 452.
51. Though Meillassoux puts this discussion in the mouth of a "theist," it's clear that he agrees that this is the proper *ethical* response to all that haunts us.
52. Ibid., p. 453.
53. Jacques Derrida, *The Work of Mourning*, trans. Michael Naas and Pascale-Anne Brault (Chicago: University of Chicago Press, 2001), p. 143.
54. Jacques Derrida, *Chaque fois unique, la fin du monde*, eds. Pascale-Anne Brault and Michael Naas (Paris: Editions Galilée, 2003), p. 9, my emphases.
55. "Immanence of the World Beyond," p. 457.
56. Ibid., pp. 455–6.
57. Ibid., p. 458.
58. "Extracts from *L'Inexistence divine*," p. 190. I have changed the place of emphasis in this sentence.
59. "Immanence of the World Beyond," p. 458.
60. Ibid., p. 461.
61. "Interview with Quentin Meillassoux," p. 163, my emphasis.
62. "Extracts from *L'Inexistence divine*," p. 189.
63. Ibid.
64. "Immanence of the World Beyond," p. 454.
65. Ibid., p. 464.
66. Ibid., p. 463.
67. Ibid., p. 464.
68. Ibid., p. 473.
69. Ibid., p. 474.
70. Ibid., p. 477.
71. Alain Badiou touches upon this in an interview on speculative realism: "For Meillassoux, the future and perhaps the dead will make the final judgment. This is a political weakness. The question is: 'how is the Real of the present deployed for the future?' " ("Interview with Alain Badiou," *The Speculative Turn*, p. 20).
72. "Extracts from *L'Inexistence divine*," p. 195.

Chapter 4

1. Alphonso Lingis, "Detotalization and Finitude." *Philosophy Today* 51.2 (2007): 152–8, 157.
2. For reasons of space, I must for the most part leave aside the object-oriented ontologies of Levi Bryant, Ian Bogost, and Timothy Morton. First, the former

has now moved on to what he has called "machine-oriented ontology," following the work of Deleuze, while the Morton largely follows Harman's schema. Bogost's work in *Alien Phenomenology* is certainly worth notice, but it largely follows a narrative approach to discussing the phenomena of "alien" things. It is a highly recommended read, but here we must follow the core arguments of OOO found in Harman. As Morton, Bogost, and Bryant develop their work in the coming years, a thorough engagement will be necessary; for this book, which has more modest claims to be less than encyclopaedic, I will unfortunately only be able to touch on their work in certain places. Harman notes his philosophical differences from Bryant, Bogost, and Morton in "The Current State of Speculative Realism." *Speculations* 4 (2013): 26–8.

3. Emmanuel Levinas, *Totality and Infinity*, p. 46.
4. Ibid., pp. 44–5.
5. Ibid., p. 123. Rudolf Bernet gives a classical "realist" reading of Husserl in this way:

    > [T]ranscendental phenomenology is devoted to a study of the correlation between the acts of a pure consciousness and noetmatic objects, i.e., objects just in so far as they are aimed by such acts. By investigating objects as correlates of the acts of a pure consciousness, transcendental phenomenology deprives them of their autonomy, of their independence with respect to consciousness, but it does not deprive them of their transcendence. Their transcendence [that is, reality beyond the intentional correlation] is preserved not only because the object of a punctual intentional act is not itself a constitutive part of that act, but also because various acts succeeding one another in time can still relate to the unity of one and the same object. (Bernet, "Levinas's Critique of Husserl," *Cambridge Companion to Levinas* [Cambridge: Cambridge University Press, 2006], p. 83.)

6. Ibid., p. 134.
7. Ibid., p. 132.
8. John Sallis, "Levinas and the Elemental." *Research in Phenomenology* 28 (1998): 152–9, 158.
9. For more of Harman's reading of Levinas, see *Guerrilla Metaphysics*, ch. 3.
10. Harman, *Quadruple Object*, p. 38.
11. Ibid., p. 42.
12. Though Harman cites Alphonso Lingis approvingly on this reading, Lingis gives another view, namely that "the elemental" is released from an anonymous background of being only through the "enjoyment" of human beings. My reading is that Levinas is presenting us with three ways in which the things of the world are reduced to sameness—not that they are wholly reducible in the

acts of theorization (Husserl), equipmentality (Heidegger), or nourishment. In any event, Lingis asks of Levinas:

> Levinas argues that things can be detached and manipulated because they are substances, solids that hold themselves together. Appropriation precedes and makes possible utilization. He characterizes things as *meubles* moveable goods, furnishings. The term designates both their character of being detachable solids, substances, and their destination for the home. . . . Levinas thus intends to show that the environment of things is constituted as such by an initial appropriation, and that detaching things and treating them as furnishings further subjects them to us. . . . And do not things have their own existence, independent of me? They exist in the vast and uncontained realms of the elements—in the air, in the light or in the darkness, in warmth or cold, supported in their places by the ground. They can be detached and appropriated because they are solids that hold together of themselves, substances. (Alphonso Lingis, "Detotalization and Finitude," p. 157.)

13. Graham Harman, "Levinas and the Triple Critique of Heidegger." *Philosophy Today* 53.4 (2009): 407–13, 411.
14. Ibid.
15. Ibid., my emphasis.
16. *Quadruple Object*, p. 6.
17. Harman, "On the Undermining of Objects: Grant, Bruno, and Radical Philosophy," p. 23.
18. David Hume, *A Treatise on Human Nature* (Oxford: Oxford University Press, 1992), p. 220.
19. Harman, "On the Undermining of Objects," p. 23.
20. See Harman's "On Interface: Nancy's Weights and Masses," in Marie-Eve Morin and Peter Gratton (eds), *Jean-Luc Nancy and Plural Thinking Expositions of World, Ontology, Politics, and Sense* (Albany, NY: SUNY Press, 2012). For my own take on Nancy's realism, see my "The Speculative Challenge and Nancy's Post-Deconstructive Realism" in the same book.
21. Harman, "On the Undermining of Objects," p. 23.
22. Ibid.
23. *Quadruple Object*, p. 9.
24. We will ask later if Harman can so quickly dismiss the temporality of objects, since this is precisely what he must do in order to deny the work of Deleuze, for example. For more on this, see James Williams, "The Objects in Manifold Times: Deleuze and the Speculative Philosophy of Objects as Processes." *Cosmos and History: The Journal of Natural and Social Philosophy* 7.1 (2011): 62–75.

25. Harman, "On the Undermining of Objects," p. 23. As we draw this chapter to a close, it will become clear why Harman must divorce objects from their historicity.
26. He includes in this instance Whitehead. See "I am also of the opinion that materialism must be destroyed." *Society and Space* (Environment and Planning D) 28: 772–90, 773.
27. *Quadruple Object*, p. 11.
28. In his "On the Undermining of Objects," Latour is said to "undermine" them; this position changes in *Quadruple Object*, p. 12.
29. My thanks to my colleague Jay Foster for several key discussions over this. His "Ontologies without Metaphysics: Latour, Harman, and the Philosophy of Things." *Analecta Hermeneutica* 3 (2012): 1–26, is an excellent discussion of Latour's relationship to Harman's thought.
30. Harman, *Prince of Networks*, p. 14.
31. Ibid., p. 75.
32. Quoted in ibid., p. 64.
33. Ibid., p. 29.
34. See also "I am also of the opinion," p. 773.
35. *Prince of Networks*, p. 111.
36. Ibid., p. 131.
37. *Quadruple Object*, p. 12.
38. That article is available open access at http://www.envplan.com/abstract.cgi?id=d5210 (Last accessed 1 July 2013).
39. Ibid. This is not strictly true, as he notes elsewhere: it is just the case, for him, that the scientific materialism undermines, while the Marxist form does the other.
40. "I am also of the opinion," p. 775.
41. Ibid.
42. *Quadruple Object*, p. 14.
43. Ibid., p. 16.
44. "I am also of the opinion," p. 785. See also Harman, "Intentional Objects for Non-Humans," p. 2.
45. See my "After the Subject" for more on this. Harman makes a similar point in *Philosophy in the Making*, p. 142.
46. Harman, "The Road to Objects." *Continent* 3.1 (2011): 171–9, 172.
47. Ibid., p. 167.
48. *Quadruple Objects*, p. 46.
49. *Philosophy in the Making*, p. 134.
50. *Quadruple Object*, p. 47.

51. Ibid., p. viii.
52. While Stove may be right, his politics were quite reactionary, and his views on women and all manner of post-1960s' progressive movements were infamous. The stink of many such reactionary "realisms" has led many to question the politics of any realisms as just naturalizing the current societal order.
53. James Franklin, "Stove's Discovery of the Worst Argument in the World." *Philosophy* 77 (2002): 615–24, 615. See also Harman, *Quadruple Object*, p. 65.
54. *Quadruple Object*, p. viii.
55. See his discussion of the "*Transcendent* [his emphasis] hammer," *Philosophy in the Making*, 136.
56. "Road to Objects," p. 175.
57. *Philosophy in the Making*, p. 135.
58. Maurice Merleau-Ponty, "Cézanne's Doubt," in *Sense and Non-Sense* (Evanston, IL: Northwestern University Press, 1964), p. 14.
59. *Philosophy in the Making*, p. 136.
60. *Quadruple Object*, p. 75.
61. *Totality and Infinity*, pp. 189, 216.
62. "Intentional Objects for Non-Humans," p. 11.
63. *Quadruple Object*, p. 101.
64. Aristotle, *Categories*, 2b8-11 and 2b28-30.
65. Ibid.
66. "The Road to Objects," p. 176, my emphases.
67. Levi Bryant argues, "Yet where substances perpetually withdraw from other substances and from themselves such that they are characterized by closure, we encounter an ontology adequate to the critique of ontotheology and the metaphysics of presence" (Ibid.). I think he means this in the literal sense that objects are closed off and therefore not present to other objects. But the closure of objects within themselves, such as Leibniz's monadology, is precisely metaphysical in every sense. Moreover, since the term is meant firstly as a critique of a reduction of time to one temporal mode, this avoids the point. In any case, Bryant's writing offers a stunning variety of influences, and readers should attend to his *Democracy of Objects*, where he appends readings of various philosophers onto Harman's edifice.
68. *Quadruple Object*, p. 55.
69. Ibid., p. 57.
70. Heidegger, *Basic Problems of Phenomenology*, trans. A. Hofstadter (Indianapolis, IN: Indiana University Press, 1988), p. 274.
71. Harman, *Prince of Networks*, p. 147.
72. Levi Bryant, *Democracy of Objects* (Michigan: Open Humanities Press, 2011), p. 140.

73. For his discussion of Leibniz, see "Plastic Surgery for the *Monadology*: Leibniz via Heidegger." *Cultural Studies Review* 17.1 (2011): 211–29.
74. Timothy Morton, "Objects as Contemporary Autonomous Zones." *Continent* 1.3 (2011): 149–55, 150–1, my emphasis. Morton's essay is also a very clear introduction to object-oriented philosophy.
75. Harman, *Guerrilla Metaphysics*, p. 5.
76. *Quadruple Object*, p. 29.
77. Ibid., p. 108.
78. Ibid., p. 75.
79. Ibid., p. 111.
80. See *Parmenides*, 130e–133a.
81. This brings us back to the distinction between purely sensuous objects (figures of the imagination such as Popeye) and those that are not purely sensuous (real objects + sensuous qualities). Is there a distinction between a concept and an actual object? Harman doesn't seem to suggest this. But if the "Arab Street" is an object, how can one *know* it has an interiority or withdrawal, if that relation is inaccessible? What distinguishes "the Arab Street" from "Popeye" or imagined beings in this substantial sense? As of his most recent writings, this remains unclear. See his interview, "Marginalia on Radical Thinking: An Interview with Graham Harman," available at http://www.skepoet.wordpress.com/2012/06/01/marginalia-on-radical-thinking-an-interview-with-graham-harman/ (Last accessed 10 June 2013).
82. Timothy Morton suggests "If on the other hand, time is emitted by objects themselves, then it's plausible that an object could emit time in such a way as to influence the past," but it's not clear how they "emit" time, which, recall, for Harman, is only *apparent* and at the level of the *sensuous*, not in the reality of the thing. See http://www.ecologywithoutnature.blogspot.com.au/2011/10/is-causality-symmetrical.html (Last accessed 10 June 2013).
83. *Quadruple Object*, p. 75. See the previous footnote for Morton's elaboration of this "retroactive effect."
84. Graham Harman, "Speculative histories, landscapes and instruments, and Latin American landscape architecture," *faslanyic*, 1 July 2012, at http://www.faslanyc.blogspot.de/2012/07/on-landscape-ontology-interview-with.html?m=1, my emphases (Last accessed 2 July 2013).
85. Harman, "On Vicarious Causation." *Collapse* 2 (2007): 187–221.
86. "The Road to Objects," p. 176.
87. *Quadruple Object*, p. 105.
88. Ibid., p. 107.
89. Ibid., my emphasis.
90. *Philosophy in the Making*, p. viii.
91. *Quadruple Object*, p. 6.

92. A similar impasse occurs in Timothy Morton's excellent overview of object-oriented ontology, *Realist Magic*. In the introduction, Morton writes, "Aesthetic-causal nonlocality and nontemporality should not be surprising features of the Universe. Quantum physics notwithstanding, even electromagnetic fields and gravity waves are nonlocal to some extent [and so on]." Note that he quickly dispatches with how to explain the nonlocal, but one can search the rest of the introduction and the book for an explanation of the nontemporal, except for continued use of the claim. Chapter 3 discusses time at some length, but his attack is on the block universe approach to time, which he thinks is dissolved by Einstein. But the problem is that it provides a space-time where time doesn't matter itself, a problem that Einstein noted in letters to other physicists given subjective notions of time; he thus is a strange ally to say that time on the surface is nontemporal but in objects is some form of emanating temporality. As Lee Smolin notes, "Relativity strongly suggests that the whole history of the world is a timeless unity; past, present, and future have no meaning apart from human subjectivity"(*Time Reborn*, p. xxv).
93. Harman, "Time, Space, Essence, and Eidos: A New Theory of Causation." *Cosmos and History: The Journal of Natural and Social Philosophy* 6.1 (2010): 1–20, 17, my emphases.
94. This, of course, is perhaps tendentious, and as I show, it need not matter.
95. Available at http://www.bogost.com/blog/time_relation_ethics_experienc.shtml (Last accessed 1 September 2013).
96. This is no more apparent than on his oft-updated weblog, http://www.doctor-zamalek2.wordpress.com, where Harman often graciously responds to reader questions and criticisms, as well as offers all manner of writing advice for younger scholars.
97. A project in many ways amenable to my own. See my *The State of Sovereignty: Lessons from the Political Fictions of Modernity* (Albany, NY: SUNY Press, 2012).

Chapter 5

1. Jane Bennett, *Vibrant Matter: A Political Ecology of Things*, p. 6.
2. Paul Crutzen, "The 'Anthropocene'." *Global Change Newsletter* 41.1 (2000): 17–18, 17.
3. Elizabeth Grosz, "Matter, Life, and Other Variations." *Philosophy Today* 55 (2011): 17–27, 17.
4. Bennett, *Vibrant Matter*, p. 122.
5. "Matter, Life, and Other Variations," p. 17.
6. Timothy Morton, *The Ecological Thought* (Cambridge, MA: Harvard University Press, 2010), p. 3.

7. Bennett, *Vibrant Matter*, p. ix.
8. Iain Hamilton Grant, "Mining Conditions: A Response to Harman," p. 46.
9. Grant, *Philosophies of Nature after Schelling*, pp. 199–206.
10. Joseph P. Lawrence, "Review of *On an Artificial Earth: Philosophies of Nature after Schelling*," *Notre Dame Philosophical Reviews* (2007).
11. A claim disputed by Meillassoux. See *After Finitude*, p. 37.
12. Grant, *Philosophies of Nature after Schelling*, p. 30.
13. Lawrence, "Review."
14. An underlying motif in this book is the undersold influence of Schelling and Peirce (the latter of whom was quite influenced by the former) on contemporary realist thinking. I cannot devote much space to their work, but it's notable the number of thinkers, especially graduate students on various weblogs, whose work relates to one of these figures and to reading speculative realism.
15. Grant, *Philosophies of Nature*, p. 101.
16. "Mining Conditions," p. 43.
17. Ibid., p. 45.
18. Ibid., p. 46.
19. F. W. J. Schelling, *First Outline of a System of the Philosophy of Nature*, trans. Keith R. Peterson (Albany, NY: SUNY Press, 2004), p. 5.
20. *Philosophies of Nature after Schelling*, p. 18. We must leave aside the fact that Grant seems to mix together very different moments in Schelling's system, from his earliest writings to his last. For example, in precisely those early works where Schelling discusses nature (as opposed to his later terminology), he speaks of "vital forces," etc. See, e.g., *First Outline*, p. 61.
21. Ibid.
22. Ibid., p. 27.
23. Markus Gabriel, *Transcendental Ontology*, p. 17.
24. Schelling, *First Outline*, p. 13.
25. Devin Shaw, *Freedom and Nature in Schelling's Philosophy of Art* (London: Continuum, 2010), p. 94. Shaw's work is overall an excellent introduction to Schelling's difficult thought.
26. I owe this point to Devin Shaw.
27. For our own reasons of showing a continuity between Schelling and the neo-Spinozist realists such as Grosz and Bennett, we are accenting certain aspects of the early Schelling. Spinoza seems to escape the critique Schelling lodges against all of modern philosophy. Modern philosophers, for him, since Descartes "have not grasped the living center of nature; they only see nature as either a quantity of individual objects, a container, or place for these objects, or as the source of goods to be exploited" (Shaw, *Freedom and Nature*, p. 121).

We should note, however, that despite the consistency of Schelling's critiques of previous ideas of nature, his own concept of nature changes over time, from text to text, and seemingly from one page to the next in some lectures. As Frederick C. Beiser notes, from 1801 to 1806, Schelling presents several competing and even conflicting accounts of the subject-object identity that underpins his absolute idealism: a Spinozist dual-aspect doctrine, a hylozistic interpretation (like Aristotle's), and a Platonic interpretation (Beiser, *German Idealism*, pp. 560–4). Shaw's discussions of nature's productivity, for instance, focus on the Spinozist texts, while Grant prioritizes a Platonist account, though one that is closer to the orbit of Spinozism than the two-world vulgar Platonism.

28. Grant, *Philosophies of Nature*, p. 34.
29. Ibid., p. 43.
30. *Philebus*, 26d8. Cited in "Mining Conditions," p. 46.
31. Ibid., p. 180.
32. For an excellent discussion of this part of German Idealism, see Markus Gabriel's *Transcendental Ontology*, chapter one. In a sense, though Gabriel is explicitly focused on the modes of "access" to the real that would seem to fall to the critiques of Meillassoux and Harman, his point is not to think the world as separable from thought. In fact German Idealism's legacy, pace Meillassoux and Harman, was to think knowledge as ontologically a part of the real, not separate from it. This, then, leads such figures as Schelling and Hegel to ask what would the real have to be like if it is to be able to give itself over to knowledge, which also is very much a real process in the world as such.
33. This is a literal translation of *das Unbedingte*, typically translated as "the unconditional." But for Grant this "unconditional" or absolute is also that which "unthings" any stable things of the world.
34. The ground he is mentioning here, if it is to be reputed to Harman, likely comes from Harman's claim that the universe itself is an object, that is, an object that is the whole within of which all other objects would be a part.
35. Grant, "Mining Conditions," p. 41.
36. I owe this point to Karen Pinkus.
37. Of course not everyone fails to provide such claims. Tim Morton argues that correlationism is the sufficient condition for Nazism. He writes in the closing pages of *Realist Magic*: "Correlationism itself only works if there is some kind of phobia of illusion. So one trajectory of correlationism culminates in Nazism. Correlationism itself is a breeding ground for Nazism, because in order to escape its paradoxes one might retreat still further into an extreme form of anthropocentrism." *Realist Magic* (Michigan: Open Humanities Press, 2013). The book is available open access at http://www.openhumanitiespress.org/realist-magic.html, though without pagination. This is perhaps a good time to call for a moratorium for the moral blackmail that either one agrees with a given position or one accedes to "Nazism."

38. See http://www.doctorzamalek2.wordpress.com/2012/04/14/warren-ellis-on-srooo/ (Last accessed 30 June 2012).
39. For example, see *The Quadruple Object*, pp. 32, 40, 46, 47, 52.
40. Timothy Morton, "Art in the Age of Asymmetry: Hegel, Objects, Aesthetics." *Evental Aesthetics* 1.1 (2012): 121–42, 132–3, my emphases.
41. Levi Bryant, *Democracy of Objects* (Michigan: Michigan University Library's Open Humanities Press, 2011), p. 20.
42. Alexander R. Galloway, "The Poverty of Philosophy and Post-Fordism." *Critical Inquiry* 39 (Winter 2013): 364.
43. Ibid., p. 357.
44. Ibid., p. 366.
45. Frantz Fanon, *Black Skins, White Masks* (New York: Grove Press, 2008), p. 109.
46. Bennett, *Vibrant Matter*, p. 14.
47. Ibid., p. viii.
48. Spinoza, *Ethics*, Part III, preface.
49. Spinoza, *Ethics*, Part I, appendix, 243.
50. Hasana Sharp, *Spinoza and the Politics of Renaturalization* (Chicago, IL: University of Chicago Press, 2011), p. 8.
51. Timothy Morton, *Realist Magic*.
52. See Sharp, *Politics of Renaturalization*, e.g., 133–4, and Bennett, *Vibrant Matter*, pp. 22–3.
53. Ibid., p. 22.
54. Ibid., p. 23.
55. Bennett, *Vibrant Matter*, p. x.
56. Bennett, *Thoreau's Nature* (New York: Rowman and Littlefield Publishers, 2002).
57. Bennett, *Vibrant Matter*, p. 6.
58. See, for example, Deleuze and Guattari, *A Thousand Plateaus: Capitalism and Schizophrenia*, trans. Brian Massumi (Minneapolis, MN: University of Minnesota Press, 1987), p. 88. As they put it:

    > On the one hand [there is] a machinic assemblage of bodies, of actions and passions, an intermingling of bodies reacting to one another; on the other hand it is a collective assemblage of enunciation, of acts and statements, of incorporeal transformations attributed to bodies. Then on a vertical axis, the assemblage has both territorial sides, or reterritorialized sides, which stabilize it, and cutting edges of deterritorialization, which carry it away. (Ibid.)

59. Bennett, *Vibrant Matter*, p. 24.

60. Ibid., p. 34.
61. Ibid., p. 99.
62. Ibid., p. 108.
63. Ibid., p. 118.
64. Ibid., p. 121.
65. Ibid., p. 122.
66. Sharp, *Politics of Renaturalization*, p. 63. See also Bennett, *Vibrant Matter*, p. xiv.
67. Bennett, *Vibrant Matter*, pp. xiv–xv.
68. For different versions of this critique, see Markus Gabriel, "The Meaning of 'Existence' and the Contingency of Sense." *Speculations* 4 (2013): 74–83; and Jon Roffe, "The Future of an Illusion." *Speculations* 4 (2013): 48–52.
69. Elizabeth Grosz, "Matter, Life, and Other Variations." *Philosophy Today* 55 (2011): 17–27, 17.
70. Sara Brill, "The Prosthetic Cosmos: Elizabeth Grosz's Ecology of the Future." *Philosophy Today* 55 (2011): 245–54.
71. Robert Aush, Randal Doane, and Laura Perez, "Interview with Elizabeth Grosz," *Found Object*, p. 9, found at http://www.web.gc.cuny.edu/csctw/found_object/start.htm, 9 (Last accessed 20 June 2013).
72. Sharp, *Politics of Renaturalization*, p. 174.
73. Grosz, "Matter, Life, and Other Variations," p. 18.
74. Elizabeth Grosz, *Chaos, Territory, Art: Deleuze and the Framing of the Earth* (New York: Columbia University Press, 2008), p. 8.
75. Elizabeth Grosz, "Bergson, Deleuze, and the Becoming of Unbecoming." *Parallax* 11.2 (2005): 4–13, 4.
76. Grosz, "Matter, Life, and Other Variations," p. 18.
77. Elizabeth Grosz, *Chaos, Territory, Art: Deleuze and the Framing of the Earth* (New York: Columbia University Press, 2008), p. 100.
78. Grosz, *Nick of Time*, p. 7.
79. Ibid.
80. Ibid., p. 8.
81. Ibid.
82. Ibid., p. 19.
83. Grosz, "Matter, Life, and Other Variations," p. 18.
84. Dorothea Olkowski, "Travels with Darwin." *symbloké* 13.1–2 (2005): 320–9, 322.
85. As she puts it, under "constructivism," "nature came to be understood as timeless, unchanging raw material, somehow dynamized and rendered historical only through the activities of the cultural and psychical orders it generates" (*Nick of Time*, p. 45).

86. Ibid., p. 23.
87. Grosz, *Time Travels*, p. 39.
88. *Nick of Time*, p. 14.
89. Grosz, "Matter, Time, and Other Variations," p. 20.
90. She numbers these slightly differently in *Time Travels*, which I've changed for summary purposes.
91. *Time Travels*, p. 28.
92. Grosz, "A Politics of Imperceptibility." *Philosophy and Social Criticism* 28.4 (2005): 463–72, 471. For an excellent account of this part of Grosz's work, see chapter five of Hasana Sharp's *Spinoza and the Politics of Renaturalization*.
93. Ibid., p. 29.
94. Ibid.
95. Ibid., p. 184. My references to Sharp are not foreign to the concerns of other speculative realists. See Levi Bryant's discussion of Sharp at http://www.larvalsubjects.wordpress.com/2012/06/10/rhetoric-ideology-and-the-ecology-of-ideas-hasana-sharps-spinoza/ (Last accessed 30 June 2013).
96. *Time Travels*, p. 29.
97. Ibid., p. 30.
98. Ibid.
99. Slavoj Žižek, "Trouble in Paradise." *London Review of Books* 35.14 (2013): 11–12.
100. *Time Travels*, p. 31.
101. Ibid.
102. Ibid.
103. Ibid., p. 52.
104. Ibid., p. 135.
105. Ibid., p. 133.
106. Ibid., my emphasis.
107. Ibid., p. 136.
108. Ibid., p. 141.
109. Ibid., p. 144.

Chapter 6

1. Cited in Adrian Johnston, *Prolegomena to Any Future Materialism, Volume 1: The Outcome of Contemporary French Philosophy* (Evanston, IL: Northwestern University Press, 2013), p. 42.

2. Catherine Malabou and Adrian Johnston, *Self and Emotional Life: Philosophy, Psychoanalysis, and Neuroscience* (New York: Columbia University Press, 2013), p. xi.
3. John McCumber relates that in the United States in particular, there is a historical reason as well for a turn in the U.S. to scientificity during the 1950s. Existential, Marxist, and political philosophers were scandalous in an era of McCarthyism, and the scaling back of philosophy to dry science-sounding endeavors was one manner in which to protect the practice of philosophy. While this thesis is contestable and whatever we might think an idealized philosophy would be (would it operate as in 1960s' and 1970s' analytic philosophy? Would it look to be disruptive and historicist as in Continental philosophy? Or, let us not forget, have a wholly different set of methodologies and agendas, as in African or Asian philosophy, for example?), philosophy as a practice is always embedded in given institutions and in relation to cultural practices. See John M. McCumber, *Time in the Ditch: American Philosophy and the McCarthy Era* (Evanston, IL: Northwestern University Press, 2001).
4. Ray Brassier, "Ray Brassier interviewed by Marcin Rychter: I am a nihilist because I still believe in truth," *Kronos* (2011) at http://www.kronos.org.pl/index.php?23151,896 (Last accessed 10 July 2013).
5. The reader will note that I've kept the language of "man" and pronoun "he" in Sellars and Foucault, since it accents questions feminists would and have asked about both figures regarding their model for epistemological rationality.
6. Wilfrid Sellars, "Philosophy and the Scientific Image of Man," in *Science, Perception and Reality* (New York: Ridgeview Publishing Company, 1991), p. 6.
7. Ibid., p. 25.
8. Wolfendale, "The Parting of the Ways: Political Agency between Rational Subjectivity and Phenomenal Selfhood," p. 2. Available at http://www.deontologistics.files.wordpress.com/2012/05/metzinger-paper.pdf (Last accessed 1 September 2013).
9. Sellars discusses Spinoza at "Philosophy and the Scientific Image of Man," p. 8.
10. Ray Brassier, *Nihil Unbound: Enlightenment and Extinction* (London: Palgrave MacMillan, 2007), p. 8.
11. Sellars, "Empiricism and the Philosophy of Mind," §41. Available at http://www.ditext.com/sellars/epm9.html (Last accessed 1 September 2013).
12. Sellars, "Philosophy and the Scientific Image of Man," p. 18.
13. I recognize the profound differences between the two accounts: (1) what Foucault dubs at the empirical does not evenly match what Sellars means by the scientific image, and (2) Sellars would be trapped within this *episteme* for Foucault and Sellars would see Foucault's work as merely another instantiation

of the manifest image. Nevertheless, the similarities in the accounts concerning the end of "transcendental" "man" are anything but superficial.

14. Michel Foucault, *The Order of Things: An Archaeology of the Human Sciences* (New York: Routledge, 1989), p. 387.
15. See Brassier, "Solar Catastrophe: Lyotard, Freud, and the Death Drive." *Philosophy Today* 47.4 (2003): 421–34.
16. See his preface to Thomas Ligotti, *The Conspiracy against the Human Race: A Contrivance of Horror* (New York: Hippocampus Press, 2011).
17. Brassier, *Nihil Unbound*, p. xi.
18. Ibid.
19. Jean-François Lyotard, "Can Thought go on without a Body?," in *The Inhuman*, trans. Rachel Bowlby (Stanford, CA: Stanford University Press, 1992), p. 8.
20. Ibid., p. 9.
21. Ibid.
22. Ibid., p. 10.
23. Meillassoux, *After Finitude*, p. 121.
24. Lyotard, "Can Thought go on without a Body?," p. 10.
25. Ibid., p. 11.
26. *Nihil Unbound*, p. 237.
27. Ibid., p. 238.
28. Ray Brassier, "Philosophy is Not Science's Underlaborer: An Interview with Nikola Andonovski," available at http://www.speculativeheresy.files.wordpress.com/2011/04/brassier-interview-2.pdf, p. 10 (Last accessed July 10 2013).
29. Ray Brassier, "Alien Theory: The Decline of Materialism in the Name of Matter," PhD dissertation, Warwick University, Department of Philosophy (2001), p. 14.
30. This is a point made in Jacques Derrida, *Speech and Phenomena* (Evanston, IL: Northwestern University Press, 1982), where Derrida argues that self-presence, which I take to be a necessary condition for the manifest image, is both the self-evident and the evidence for anything that is considered evident: knowledge must always present itself to thought, or it is not evidence of anything.
31. Catherine Malabou and Adrian Johnston, *Self and Emotional Life: Philosophy, Psychoanalysis, and Neuroscience* (New York: Columbia University Press, 2013), p. 55.
32. Brassier, "Ray Brassier interviewed by Marcin Rychter."
33. Thomas Metzinger, *Being No One: The Self-Model Theory of Subjectivity* (Cambridge, MA: MIT University Press, 2003), p. 16. Metzinger specifically calls on Paul Churchland in the passage cited.
34. Metzinger discusses Sellars' "manifest image" quickly at *Being No One*, p. 190. However Metzinger would think the manifest image but a "folk psychology" without the sophistication Sellars describes.

35. For Graham Harman's critique of Metzinger, in particular his dismissal of objects as a similar conceptual mistake, see "The Problem With Metzinger." *Cosmos and History: The Journal of Natural and Social Philosophy* 7.1 (2011): 7–36. Sellars, for his part, argued, "there are really no such things as the physical objects and processes of the common sense framework" (Wilfrid Sellars, *Philosophical Perspectives* [New York: Ridgeview Publishers, 1967], p. 354.

36. While many have claimed that Metzinger only dispenses with a *cogito* that long ago fell under the knife of Hume, Kant, and Nietzsche, the same claim cannot be made for Brassier, who in coming publications shows how such projects as phenomenology, founded on the transcendental and therefore a *non*-substantial ego, fall under the "Myth of the Given" (Ray Brassier, "The View from Nowhere: Sellars, Habermas, Metzinger," pp. 26–33). In fact, while critiques of the "given" go back to Hegel's sense-certainty (and in fact are central, for example, to Derrida's critique of the transcendental signifier), Brassier shows how Sellars' "myth of the given" can be widely applied beyond the empiricism that was Sellars' target, including the very givenness of the noetico-noema relation central to phenomenology (Brassier, "The View from Nowhere," pp. 26–32).

37. Metzinger, *Being No One*, pp. 549–50.

38. Ibid., p. 337.

39. Wilfrid Sellars, *Empiricism and the Philosophy of Mind* (Cambridge, MA: Harvard University Press, 1997), pp. 75–6.

40. Ibid., p. 558.

41. Thomas Metzinger, *The Ego Tunnel: The Science of the Mind and the Myth of the Self* (New York: Basic Books, 2009), p. 127.

42. Ray Brassier, "The View from Nowhere: Sellars, Habermas, Metzinger," p. 22.

43. Ibid.

44. Ibid., p. 23.

45. At least in the sense of making direct identifications between mental and neurological states. Metzinger's naturalized theory of representation provides distinct levels of internal, mental, and phenomenal representations that are "correlated" to events at the physical level, yet these levels of description are irreducible, since each type of representation has "structural properties and features specific to each" (Ibid., p. 14).

46. Ibid., p. 22.

47. Ibid., p. 24.

48. See Wolfendale, "Ray Brassier," in *The Meillassoux Dictionary* (Edinburgh: Edinburgh University Press, 2014).

49. *Nihil Unbound*, p. 4.

50. Brassier, "View from Nowhere," p. 6, my emphases.

51. Ibid., pp. 4–5.

52. Ibid., p. 5.

53. Ibid., p. 33.
54. Ray Brassier, "Concepts and Objects," *The Speculative Turn*, eds. G. Harman, L. Bryant, and N. Srnicek (Melbourne: Re.Press, 2011), p. 49.
55. Ibid., p. 47.
56. Ibid.
57. Ibid., p. 49.
58. Peter Wolfendale, "Essay on Transcendental Realism," available at http://www.academia.edu/1146988/Essay_on_Transcendental_Realism, p. 11 (Last accessed 11 July 2013).
59. Ray Brassier and Bram Ieven, "Against an Aesthetics of Noise," available at http://www.ny-web.be/transitzone/against-aesthetics-noise.html (Last accessed 11 July 2013).
60. Brassier, "Concepts and Objects," pp. 49–50.
61. Daniel Sacilotto, "Realism and Representation: On the Ontological Turn." *Speculations* 4 (2013): 53–62, 55.

Chapter 7

1. Adrian Johnston, *Badiou, Žižek, and Political Transformations: The Cadence of Political Change* [Evanston, IL: Northwestern University Press, 2009], p. 25.
2. See my "New Directions in the Study of Sartre," in Jack Reynolds, Ashley Woodward, and Felicity Joseph (eds), *Continuum Companion to Existentialism* (London: Bloomsbury Press, 2011).
3. Jean-Paul Sartre, *Search for a Method*, trans. Hazel Barnes (New York: Vintage Books, 1968), p. 30.
4. Ibid., p. 21.
5. Ibid., p. 133.
6. Adrian Johnston, "Points of Forced Freedom: Eleven (More) Theses on Materialism." *Speculations* 4 (2013): 97.
7. It's notable, of course, that Sartre's *Critique of Dialectical Reason* was highly influential over Alain Badiou's early work on subjectivity, which in turn is influential in Johnston's own writings on Badiou. (See especially Adrian Johnston, *Badiou, Žižek, and Political Transformations: The Cadence of Political Change* [Evanston, IL: Northwestern University Press, 2009], pp. 78–81.)
8. "Materialism, Subjectivity, and the Outcome of French Philosophy," p. 174, my emphasis.
9. "Points of Forced Freedom," p. 94.
10. Adrian Johnston, *Prolegomena to Any Future Materialism*, p. 75.
11. Adrian Johnston, *Žižek's Ontology: A Transcendental Materialist Theory of Subjectivity* (Evanston, IL: Northwestern University Press, 2008), p. 102.

12. Ibid.
13. Žižek, *Hegel Book*, p. 555.
14. Johnston, "Materialism, Subjectivity and the Outcome of French Philosophy."
15. Slavoj Žižek, *The Parallax View* (Cambridge, MA: MIT University Press, 2006), p. 205.
16. Johnston, *Žižek's Ontology*, p. 120.
17. Johnston, *Prolegomena*, p. 34.
18. Johnston, *Žižek's Ontology*, p. 286.
19. Johnston, *Badiou, Žižek, and Political Transformations: The Cadence of Change* (Evanston, IL: Northwestern University Press, 2009), pp. 286–7.
20. Ibid., p. xxviii.
21. Ibid., pp. 21–30.
22. Cited at Ibid., p. 13.
23. Ibid., p. 30.
24. Ibid., p. 59.
25. Ibid., pp. 57–9.
26. Ibid., p. 79.
27. Ibid., p. 78.
28. Ibid., pp. 78–9, my emphasis.
29. Johnston, *Prolegomena*, p. 24.
30. Johnston, "Materialism, Subjectivity, and the Outcome of Philosophy."
31. Johnston, "Points of Forced Freedom," p. 96.
32. See Žižek, *Parallax View*, pp. 369–71.
33. Ibid., p. 370. See, e.g., G. W. F. Hegel, *The Science of Logic*, trans. G. di Giovanni (Cambridge: Cambridge University Press, 2010), p. 472.
34. Johnston, "Materialism, Subjectivity, and the Outcome of Philosophy."
35. Michael Marder, *Plant-Thinking: A Philosophy of Vegetal Life* (New York: Columbia University Press), pp. 2–3.
36. Ibid., p. 42.
37. In *The Animal that Therefore I am*, Derrida argued neither for continuinism nor absolute divergence between animal and human life, deconstructing the human-animal distinction while testifying to the specificity of particular animals, including the animal that the human is. Such a lack of subtle differentiation is seemingly lost in Marder's account, as can be seen when he links the neo-Platonism to capitalist accumulation and the degradation of the environment. But this fails to see the post-Cartesian view of nature as fundamentally different from neo-Platonic accounts (a point Marder himself suggests in his work on Plotinus). But it's also the case that capitalism does not simply spring from Western metaphysics, not least because capitalism shares a nihilist equation of everything that is foreign to neo-Platonic transcendentalism. As in many things, this quasi-Heideggerian

philosophical determinism—violence of metaphysics can only end in actual violence unleashed upon the world—makes for history reduced to an idea.

38. See for example, ibid., pp. 21, 149.
39. Johnston, "Points of Forced Freedom," p. 96.
40. Ibid., p. 93.
41. Johnston, *Prolegomena*, p. 34.
42. Ibid.
43. Ibid., p. 64.
44. Ibid., p. 34.
45. Ibid., p. 37, my emphases.
46. Ibid., p. 25.
47. Johnston/Malabou, *Self and Emotional Life*, p. 204. Repeated at *Prolegomena*, p. 57.
48. *Prolegomena*, p. 22.
49. Ibid., p. 53.
50. Ibid., p. 57.
51. Ibid., p. 53.
52. Ibid., p. 180.
53. Ibid., p. 57.
54. Ibid., p. 26.
55. Ibid., p. 209.
56. Johnston, "Points of Forced Freedom," p. 96.
57. Ibid.
58. Ibid.
59. See *Prolegomena*, p. 193.
60. Ibid., p. 188.
61. Johnston, "Materialism, Subjectivity, and the Outcome of French Philosophy."
62. Ibid.
63. Johnston/Malabou, *Self and Emotional Life*, p. 204.
64. Johnston, *Time Driven*, pp. 340–1.

Chapter 8

1. Johnston's introduction to *Self and Emotional Life* goes over well the differences between the two.
2. Catherine Malabou, *The New Wounded: From Neurosis to Brain Damage*, trans. Steven Miller (New York: Fordham University Press, 2012), p. xv.

3. See, for example, her contribution to *Self and Emotional Life*, especially Chapter 7.
4. "Interview with Catherine Malabou," available at http://www.groundwork-philosophy.wordpress.com/2012/02/17/interview-with-catherine-malabou/ (Last accessed 1 September 2013).
5. Sarah Kizuk raises good questions about this in her review of *Changing Difference* in *Society and Space*. See http://www.societyandspace.com/reviews/reviews-archive/malabou_kizuk/ (Last accesses 1 September 2013). The problem in general is that Malabou revisits few works in recent feminist discourses, which has dealt widely with essentialism and anti-essentialism in ways that have changed ontological discussions of this topic beyond and still alongside supposed "feminist" concerns.
6. Catherine Malabou and Noël Vahanian, "A Conversation with Catherine Malabou." *Journal for Cultural and Religious Theory* 9.1 (2008): 1–13.
7. See Ian James, *The New French Philosophy* (London: Polity, 2012), pp. 83–109.
8. *The New Wounded*, p. xix.
9. Ibid.
10. Ibid.
11. Malabou, *The Heidegger Change*, trans. Peter Skafish (New York: SUNY Press, 2004), pp. 279–85.
12. See *Plasticity at the Dusk of Writing*, for example.
13. Catherine Malabou, *What Should We Do with Our Brain?*, trans. Sebastian Rand (New York: Fordham University Press, 2008), pp. 17–26.
14. Catherine Malabou, *The Future of Hegel: Plasticity, Temporality and Dialectic*, trans. L. During (London: Routledge, 2004), p. 9.
15. Malabou quotes Marx's dictum at the beginning of her introduction to *What should We do with our Brain?*, p. 1.
16. Ian James, *The New French Philosophy*, p. 107.
17. See Malabou, *Ontology of the Accident*, pp. 99–105.
18. Catherine Malabou, *Self and Emotional Life*, pp. 27–8.
19. Catherine Malabou, *The New Wounded*, p. 48.
20. Ibid., p. 34.
21. Malabou, *Plasticity at the Dusk of Writing*, p. 57.
22. Ibid., p. 13.
23. Ibid., p. 59.
24. Malabou, *Brain?*, p. 6.
25. Malabou, *Plasticity at the Dusk of Writing*, p. 60.
26. Ibid., p. 59.
27. Ibid., p. 81.
28. *Brain?*, p. 12.

29. Catherine Malabou and Noëlle Vahanian, "A Conversation with Catherine Malabou." *Journal for Cultural and Religious Theory* 9.1 (Winter 2008): 1–13, 6.
30. Jacques Derrida, *Of Grammatology*, trans. G. Spivak (Baltimore: The Johns Hopkins University Press, 1977), p. 4.
31. *Brain?*, p. 6.
32. *EW*, p. 434.
33. Ibid., p. 431.
34. Ibid., p. 427.
35. *PDW*, p. 50.
36. Derrida's most sustained discussion of form is to be found in "Form and Meaning: A Note on the Phenomenology of Language," *Margins of Philosophy*, trans. Alan Bass (Chicago, IL: University of Chicago Press, 1982).
37. "*Différance*," Margins *of Philosophy*, trans. Alan Bass (Chicago, IL: University of Chicago Press, 1982), p. 13.
38. Catherine Malabou, *The New Wounded*, p. xii.
39. Catherine Malabou, *Self and Emotional Life*, p. 72.
40. Catherine Malabou, *The New Wounded*, p. 9.
41. Ibid., p. 17.
42. Ibid., p. xviii.
43. Stacey Smith, "Review of *Ontology of the Accident*," available at http://societyandspace.com/reviews/reviews-archive/malabou_smith/ (Last accessed 1 September 2013).
44. Catherine Malabou, *Self and Emotional Life*, p. 29.
45. Catherine Malabou, *The New Wounded*, p. 211.
46. Ibid., p. 205.
47. Ibid.
48. Ibid.
49. For a summary of these, see my *The State of Sovereignty*, pp. 138–41.
50. Hannah Proctor, "Neuronal Ideologies: Catherine Malabou's Explosive Plasticity in Light of the Marxist Psychology of A. R. Luria." *Dandelion* 2.1 (2011), available at http://www.dandelionjournal.org/index.php/dandelion/article/view/24/81 (Last accessed 1 September 2013).
51. Michel Foucault, "What is Enlightenment?," in Paul Rabinow (ed.), *The Foucault Reader* (New York: Pantheon Books, 1984), pp. 32–50, 45.
52. Malabou, *Brain?*, pp. 1–12. Malabou's repeated refrain in those pages is that we have a brain and do not know it, yet, by repeating this, the text itself can only be

announcing that it does have this knowledge, one the book is meant to impart to those with the brains to understand it.

53. Ibid., p. 3.
54. Malabou, Catherine and Xavier Emmanuelli, *La grande exclusion: L'urgence sociale, symptôme et thérapeutique* (Paris: Bayard, 2009), p. 37.
55. Paul Gilroy, *After Empire: Melancholia or Convivial Culture* (London: Routledge, 2004).
56. In this, Malabou is not alone: in the past decade, Julia Kristeva, Giorgio Agamben, and Bernard Stiegler have all published works that discuss popular "docility" specifically as it links to the faculties of the mind. See my *The State of Sovereignty*, pp. 188–9.
57. Malabou, *Brain?*, p. 11.
58. Ibid., p. 46.
59. Thomas Friedman, "How to Get A Job," *New York Times*, 29 May 2013, A23.
60. Thomas Friedman, "The Internship: Not the Movie," *New York Times*, 9 June 2013, SR11.
61. Malabou, *What should we do with our Brain?*, p. 46.
62. Ibid., p. 9.
63. *New Spirit of Capitalism* (London: Verso, 2006), p. 149.
64. Catherine Malabou, *Plasticity at the Dusk of Writing*, p. 57, my emphasis.
65. Ibid., pp. 70–1.
66. "A Conversation with Catherine Malabou," p. 11.
67. Ibid.
68. "Interview with Catherine Malabou."

Time for a Conclusion

1. Janicaud, *Chronos: Pour l'intelligence du partage temporal* (Paris: Grasset, 1997), p. 43.
2. For a clear survey of these views, see Chapter 4, "Does Time Pass?," in Adrian Bardon (ed.), *A History of the Philosophy of Time* (Oxford: Oxford University Press, 2013).
3. *Time Reborn*, pp. 3–24.
4. Paul Davies, "The Mysterious Flow of Time," *Scientific American* (September 2002), p. 36.
5. Sellars, "Time and World Order," in H. Feigl and G. Maxwell (eds), *Minnesota Studies in the Philosophy of Science*, Vol. III (Minneapolis: University of Minnesota Press, 1962), pp. 527–616.

6. If the language is strong here, I invite you to read the work of popular explainers of physics on the notion of time: the human who thinks in such a way is always portrayed as the rube to be enlightened, and yet, as Adrian Johnston remarks about Metzinger: why is it that these illusions remain so implacable?
7. Readers will note that I'm leaving aside the work of Gilles Deleuze. It's true that Deleuze argues for what can be called a temporal realism in his works of the 1960s but my task here is to show the non-correlationism of those most castigated by the speculative realists.
8.

> Peirce's semiology constitutes a rejection of Saussure: because Saussure's structuralism operates only in terms of a binary or dyadic relation of signifier (words) and signified (concepts), his account of communication is nominalist (concepts say nothing about the world) and subjective-idealist (communication is a matter of linguistic structures alone). Deconstruction takes this subjective idealism to its extreme limit by treating communication as nothing more than *the differential plurality of signifiers* [my emphasis]—a paradoxical form of monism. Jim Bradley, "Beyond Hermeneutics," p. 56.

9. Jacques Derrida, *Of Grammatology*, trans. Gayatri Spivak (Baltimore: Johns Hopkins University Press, 1976), p. 158.
10. Lee Braver, *Thing of this World* (Evanston, IL: Northwestern University Press, 2007), p. 495.
11. See Braver's discussion in *Thing of This World*, pp. 464–6.
12. Clearly here I am privileging the temporal, though Derrida would rightly note that *différance* is temporal-spatial, or the opening of the temporal-spatial. But this "momentary" privileging of a "real temporalization" in Derrida's text is meant—as Derrida often did himself—to overturn a thinking that emphasizes the spatiality of the *topos* in Heidegger and the textual readings of his own texts.
13. Derrida, *Limited Inc.*, trans. Samuel Weber (Evanston, IL: Northwestern University Press, 1988), p. 137.
14. Derrida, "As If It Were Possible, 'Within Such Limits' . . ." *Negotiations: Interviews and Interviews*, trans. Elizabeth Rottenberg (Stanford, CA: Stanford University Press, 2002). See also Derrida, *Séminaire: La bête et le souverain: Vol. 1 (2001–2002)* (Paris: Éditions Galilée, 2008), p. 113.
15. For an excellent discussion of this latter claim, see Jack Reynold's "Analytic and Continental Philosophy: A Contretemps" in his *Chronopathologies: Time and Politics in Deleuze, Derrida, Analytic Philosophy, and Phenomenology* (London: Lexington Books, 2012), pp. 17–34.
16. Huw Price, *Time's Arrow and Archimedes' Point: New Directions for the Physics of Time* (Oxford: Oxford University Press, 1996), pp. 3–18.

17. Heidegger, *On Time and Being*, trans. Joan Stambaugh (New York: Harper and Row, 1972), p. 5.
18. Emmanuel Levinas, *God, Death, and Time*, trans. Bettina Bergo (Stanford, CA: Stanford University Press, 2000), p. 115.
19. Of course, we must recognize a Plato beyond or before Platonism, while demonstrating the historical-philosophical effects of a Platonism beyond the letter and the page of Plato's texts. Such a reading would begin at the beginning of Plato, namely in the *Timaeus* with the (non)place and (non)time of the *khora*, which is neither sensible nor intelligible and thus is irreducible to what gets named Platonism.
20. Augustine, *Confessions*, trans. William Watts (Cambridge, MA: Harvard University Press [Loeb edition], 1912), Book xi, Chapter xiv, translation adjusted slightly.
21. *Hamlet*, act I, scene v, 189–90.
22. Jacques Derrida, "*Différance*," *Margins of Philosophy*, trans. Alan Bass (Chicago, IL: University of Chicago Press, 1979), p. 19.
23. Heidegger, "Time and Being," p. 8.
24. Derrida, "*Ousia* and *Grammē*," *Margins of Philosophy*, p. 59.
25. Derrida is thinking of Aristotle's *Physics* (217b-18a): "Some of it has been and is not, some of it is to be and is not yet. From these both infinite time [*apeiros*] and time in its incessant return are composed. But it would seem to be impossible that what is composed of things that are not should participate in being [*ousia*]."
26. Derrida, *Given Time: I Counterfeit Money*, trans. Peggy Kamuf (Chicago, IL: University of Chicago Press, 1992), p. 28.
27. Derrida, "*Ousia* and *Grammē*," pp. 66–7.
28. Derrida, *Of Grammatology*, p. 86.
29. Derrida, "*Différance*," p. 8.
30. Ibid.
31. Derrida, *Of Grammatology*, p. 5.

BIBLIOGRAPHY

Agamben, Giorgio (2000), *Potentialities: Collected Essays in Philosophy*, trans. Daniel Heller-Roazen. Stanford, CA: Stanford University Press.

Augustine (1912), *Confessions*, Vol. 2: Books 9–13. Cambridge, MA: Harvard University Press.

Aush, Robert, Randal Doane, and Laura Perez, "Interview with Elizabeth Grosz." *Found Object*, p. 9, found at http://web.gc.cuny.edu/csctw/found_object/start.htm, 9 (Last accessed 30 June 2013).

Badiou, Alain (2005), *Being and Event*. Trans. Oliver Feltham. London: Continuum.

—(2011), "Interview with Alain Badiou," in G. Harman, N. Srncek, and L. Bryant (eds), *The Speculative Turn*. Melbourne: Re.Press.

Bennett, Jane (2002), *Thoreau's Nature*. New York: Rowman and Littlefield Publishers.

—(2010), *Vibrant Matter: A Political Ecology of Things*. New York: Duke University Press.

Berkeley, George (1999), *Principles of Human Knowledge: Three Dialogues*. London: Oxford University Press.

Bernet, Rudolf (2006), "Levinas's Critique of Husserl," in Simon Critchley and Robert Bernasconi (eds), *Cambridge Companion to Levinas*. Cambridge: Cambridge University Press.

Blattner, William (1999), *Heidegger's Temporal Idealism*. Cambridge: Cambridge University Press.

Brassier, Ray (2001), "Alien Theory: The Decline of Materialism in the Name of Matter," PhD dissertation, Warwick University, Department of Philosophy.

—(2003), "Solar Catastrophe: Lyotard, Freud, and the Death Drive." *Philosophy Today* 47(4): 421–34.

—(2007), *Nihil Unbound: Enlightenment and Extinction*. New York: Palgrave Macmillan.

—(2010), Bram Ieven, "Against an Aesthetics of Noise," available at http://ny-web.be/transitzone/against-aesthetics-noise.html (Last accessed 11 July 2013).

—(2011a), "Concepts and Objects," in Levi Bryant, Nick Srnicek and Graham Harman (eds), *The Speculative Turn*. Melbourne: Re.Press, pp. 47–65.

—(2011b), "Philosophy is Not Science's Underlaborer: An Interview with Nikola Andonovski," available at http://speculativeheresy.files.wordpress.com/2011/04/brassier-interview-2.pdf, p. 10 (Last accessed 10 July 2013).

—(2011c), "Preface," in Thomas Ligotti (ed.), *The Conspiracy against the Human Race: A Contrivance of Horror*. New York: Hippocampus Press, pp. 1–7.

—(2011d), "Ray Brassier interviewed by Marcin Rychter: I am a nihilist because I still believe in truth," *Kronos*, available at http://www.kronos.org.pl/index.php?23151,896 (Last accessed 10 July 2013).

—(2012), "The View from Nowhere: Sellars, Habermas, Metzinger," "Myth of the Given," provided to author.

Braver, Lee (2007), *A Thing of this World*. Evanston, IL: Northwestern University Press.

Brill, Sara (2011), "The Prosthetic Cosmos: Elizabeth Grosz's Ecology of the Future." *Philosophy Today* 55: 245–54.

Brown, Nathan (2011), "The Speculative and the Specific: On Hallward and Meillassoux," in G. Harman, N. Srncek, and L. Bryant (eds), *The Speculative Turn*. Melbourne: Re.Press, pp. 142–62.

Bryant, Levi (2010), "Lexicon of Onticology," available at http://larvalsubjects.wordpress.com/2010/05/22/a-lexicon-of-onticology/ (Last accessed 1 September 2013).

—(2011), *Democracy of Objects*. Michigan: Michigan University Library's Open Humanities Press.

Cerbone, Michael (1995), "World, World-Entry, and Realism in Early Heidegger." *Inquiry* 38: 401–21.

Coole, Diana and Samantha Frost (eds) (2010), *New Materialisms: Ontology, Agency, and Politics*. Durham, NC: Duke University Press.

Crutzen, Paul (2000), "The 'Anthropocene.'" *Global Change Newsletter* 41(1): 17–18.

Davies, Paul (September 2002), "The Mysterious Flow of Time." *Scientific American*, p. 36.

Deleuze, G. and F. Guattari (1987), *A Thousand Plateaus: Capitalism and Schizophrenia*. Trans. Brian Massumi. Minneapolis, MN: University of Minnesota Press.

Derrida, Jacques (1967), *De la Grammatologie*. Paris: Éditions de Minuit. English translation by Gyatri Spivak. 1998. Of Grammatology. Corrected ed. Baltimore, MD: Johns Hopkins University Press.

—(1973), *Speech and Phenomena*. Trans. David Allison. Evanston, IL: Northwestern University Press.

—(1982a), "Différance," in *Margins of Philosophy*. Trans. Alan Bass. Chicago, IL: University of Chicago Press, pp. 1–27.

—(1982b), "Form and Meaning: A Note on the Phenomenology of Language," in *Margins of Philosophy*. Trans. Alan Bass. Chicago, IL: University of Chicago Press, pp. 155–74.

—(1982c), "*Ousia* and *Grammē*," in *Margins of Philosophy*. Trans. Alan Bass. Chicago, IL: University of Chicago Press, pp. 29–67.

—(2001), *The Work of Mourning*. Trans. Michael Naas and Pascale-Anne Brault. Chicago: University of Chicago Press.

—(2003), *Chaque fois unique, la fin du monde*. Eds. Pascale-Anne Brault and Michael Naas. Paris: Editions Galilée.

Dummett, Michael (1981), *The Interpretation of Frege's Philosophy*. Cambridge, MA: Harvard University Press.

—(1982), "Realism." *Synthese* 52: 55–112.
Ennis, Paul J. (2011), *Continental Realism*. Winchester, UK: Zero Books.
Fanon, Frantz (2008), *Black Skins, White Masks*. New York: Grove Press.
Fish, William (2010), *A Philosophy of Perception: A Contemporary Introduction*. London: Routledge.
Foster, Jay (2012), "Ontologies without Metaphysics: Latour, Harman, and the Philosophy of Things." *Analecta Hermeneutica* 3: 1–26.
Foucault, Michel (1984), "What is Enlightenment?," in Paul Rabinow (ed.), *The Foucault Reader*. New York: Pantheon Books, pp. 32–50.
—(1989), *The Order of Things: An Archaeology of the Human Sciences*. New York: Routledge.
Franklin, James (2002), "Stove's Discovery of the Worst Argument in the World." *Philosophy* 77: 615–24.
Friedman, Thomas, "How to Get A Job." *New York Times*, 29 May 2013, A23.
—, "The Internship: Not the Movie." *New York Times*, 9 June 2013, SR11.
Gabriel, Markus (2011), *Transcendental Ontology: Essays in German Idealism*. London: Continuum.
—(2013), "The Meaning of 'Existence' and the Contingency of Sense." *Speculations* 4: 74–83.
Galloway, Alexander R. (2013), "The Poverty of Philosophy and Post-Fordism." *Critical Inquiry* 39: pp. 347–66.
Gilroy, Paul (2004), *After Empire: Melancholia or Convivial Culture*. London: Routledge.
Grant, Iain Hamilton (2008), *Philosophies of Nature after Schelling*. London: Continuum.
—(2011), "Mining Conditions: A Response to Harman," in *Speculative Turn*, pp. 41–6.
Gratton, Peter (2009), "Review of *After Finitude*." *Philosophy in Review* 29(6).
—(2011), "New Directions in the Study of Sartre," in Jack Reynolds, Ashley Woodward, and Felicity Joseph (eds), *Continuum Companion to Existentialism*. London: Bloomsbury Press.
—(2012a), "Review of *Spinoza and the Politics of Renaturalization*," in *Society and Space*. Available at http://societyandspace.com/reviews/reviews-archive/hasana-sharp-spinoza-and-the-politics-of-renaturalization-reviewed-by-peter-gratton/ (Last accessed 1 June 2013).
—(2012b), "The Speculative Challenge and Post-Deconstructive Realism," in Peter Gratton and Marie-Eve Morin (eds), *Jean-Luc Nancy and Plural Thinking*. Albany, NY: SUNY Press, pp. 109–28.
—(2012c), *The State of Sovereignty: Lessons from the Political Fictions of Modernity*. Albany, NY: SUNY Press.
Grosz, Elizabeth (2005a), "Bergson, Deleuze, and the Becoming of Unbecoming." *Parallax* 11(2): 4–13.
—(2005b), "A Politics of Imperceptibility." *Philosophy and Social Criticism* 28(4): 463–72.
—(2008), *Chaos, Territory, Art: Deleuze and the Framing of the Earth*. New York: Columbia University Press.

—(2011), "Matter, Life, and Other Variations." *Philosophy Today* 55: 17–27.

Hacking, Ian (2000), *The Social Construction of What?*. Cambridge, MA: Harvard University Press.

Hallett, Michael (1986), *Cantorian Set Theory and Limitation of Size*. Oxford: Clarendon.

Hallward, Peter (2008), "Anything Is Possible: Book Review of *After finitude* by Quentin Meillassoux." *Radical Philosophy* 152: 56–7.

Harman, Graham (2002), *Tool-Being: Heidegger and the Metaphysics of Objects*. Chicago, IL: Open Court Press.

—(2005), *Guerrilla Metaphysics: Phenomenology and the Carpentry of Things*. Chicago, IL: Open Court Press.

—(2007), "On Vicarious Causation." *Collapse* 2: 187–221.

—(2009), "Levinas and the Triple Critique of Heidegger." *Philosophy Today* 53(4): 407–13.

—(2010a), "Time, Space, Essence, and Eidos: A New Theory of Causation." *Cosmos and History: The Journal of Natural and Social Philosophy* 6(1): 1–20.

—(2010b), *Toward Speculative Realism: Essays and Lectures*. Washington, DC: Zero Books.

—(2011a), "I am also of the opinion that materialism must be destroyed." *Society and Space* (Environment and Planning D) 28: 772–90.

—(2011b), "Plastic Surgery for the *Monadology*: Leibniz via Heidegger." *Cultural Studies Review* 17(1): 211–29.

—(2011c), "The Problem with Metzinger." *Cosmos and History: The Journal of Natural and Social Philosophy* 7(1): 7–36.

—(2011d), *The Quadruple Object*. Washington, DC: Zero Books.

—(2011e), *Quentin Meillassoux: Philosophy in the Making*. Edinburgh: Edinburgh University Press.

—(2011f), "The Road to Objects." *Continent* 3(1): 171–9.

—(2012a), "Marginalia on Radical Thinking: An Interview with Graham Harman," available at http://skepoet.wordpress.com/2012/06/01/marginalia-on-radical-thinking-an-interview-with-graham-harman/ (Last accessed 10 June 2013).

—(2012b), "On Interface: Nancy's Weights and Masses," in Marie-Eve Morin and Peter Gratton (eds), *Jean-Luc Nancy and Plural Thinking Expositions of World, Ontology, Politics, and Sense*. Albany, NY: SUNY Press, pp. 95–108.

—(2012c), "Speculative histories, landscapes and instruments, and Latin American landscape architecture," *faslanyic*, 1 July 2012, available at http://faslanyc.blogspot.de/2012/07/on-landscape-ontology-interview-with.html?m=1 (Last accessed 2 July 2013).

—(2013), "The Current State of Speculative Realism." *Speculations* 4: 26–8.

Hegel, G. W. F. (2010), *The Science of Logic*. Trans. G. di Giovanni. Cambridge: Cambridge University Press.

Heidegger, Martin (1962), *Being and Time*. Trans. John Macquarrie and Edward Robinson. San Franciso, CA: Harper & Row. Published in German as *Sein und Zeit*, 7th edn. Tübingen: Neomarius Verlag, 2001.

—(1969), "The Onto-Theo-Logical Constitution of Metaphysics," in *Identity and Difference*. Trans. Joan Stambaugh, New York: Harper & Row.

—(1971), "The Thing," in *Poetry, Language, Thought*. Trans. A. Hostadter. New York: Harper & Row.

—(1988), *The Basic Problems of Phenomenology*. Trans. Albert Hofstadter. Bloomington: Indiana University Press.

—(1995), *The Fundamental Concepts of Metaphysics: World, Finitude, Solitude*. Trans. William McNeill and Nicholas Walker. Bloomington: Indiana University Press. Originally published as *Die Grundbegriffe der Metaphysik. Welt—Endlichkeit—Einsamkeit*. Frankfurt am Main: Vittorio Klostermann, 1992.

—(2005), "*Einblick in das was ist. Bremer Vorträge*," in *Gesamtausgabe 79*, 2nd edn. Frankfurt am Main: Vittorio Klosterman.

—(2008), "Introduction to 'What is Metaphysics?'," in *Pathmarks*. Trans. William McNeill. Cambridge: Cambridge University Press.

Hume, David (1992), *A Treatise on Human Nature*. Oxford: Oxford University Press.

Husserl, Edmund (1981), "'Phenomenology', Edmund Husserl's Article for the *Encyclopaedia Britannica*," in Peter McCormick and Frederick A. Elliston (eds), *Husserl: Shorter Works*. Notre Dame, IN: University of Notre Dame Press, pp. 21–35.

—(1983), *Ideas Pertaining to a Pure Phenomenology and to a Phenomenological Philosophy, First Book: General Introduction to a Pure Phenomenology*. Trans. F. Kersten. The Hague: Martinus Nijhoff.

Janicaud, Dominique (1997), Chronos, pour l'intelligence du partage temporel. Paris: Grasse.

Johnston, Adrian (2005), *Time Driven: Metapsychology and the Splitting of the Drive*. Evanston, IL: Northwestern University Press, 2007.

—(2008), *Zizek's Ontology: A Transcendental Materialist Theory of Subjectivity*. Evanston, IL: Northwestern University Press.

—(2009a), *Badiou, Žižek, and Political Transformations: The Cadence of Political Change*. Evanston, IL: Northwestern University Press.

—(2009b), "The World before Worlds: Quentin Meillassoux and Alain Badiou's Anti-Kantian Transcendentalism." *Contemporary French Civilization* 33(1): 73–99.

—(2011a), "Hume's Revenge: à Dieu, Meillassoux?," in Levi Bryant, Nick Srnicek and Graham Harman (eds), *The Speculative Turn*. Melbourne: Re.Press, pp. 92–113.

—(2011b), "Materialism, Subjectivity, and the Outcome of French Philosophy." *Cosmos and History: The Journal of Natural and Social Philosophy* 7(1): 167–81.

—(2013a), "Points of Forced Freedom: Eleven (More) Theses on Materialism." *Speculations* 4: pp. 91–9.

—(2013b), *Prolegomena to Any Future Materialism, Volume 1: The Outcome of Contemporary French Philosophy*. Evanston, IL: Northwestern University Press.

Kant, Immanuel (1996), *Critique of Pure Reason*. Trans. Werner S. Pluhar. New York: Hackett.

Kearney, Richard (2001), *The God Who May Be: A Hermeneutics of Religion*. Indianapolis, IN: Indiana University Press.

Kizuk, Sarah (2013), "Review of *Changing Difference*," *Society and Space*. Available at http://societyandspace.com/reviews/reviews-archive/malabou_kizuk/ (Last accessed 1 September 2013).

Landes, Donald A. (2013), *Merleau-Ponty and the Paradoxes of Expression*. London: Bloomsbury.

Lawrence, J. P. (2007), "Review of *On an Artificial Earth: Philosophies of Nature after Schelling*," *Notre Dame Philosophical Reviews*, available at https://ndpr.nd.edu/news/25292-on-an-artificial-earth-philosophies-of-nature-after-schelling/ (Last accessed 20 February 2014).

Levinas, Emmanuel (1972), *Totality and Infinity: An Essay on Exteriority*. Trans. A. Lingis. Pittsburgh, PA: Duquesne University Press.

Lingis, Alphonso (2007), "Detotalization and Finitude." *Philosophy Today* 51(2): 152–8.

—(2009), "The Voice of Things." *Senses and Society* 4(3): 273–82.

Lyotard, Jean-François (1992), "Can Thought go on without a Body?," in *The Inhuman*. Trans. Rachel Bowlby. Stanford, CA: Stanford University Press.

Malabou, Catherine (2004), *The Heidegger Change*. Trans. Peter Skafish. New York: SUNY Press.

—(2005), *The Future of Hegel: Plasticity, Temporality and Dialectic*. Trans. Lisabeth During. London: Routledge.

—(2008), *What Should We Do with Our Brain?*. Trans. Sebastian Rand. New York: Fordham University Press.

—(2010), *Plasticity at the Dusk of Writing: Dialectic, Destruction, Deconstruction*. Trans. Carolyn Shread. New York: Columbia University Press.

—(2012a), "Interview with Catherine Malabou," available at http://groundwork-philosophy.wordpress.com/2012/02/17/interview-with-catherine-malabou/ (Last accessed 1 September 2013).

—(2012b), *The New Wounded: From Neurosis to Brain Damage*. Trans. Steven Miller. New York: Fordham University Press.

Malabou, Catherine and Adrian Johnston (2013), *Self and Emotional Life: Philosophy, Psychoanalysis, and Neuroscience*. New York: Columbia University Press.

Malabou, Catherine and Noël Vahanian (2008), "A Conversation with Catherine Malabou." *Journal for Cultural and Religious Theory* 9(1): 1–13.

Malabou, Catherine and Xavier Emmanuelli (2009), *La grande exclusion: L'urgence sociale, symptôme et thérapeutique*. Paris: Bayard.

Marder, Michael (2013), *Plant-Thinking: A Philosophy of Vegetal Life*. New York: Columbia University Press.

McCumber, John M. (2001), *Time in the Ditch: American Philosophy and the McCarthy Era*. Evanston, IL: Northwestern University Press.

McDowell, John (1996), *Mind and World*, 2nd edn. Cambridge, MA: Harvard University Press.

McNeill, William (1997), *Glance of the Eye*. Albany, NY: SUNY Press.

Meillassoux, Quentin (2007), "Potentiality and Virtuality," in Robin Mackay (ed.), *Collapse Volume II: Speculative Realism*. Oxford: Urbanomic, pp. 55–81.

—(2008a), *After Finitude. An Essay on the Necessity of Contingency*. Trans. Ray Brassier. London: Continuum.

—(2008b), "Spectral Dilemma," in Robin Mackay (ed.), *Collapse Volume IV: Concept Horror*. Falmouth: Urbanomic, pp. 261–75.

—(2008c), "Time without Becoming," lecture at Middlesex University, London, 8 May 2008. Accessed at http://speculativeheresy.wordpress.com/resources/, p. 1 (1 May 2013).

—(2010), "The Immanence of the World Beyond," in Connor Cunningham and Peter Candler (eds), *The Grandeur of Reason: Religion, Tradition, and Universalism*. London: SCM Press, pp. 444–78.

—(2011a), "Continency & Absolutization of the One," lecture delivered at the Sorbonne, Trans. Benjamin James Lozano. Accessed at http://speculativeheresy.files.wordpress.com/2011/03/contingency-and-absolutization-of-the-one.pdf, p. 6 (1 May 2012).

—(2011b), "Excerpt from *Divine Inexistence*," in Graham Harman (ed.), *Quentin Meillassoux: Philosophy in the Making*. Edinburgh: Edinburgh University Press.

—(2012), "Iteration, Reiteration, Repetition: A Speculative Analysis of the Meaningless Sign," Paper presented at the Freie Universität, Berlin, Germany, 20 April 2012. Available at oursecretblog.com/txt/QMpaperApr12.pdf (Last accessed 1 September 2013).

Merleau-Ponty, Maurice (1964), "Cézanne's Doubt," in *Sense and Non-Sense*. Evanston, IL: Northwestern University Press.

—(1968), *The Visible and the Invisible*. Trans. Alphonso Lingis. Evanston, IL: Northwestern University Press.

—(2013), *Phenomenology of Perception*, trans. Donald Landes. London: Routledge.

Metzinger, Thomas (2003), *Being No One: The Self-Model Theory of Subjectivity*. Cambridge, MA: MIT Press.

—(2009), *The Ego Tunnel: The Science of the Mind and the Myth of the Self*. New York: Basic Books.

Morin, Marie-Eve (2014), "Martin Heidegger," in Peter Gratton and Paul Ennis (eds), *The Meillassoux Dictionary*. Edinburgh University Press.

Morton, Timothy (2010), *The Ecological Thought*. Cambridge, MA: Harvard University Press.

—(2011), "Objects as Contemporary Autonomous Zones." *Continent* 1(3): 149–55.

—(2012), "Art in the Age of Asymmetry: Hegel, Objects, Aesthetics." *Evental Aesthetics* 1(1): 121–42.

—(2013), *Realist Magic: Objects, Ontology, and Causality*. Michigan: Open Humanities Press.

Nirenberg, Ricardo L. and David Nirenberg (2011), "Badiou's Number: A Critique of Mathematics as Ontology." *Critical Inquiry* 37(4): 583–614.

Nolt, John (2004), "An Argument for Metaphysical Realism." *Journal for General Philosophy of Science* 35: 71–90.

Noys, David C. (2009), *The Time of Our Lives: A Critical History of Temporality*. Cambridge, MA: MIT Press.

Olkowski, Dorothea (2005), "Travels with Darwin." *symbloké* 13(1–2): 320–9.

Peirce, Charles S. (1891), "The Architecture of Theories." *The Monist* 1(2): 161–76.

Philo (1855), *The Works of Philo Judaica: Vol. 1*. Trans. C. D. Younge. London: Hadden Brothers.

Price, Hew (1996), *Time's Arrow and Archimedes' Point: New Directions for the Physics of Time*. New York: Oxford University Press.

Proctor, Hannah (2011), "Neuronal Ideologies: Catherine Malabou's Explosive Plasticity in Light of the Marxist Psychology of A. R. Luria." *Dandelion* 2(1), available at http://www.dandelionjournal.org/index.php/dandelion/article/view/24/81 (Last accessed 1 September 2013).

Putnam, Hilary (1978), *Meaning and the Moral Sciences*. London: Routledge.

—(1988), *Reality and Representation*. Cambridge, MA: MIT Press.

—(2002), "A Problem about Reference," in Michael J. Loux (ed.), *Metaphysics: Contemporary Readings*. London: Taylor & Francis, pp. 496–524.

Roffe, Jon (2013), "The Future of an Illusion." *Speculations* 4: 48–52.

Sacilotto, Daniel (2013), "Realism and Representation: On the Ontological Turn." *Speculations* 4: 53–62.

Sallis, John (1998), "Levinas and the Elemental." *Research in Phenomenology* 28: 152–9.

Sartre, Jean-Paul (1968), *Search for a Method*. Trans. Hazel Barnes. New York: Vintage Books.

Schelling, F. W. J. (2004), *First Outline of a System of the Philosophy of Nature*. Trans. Keith R. Peterson. Albany, NY: SUNY Press.

Sellars, Wilfred (1962), "Time and World Order," in H. Feigl and G. Maxwell (eds), *Minnesota Studies in the Philosophy of Science*, Vol. III. Minneapolis: University of Minnesota Press, pp. 527–616.

—(1967), *Philosophical Perpectives*. New York: Ridgeview Publishers.

—(1991), "Philosophy and the Scientific Image of Man," in *Science, Perception and Reality*. New York: Ridgeview Publishing Company.

—(1997), *Empiricism and the Philosophy of Mind*. Cambridge, MA: Harvard University Press.

Sharp, Hasana (2011), *Spinoza and the Politics of Renaturalization*. Chicago, IL: University of Chicago Press.

Shaw, Devin (2010), *Freedom and Nature in Schelling's Philosophy of Art*. London: Continuum.

Smith, John and Sharyn Ward (1984), "Are We Only Five Minutes Old? Acock on the Age of the Universe." *Philosophy of Science* 51: 511–13.

Smith, Stacey (2013), "Review of *Ontology of the Accident*," available at http://societyandspace.com/reviews/reviews-archive/malabou_smith/ (Last accessed 1 September 2013).

Smolin, Lee (2013), *Time Reborn: From the Crisis in Physics to the Future of the Universe*. New York: Houghton Mifflin Harcourt.

Williams, James (2011), "The Objects in Manifold Times: Deleuze and the Speculative Philosophy of Objects as Processes." *Cosmos and History: The Journal of Natural and Social Philosophy* 7(1): 62–75.

Wolfendale, Pete (2012), "Essay on Transcendental Realism," available at http://www.academia.edu/1146988/Essay_on_Transcendental_Realism, p. 11 (Last accessed 11 July 2013).

Žižek, Slavoj (2006), *The Parallax View*. Cambridge, MA: MIT University Press.

—(2011), Ecology as the New Opium of the Masses," available at http://www.lacan.com/zizecology2.htm (Last accessed 1 May 2012).

—(2013), "Trouble in Paradise." *London Review of Books* 35(14): 11–12.

INDEX